REFLECTIONS ON PRECISION TEACHING

RICHARD M. KUBINA JR.

Greatness Achieved Publishing Company
Pittsburgh, PA
2021

Copyright © 2021 by Greatness Achieved Publishing Company

All rights reserved.

For information about permission to reproduce selections from this book, write to greatnessachievedpubcom@gmail.com

http://greatnessachieved.com/

ISBN 978-1-7336675-1-7

Dedication

To every learner working to better themselves through education or performance enhancement, I salute you. Your efforts will make you a better person and lead to a better world.

–RMK

Contents

0. Introduction	1
1. On Precision Teaching	5
Entry: First blog post	5
Entry: All learning boundaries are conventions	7
Entry: We desperately need standards	11
Entry: We desperately need standards	13
Entry: The Big Heart	19
Entry: Information and knowledge	22
Entry: The power of celeration metrics	25
Entry: Precision Teaching: Misconceptions, Misunderstanding, and Myths	29
Entry: An ode to Og	36
2. The Keystone of Precision Teaching - Pinpointing	39
Entry: Classification in the sciences and PT	39
Entry: Pinpoint detection	41
What to do	42
Entry: Agents of precision	44
Entry: Pinpointing and PEAK	46
3. Counting Behavior	51
Entry: Counting and timing behavior	51
Entry: Moving frequencies	52
Entry: The 'record ceiling'	55
Entry: Stop hating on percent	57
4. Linear Graphs versus Standard Celeration Charts?	61
Entry: Four warning signs of a poorly constructed line graph	61
Entry: Quick fact: Linear graphs can fool you	67
Entry: Why NSLGs stink	69
Entry: Counts and visual displays	76
Entry: Nonstandard linear graphs or Standard Celeration Charts?	79
Entry: The king of all time-series visual displays	82
5. Inside the SCC	85
Entry: Charting zero	86
Entry: Condition change or phase change?	91
Entry: Celeration – Why growth rates matter	94
Entry: Decay rates and celeration	97

Entry: Why the world needs celeration	101
Entry: The celeration period	107
Entry: Bounce on the SCC	109
Entry: Do you know bounce?	111
Entry: A behavioral metric for quantifying improvement	114
Entry: How bizarre	116
Entry: Illegal Oscar Screeners: The Standard Celeration Chart projects an end to piracy	119
Entry: Jaws, Snowplows, and Dives: Using Learning Pictures for decision making	125

6. More SCC Goodness — 137

Entry: More on relative change	137
Entry: Powers of 10 are sexy	139
Entry: Metrics and analytics: The key to better understanding behavior	141
Entry: Multipliers	146
Entry: What Southwest's Flight Tracker reminds us about tracking behavior	150

7. Behavioral Production — 155

Entry: Don't 'drill' but do "practice"	156
Entry: Three simple steps for better practice	158
Entry: Practice - The key to success in school and life	162
Entry: A behavioral complexity checklist	167
Entry: To write better chart better	172
Entry: SAFMEDS	178

8. PT Inspiration — 185

Entry: All testing is not evil	185
Entry: On individuality	188
Entry: What is accountability?	190
Entry: We have an answer	197
Entry: Using Precision Teaching for a better future	200

9. PT Miscellany — 203

Entry: Which trial should I chart?	203
Entry: Data, variables, applied science, and Precision Teaching	208
Entry: Inners	214
Entry: Chart shares are fun	217
Entry: Cumulative Record → Standard Celeration Chart	221
Entry: ABA and PT	224

References — 229
Index — 235

Chapter 0

Introduction

At some level every person wants to change behavior for the better. The behavior change may fall under the realm of self-improvement. Self-improvement refers to any change in knowledge, skill, or betterment in one's own life. The appetite for self-improvement appears quite healthy in society. For example, at the time of this writing a search of amazon.com yields a result of over 80,000 results for books under self-improvement.

Beyond self-improvement, businesses seek to apply performance improvement. Performance improvement focuses on changing people, processes, organizations, and performance (Van Time, Moseley, & Dessiger, 2012). Performance, of course, just means behavior. And changing people, changing a business process, or changing how an organization functions all boil down to the behavior of people.

The information offered to enact self-improvement or performance improvement lives in books, book chapters, peer-reviewed journal articles, webinars, blog posts, and a host of other sources. In fact, information for behavior change seems overwhelming by the sheer magnitude of contributions found in print and digital media. While content on the topic of specific programs and approaches to behavior change has tremendous value, an equally important topic holds as much meaning: how to measure behavior change and make effective decisions surrounding program or intervention effectiveness.

Precision Teaching (PT) offers such incredible value to anyone interested in changing their own behavior or helping someone else reach their own goals. PT started in the 1960s and thrives to this day due to its elegant and powerful process. The process simply tells the person interested about how some intervention or program, or lack thereof, has affected a behavior. As a result, the person can decide whether they should continue with their present course of action or make a change. The lack of change information can significantly hinder someone's progress. In some cases, the person may never reach their goals.

This book will showcase what has taken me a lifetime to learn. I lay bare my thinking from early in my career to the present day (the time of this writing). The following book captures many posts from my days as a blogger. Every blog I wrote spoke to something important to me at the time or a topic someone asked me to discuss. All of the content can aid people interested in behavior change and how a precision measurement/decision making system can foster superior outcomes. Figure 0 shows what I have learned about PT as a process.

Precison Teaching Process

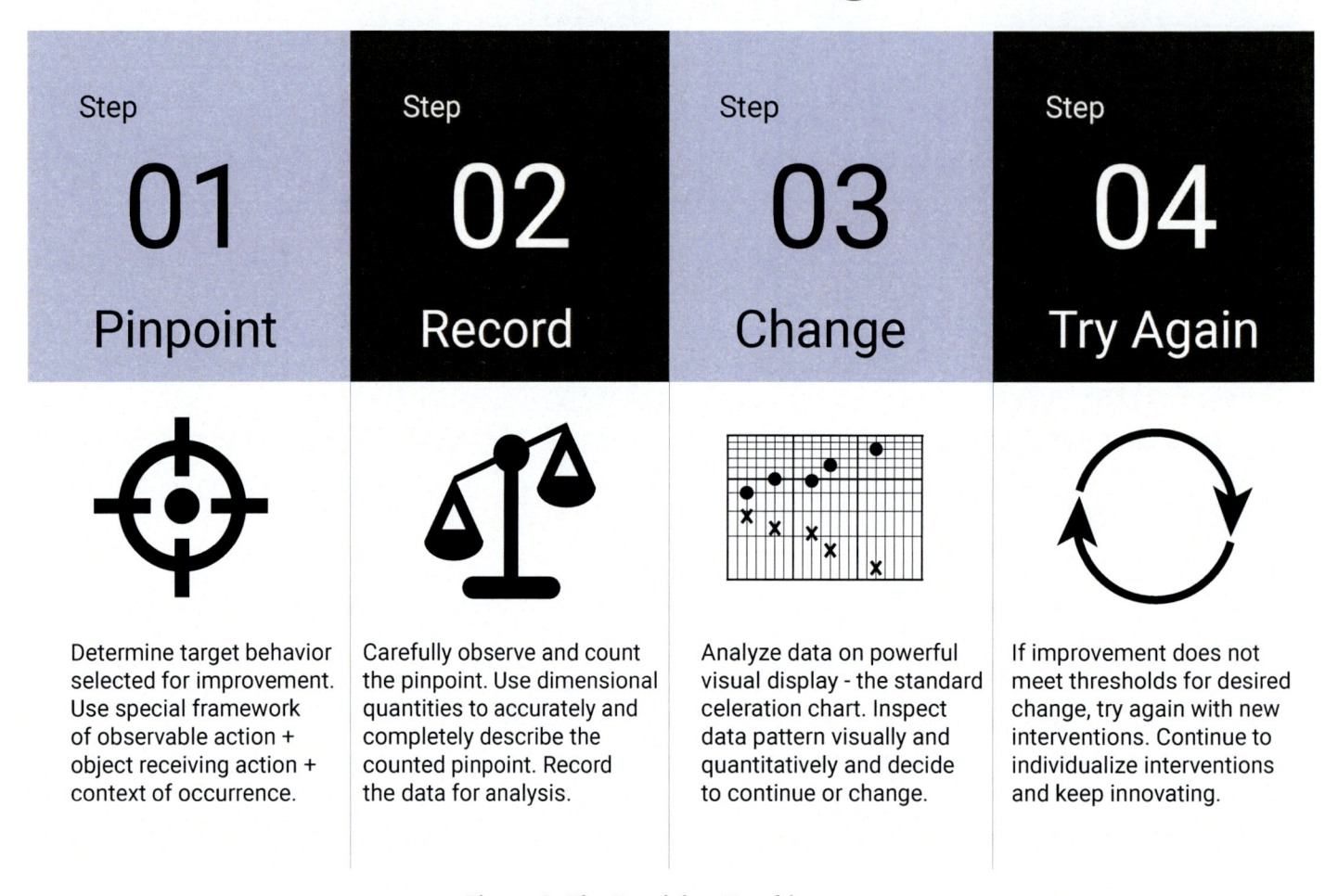

Step 01 Pinpoint	Step 02 Record	Step 03 Change	Step 04 Try Again
Determine target behavior selected for improvement. Use special framework of observable action + object receiving action + context of occurrence.	Carefully observe and count the pinpoint. Use dimensional quantities to accurately and completely describe the counted pinpoint. Record the data for analysis.	Analyze data on powerful visual display - the standard celeration chart. Inspect data pattern visually and quantitatively and decide to continue or change.	If improvement does not meet thresholds for desired change, try again with new interventions. Continue to individualize interventions and keep innovating.

Figure 0. The Precision Teaching process.

Reflections of Precision Teaching began in 2007 with the publication of my first blog. I had a general Precision Teaching blog. My original efforts did not serve as a good model for blogging. Across 5 years I wrote about 12 blogs. Next, I wrote several blogs for the Precision Teaching Book website. There I produced 25 blogs across three years. From there I started coming into my own writing over 50 blogs for the Chartlytics website. I still blog to this day at the CentralReach website but share blogging duties with fellow colleagues who write about other topics such as behavior analysis, practice management, and technology.

For the present book, I followed a specific format. I took all of the blogs I have ever written and then sorted them into categories. The categories became chapters based on similar content.

Chapter 0: Introduction

In each chapter I wrote an introduction about the blog and shared the meaning it had for me or others interested in PT content. Then I reviewed what I wrote, edited the content, created new figures where needed, and delighted in contemplating my old thoughts and how they changed throughout the years as I became more knowledgeable about the field.

I hope readers find the subject matter and themes in *Reflections of Precision Teaching* as useful and compelling as when I originally wrote them. Some blogs include my unlikely attempts at humor while all share my deep respect and love of Precision Teaching; I hope all readers feel that undercurrent reverence.

Chapter 1

On Precision Teaching

A REFLECTION ON ONE'S history of writing brings back thoughts and concerns of the past. The first blog post I wrote expresses themes that would come to dominate my professional writing, research efforts, and entrepreneurial adventures. Early in my career I spent almost all my time in schools and wrote about education. As my career progressed, I shifted to discuss how Precision Teaching (PT) also had a home in other disciplines. Still, wherever one applies the tried and true PT process, success will soon follow.

Entry: First blog post

First blog post, what to say? Do I start by pointing out that our education system fails too many learners and is more of an art than a science? No, that seems a little negative. Perhaps I can draw attention to the booming cottage industry of people selling faux performance/learning enhancing products like Baby Einstein and Power Balance bracelets? No, again that falls on the pessimist side of the ledger. Maybe the best way to start my first blog is to say "Welcome!" and "Your journey for discovering a world class scientific measurement system for human behavior and learning has ended." I would also say, however, learning about Precision Teaching and Standard Celeration Charting means your journey has also just begun.

We live in a rapidly changing world. Part of surviving and thriving is the ability to learn and master new concepts and skills. By the way, true mastery of any skill does not mean 100%; percent correct can only tell us about accuracy and acquisition, but more on that later. Our world has become increasingly technological, therefore, fully harnessing the power of the information age requires us to maximize all opportunities for learning. If you have ever been in a classroom, seen a classroom, or know someone in a classroom, you have already realized at some point in time people struggle to learn. Enter Precision Teaching.

Precision Teaching represents a measurement and decision making system. PT is not a curriculum that tells people what to teach. Instead, Precision Teaching offers an unparalleled system for (1) defining behavior; (2) measuring and recording behavior; (3) showing whether a change is, or is not, needed and suggesting methods for change; and (4) not giving up on the learner by providing strategies for continued problem-solving.

The four PT steps previously described, Pinpoint-Record-Change-Try Again, may appear simple, but the full application is rigorous, technically demanding, and a precise science (a process akin to the scientific method). Imagine the great care and meticulousness applied to measurement in mature sciences like physics and chemistry. Indeed, physics and chemistry would not command the universal respect they do without having applied the high standards for measuring their respective subject matters. In particle physics scientists are on the verge of discovering the Higgs boson, a subatomic particle hypothesized to be a fundamental building block of the universe (*Author's note*: Since the time of the post, scientists did confirm the presence of the Higgs boson with the Large Hadron Collider and received the Nobel prize in physics). Precise measurement will allow humanity to peer into the creation of the Universe! If such a discovery is not a titanic score for our species, then I don't know what is.

In education, high degrees of measurement by standard units are unfortunately rare. Even more scarce, the use of high-quality visual display systems for time series data. The name "time series" data almost explains itself; data that occur across a dimension of time are scrutinized for change. The Precision Teaching system uses the most powerful and informative graphic for time series data I am aware of – the Standard Celeration Chart (SCC). The SCC has so much to offer those interested behavior change it seems only a matter of time before it becomes institutional standard. Of course, for the SCC to be adopted widescale would mean education has embraced science and high-quality measurement as a common practice.

So why care about PT? If you want to improve a behavior for yourself, a loved one, or client, then learning and using Precision Teaching is a must. Measuring behavior as precisely as possible is like watching a Blue Ray movie on high definition television – the clarity is unbelievable and you see all the subtle and important details (*Author's note*: Yikes this seems outdated now but that will always happen by referencing technology of the day, it will inevitably become obsolete). Without PT, the picture may be in black white, grainy, and difficult to see. You might get part of the picture, but without the extreme precision critical details are missed. And when critical details are missed decision making is negatively affected. As part of the heritage of PT, teachers have been watching the high definition TV for years and have discovered amazing things. Some of the findings fall under behavioral fluency which I will write about frequently. There are many others.

Indeed, my intention of writing blogs, books, conducting research, and working directly with learners is to be a small part of the movement already underway. Namely, to usher in an age of spectacular precision in measurement of human behavior and enhanced decision making. The good news is we already know how to measure behavior with the resolve of the strictest natural scientists out there. Furthermore, we have a visual display system, the SCC, that allows us to determine consistent, genuine significance of behavior change. I hope I can join you on your journey to discovering the elegant and strikingly robust measurement system that is Precision Teaching. If you are reading this, you may have specific problems that need solved or are curious how to do even better measuring behavior. I hope to interact with you in the future and welcome all your comments, questions, and suggestions.

I wrote several blogs explaining PT. In some of those blogs I also described different components of the PT system. I wrote the following blog while listening to the Cloud Atlas soundtrack. In the score, a song stuck out and moved me, "All boundaries are conventions." I love the song and title so much I took the name added "learning." The song has a sweeping, majestic feel, exactly the feelings I have about Precision Teaching.

Entry: All learning boundaries are conventions

People we care for can struggle when learning. Sometimes those challenges rise to a level signaling deep concern. A student who cannot read, for instance, will have very limited career avenues not to mention limited participation in much of what our technological society has to offer. What can we do?

For starters, potential solutions will result from how a teacher views learning. Unfortunately, all too often the learner is blamed for the failure. Convenient labels communicate the problem resides within the student themselves and the teacher must fix the learner. As an example, auditory processing disorder states a person cannot process information auditorily like other people do. The disorder means the person has difficulty with sounds that compose speech. Fixing the underlying speech processing mechanism then would lead to improved academic performance. The following example illustrates the line of reasoning applied to a math problem.

Problem: Student struggles to learn adding fractions ½ + ⅔ = ?

Diagnosis of problem: Student has auditory processing disorder and cannot understand the instructions provided by the teacher or student cannot engage in "mental math" because he or she has trouble hearing their own voice.

Solution: Fix the underlying problem (auditory processing disorder) or provide accommodations so the student can overcome problem.

Teachers who embrace the previously mentioned problem with an indirect cause will likely focus much energy and effort at marginally useful exercises. For example, a solution may involve "Right Brain Math Strategies," presenting information at a slow pace, giving the student one problem at a time, or strengthening note-taking skills.

Students with auditory processing disorders (or any other underlying problem like Attention Deficit Hyperactivity Disorder) have a clearly defined learning boundary; they cannot escape who they are.

Precision Teaching

How does Precision Teaching differ from methods that establish the problem as a characteristic of the learner? The answer lies in the structure of the PT system:

Pinpoint > Record > Change > Try Again.

Step 1 = *Pinpoint*. Pinpointing means selecting the most precise, representative label of behavior. Pinpointing follows a specific method:

1. Select an action verb.
2. Select object used with action verb (keep it singular).
3. Add "s" to the end of action verb (Present tense).
4. Check the pinpoint for observability and cyclicality (repeatability).
5. Add context important to the pinpoint.

Let's take the previous problem: Student struggles to learn adding fractions: ½ + ⅔ =

According to the pinpointing steps above we have the following:

1. Write (action verb for this particular behavior involves writing, though it could also involve keyboarding, saying, or selecting, all different behaviors).
2. Fraction answer
3. Writes
4. "Writes fraction answer" passes the test for observability and cyclicality – anyone can clearly observe it and the student can repeat the behavior.
5. Writes fraction answer on practice sheet (the added context further clarifies the exact nature of the pinpoint).

With the pinpoint, "Writes fraction answer on practice sheet," the focus of the problem centers solely on behavior, not a processing problem or some other indirect cause. Of course, pinpointing behavior does not mean the teacher ignores issues that may affect the behavior. For instance, if a student has poor handwriting, the handwriting would factor into how well the student can write and perform the pinpoint "Writes fraction answer on practice sheet."

Step 2 = Record. The second step means the teacher records the student's pinpoint "Writes fraction answer on practice sheet" via frequency. Frequency refers to a count in a time interval. In the practice sheet (Figure 1), a teacher or other person can count the number of correct and incorrect written fraction answers on the practice sheet. The student wrote a total of 4 correct digits and 9 incorrect digits. An inspection of the performance shows a clear strategy the student has used: just adding the digits from left to right. By using the straight adding strategy, the student did write some correct digits. However, each correct digit appeared in the correct placement by happenstance, not because the student applied the necessary strategy to understand and complete the addition algorithm properly.

If the student completed the performance in 1 minute, we now have a frequency: 4 correct and 9 incorrect digits per minute. Recording the frequency of the pinpoint each day brings us to the third step in Precision Teaching, Change.

Name: Sarah   Score: _____
Teacher: _____   Date: _____

Adding Fractions

1) $\frac{3}{5} + \frac{3}{10} = \frac{6}{15}$ — 1 incorrect digit written / 1 correct and 1 incorrect digit written

2) $\frac{8}{10} + \frac{2}{3} = \frac{10}{13}$ — 2 incorrect digits written / 1 correct and 1 incorrect digit written

3) $\frac{1}{2} + \frac{2}{10} = \frac{3}{10}$ — 1 incorrect digit written / 2 correct digits written

4) $\frac{1}{10} + \frac{1}{2} = \frac{2}{12}$ — 1 incorrect digit written / 2 incorrect digits written

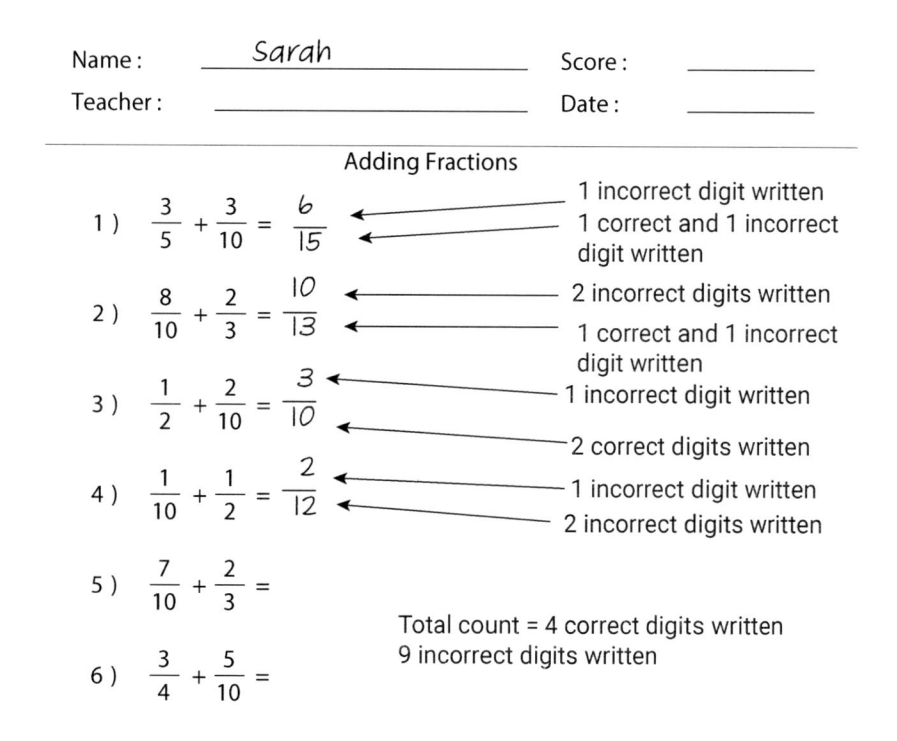

5) $\frac{7}{10} + \frac{2}{3} =$

6) $\frac{3}{4} + \frac{5}{10} =$

Total count = 4 correct digits written
9 incorrect digits written

Figure 1. Adding fractions practice sheet.

Step 3 = Change. The student will perform the pinpoint each day. The teacher will record the correct and incorrect frequency. Then the student or teacher (best when done by the student) will chart data on a Standard Celeration Chart or SCC.

The SCC in Figure 2 displays the first recorded frequency (discussed above in step 2) and four more frequencies taken each day of the week. An examination of the trends for corrects and incorrects present a troubling learning picture. The number of corrects appear below incorrects and have not grown. Incorrects, on the other hand, accelerated suggesting Ivan has tried harder (i.e., completed more problems in the same amount of time) but has not applied a strategy that leads to more correct answers.

The SCC paints a vivid picture for the teacher who will decide whether to institute a change or continue the present course of behavior. Clearly the teacher will make a change due to poor and deteriorating performance. Additionally, PT involves the student. When students self-chart, ownership of the pinpoint rises. Students can then self-monitor and contribute to decision making.

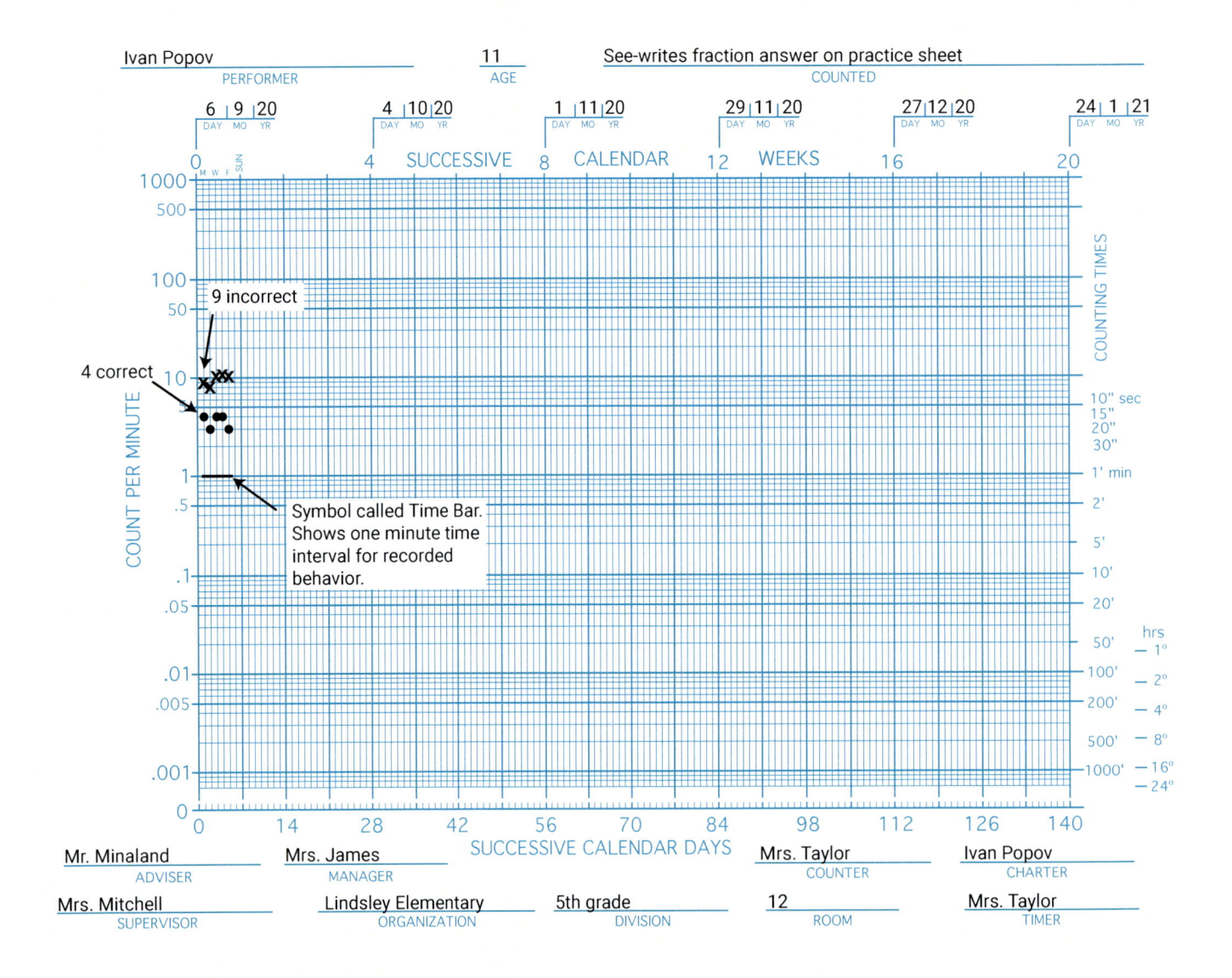

Figure 2. The SCC and data.

Step 4 = Try Again. Try Again refers to a Precision Teacher's marching orders; keep trying interventions until a solution exists for the problem. Several different intervention tactics have emerged from the 1,000s of teachers and students who have used PT through the years. As one example, the teacher could use the tactic, "Try-3-at-once." The teacher gives the student three different tasks, like writing multiplication fact answers on a practice sheet, saying multiplication fact answers to flashcards, or keyboarding multiplication fact answers on a computer screen. After giving the student daily, timed assessments for a week, the task in which the student learned best in (as shown by the steepest trend or celeration line on a SCC) would become the preferred method of instruction. Many other Try Again problem solving tactics exist to help the student, all directly governed by the student's observable behavior.

Recap. The Precision Teaching process focuses directly on behavior. A pinpointed behavior, precisely measured as a frequency, and then charted and displayed on a specially designed visual graphic that unambiguously depicts the course of behavior. Reexamining the earlier described problem and solution in a Precision Teaching perspective looks like the following:

Problem: Student struggles to learn adding fractions: ½ + ⅔ =

Diagnosis of problem: Student does not know the proper algorithm for adding fractions.

Solution: Fix the problem by teaching and then having the student practice the algorithm for adding fractions. The teacher closely monitors the student's daily performance and knows immediately how well the student has learned the algorithm.

If you root for the underdog, believe applied science can solve the most inveterate problems, and hold the conviction that we should never give up on the learner, then you share the core beliefs of a Precision Teacher.

※

The use of standards always seemed an incredibly important ingredient of the PT system. Standards make life better and they exist throughout civilized society. Contrast something that has a nonstandard nature with a standard. The difference will appear as striking as comparing chaos to order. The following entry marked my attempt to express the power of a standard as embodied in PT.

Entry: We desperately need standards

Standards

Think about the order in human endeavors like business, science, and even social clubs. Order emanates from standards. Business has standards in commerce like money. And science has many standards for measurement (e.g., units for weight, length, time). How would business operate without a standard currency? How would science work without standard units of measurement? In both cases, not so well.

A standard "is a criterion, unit of reference, model, or process approved or accepted as correct by common consent, established custom, or recognized authority" (Schmid, 1976). Standards facilitate access to a common scale and frame of reference. For example, standards transformed the New York subway from confusion and chaotic system into one of clarity and dependable utility.

In 1976 Schmid delivered a wonderfully informational piece on standards. In his presentation he listed 5 reasons why everyone should use standards. He made the following excellent points about standards:

1. "They serve as important guides in maintaining uniformity and consistency for many repetitive and recurring procedures.
2. They represent an important educational tool by facilitating the training and indoctrination of new employees, thereby relieving the supervisory staff of time and effort.
3. They can be helpful in enhancing the quality of work by developing procedures based on experience, collaboration, and consensus.
4. They can reduce costs by increasing the efficiency and economy of basic procedures.
5. "Standards represent a distillation of experience which can be retained and perpetuated without dissipating time and energy in constantly retracing or reinventing certain procedures" (Schmid, 1976, p. 75-76).

Unpacking Schmid's message makes one wonder why everyone doesn't go out and find a standard and give it a big hug. We certainly have with PT!

1. People who learn how to create pinpoints have a system for always selecting behavior in a consistent and productive manner.
2. New people learning how to help others master and become fluent with content can learn systematic practice routines quickly and efficiently.
3. Once people become proficient with the Standard Celeration Chart they can make decisions with fewer errors, more speed, and greater effectiveness.
4. Greatly reduced expenditures go to training because once people learn PT, they can quickly teach others. A community of people rallying around standard procedures and standard measures allows users to harness the full power of the science of performance improvement and measurement.
5. When an organization learns how to successfully foster positive change experiences, even one in that system benefits from the shared knowledge of the discovery.

No standards? Prepare for distress and frustration

Take what Schmid said in his five reasons above stating why standards work. People who don't embrace standards live in a world ruled by the inconsistent procedures, recurring problems, lengthy and involved indoctrination procedures, high training expenses, and a lack of institutional knowledge. Who wants any of that?

PT uses standards to help people achieve their personal goals of performance and learning improvement.

Standards and specifically how they impact the field of education, psychology, behavior analysis, and other disciplines concerned with behavior change distinguished a significant portion of my writing. I felt a need to come up with different ways to champion standards because of their conspicuous absence in almost all fields focusing on behavior change.

Entry: We desperately need standards

Years ago, I spent time in the US Navy as a Seabee. I had a job as an equipment operator. Driving different heavy equipment seemed easy enough. See me in the picture below with my rough-terrain forklift.

Figure 3. Rick in his younger years serving his country.

At times, I got to hang out with my Seabee buddies during construction tasks. A friend of mine became a construction electrician. At a work site I remember asking him why it took so long to do the wiring (I wanted to get back to our barracks). He made some remark about electrical currents, materials, and standards. My brilliant remark? "Standards, who needs them?"

Funny how education changes us! If present-day, older Rick could meet past, younger Rick I might try and talk some sense into him about standards. But then again, I might just tell him to invent Google or Facebook, or maybe Googlebook.

Standards

Over time I have come to appreciate standards like nobody's business. Our modern society owes so much to standards that I can hardly do justice to the topic in one post.

Standardization describes the process of employing world-class specifications that govern the construction and delivery of services, systems, and products (International Organization for Standardization, 2014). This process results in a standard, or "...an agreed-upon way of doing something" (Spivak & Brenner, 2001, p.1).

Standards occur in industry and commerce, health care, and almost every mature scientific discipline. Standards have brought us, literally, from the dark age to the digital age. Everywhere you look you can see the power of standards. Examples:

The smart phone we can't live without has a standard operating system that allows app makers to construct everything from Angry Birds to Lose It!

The houses in which we live and the buildings in which we shop and work came into existence through a series of standards: (1) construction workers using materials born of adhesive, cement, and concrete standards; (2) builders following masonry standards, roofing standards, and wood standards; and (3) inspections to ensure the structure met fire standards, insulation standards, and engineering standards.

When we visit medical professionals, they use standards to determine if our vision, hearing, heart rate, and temperature indicate health or that we need help.

The list could go on and on. As stated by Thomas, the then President of American Society for Testing and Materials: "Standardization is indispensable to life in this century. It is virtually as indispensable as the air we breathe. And like the air we breathe, it is invisible to all except its technicians" (Spivak & Brenner, 2001, p.v).

Complete lack of standards in graphs

Take a moment and look at time series graphs from any education, behavior analytic, psychology, sociology, economics, or other social science journal. The line graphs will show change across time. The line graphs will also showcase the rampant nonstandardization across the fields.

Variability starts at the conception of graphs thanks to nonstandardization. Take the example of three figures constructed by graduate students experienced in graph construction. No doubt you will immediately notice the graphs vary in construction even though they have the same data. And while one may feel tempted to blame the different physical dimensions on inexperience, the same phenomenon will occur with any graph in any behavioral journal.

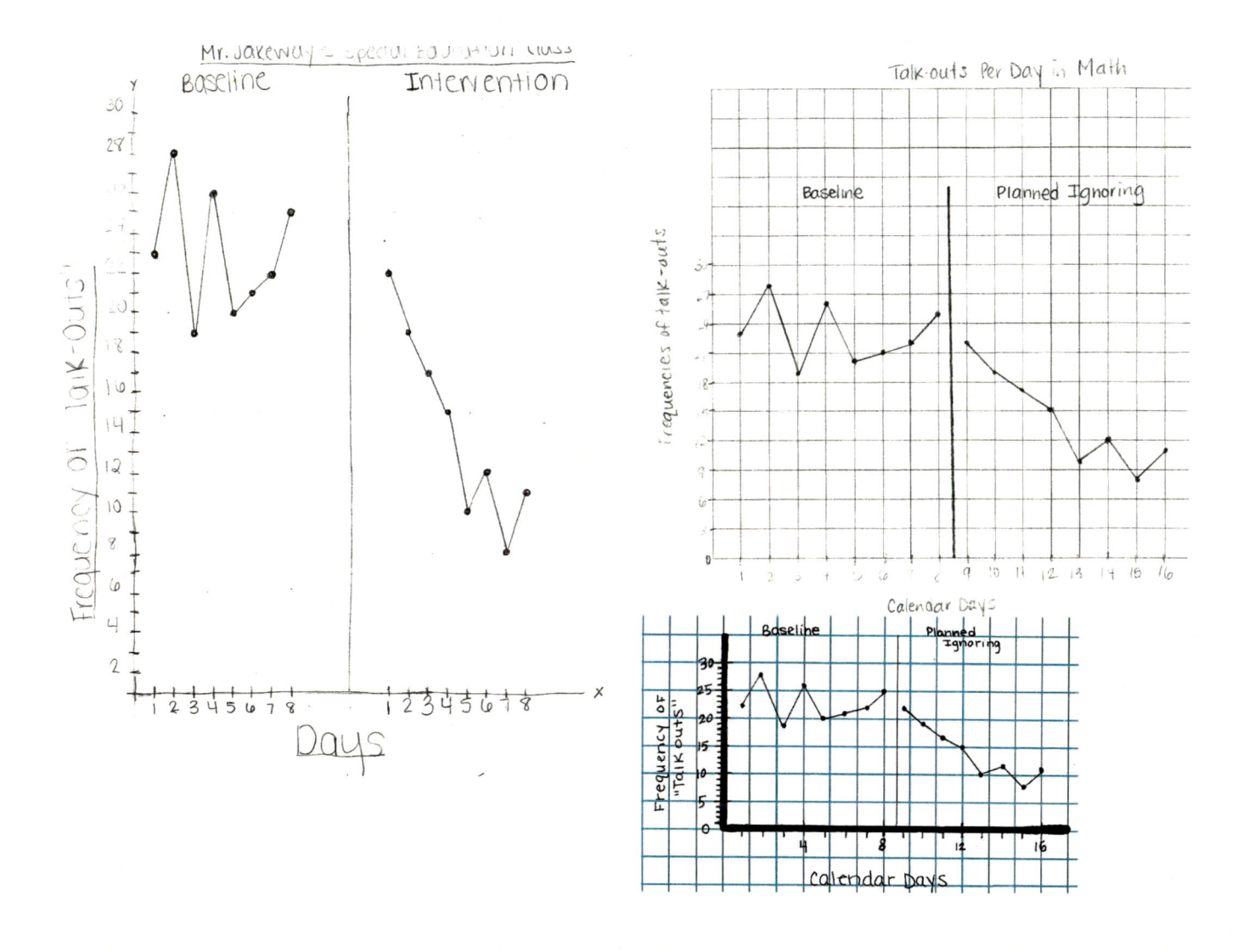

Figure 4. Three nonstandard linear graphs.

Why should it matter? Why should any of us care that almost everyone uses nonstandard linear graphs? Let's answer the question with another set of questions. Would we care if our smart phones used nonstandard operating systems? Yes, because nonstandardization affects all the gaming, productively, and photograph apps we like.

Should we care if our buildings fell under the domain of nonstandardization? Yes! They might fall over in high winds, bombard us with noxious gases due to improper building materials, or have roofs that can't keep the water out when it rains.

And what if our health care professionals employ nonstandardization with the devices they use to measure different health indicators? If we don't care about quality health care service then yes, let's embrace the lack of standards and let every single health care device maker rig their own technical specs.

We use graphs to make decisions, in most cases high stake decisions. Professionals and nonprofessionals alike use time series graphs such as the line graph to detect subtle and dramatic changes in a measured quantity across time. Having nonstandard linear graphs serve as the basis of our main decision making/evaluative tool comes with its hazards. For this blog, I will not lay out all the inherent limitations with a linear graph; they exist, and many have pointed out their informational shortcomings (shameless plug: The Precision Teaching Book). But I will discuss two problems with nonstandardization.

Two basic problems *always* exist with graphs that live in the land of nonstandardization:

1. Slope changes based on the size and proportions of the graph
2. Variability changes based on the size and proportions of the graph

The graphs below illustrate the differences in slope changes. Each nonstandard linear graph has the same data, but the axes underwent manipulation (by the way, you find textbooks that encourage graph makers to play with the data and see what looks best - Oy vey!).

Same data on two nonstandard graphs

Two radically different slopes of trend lines due to nonstandardization

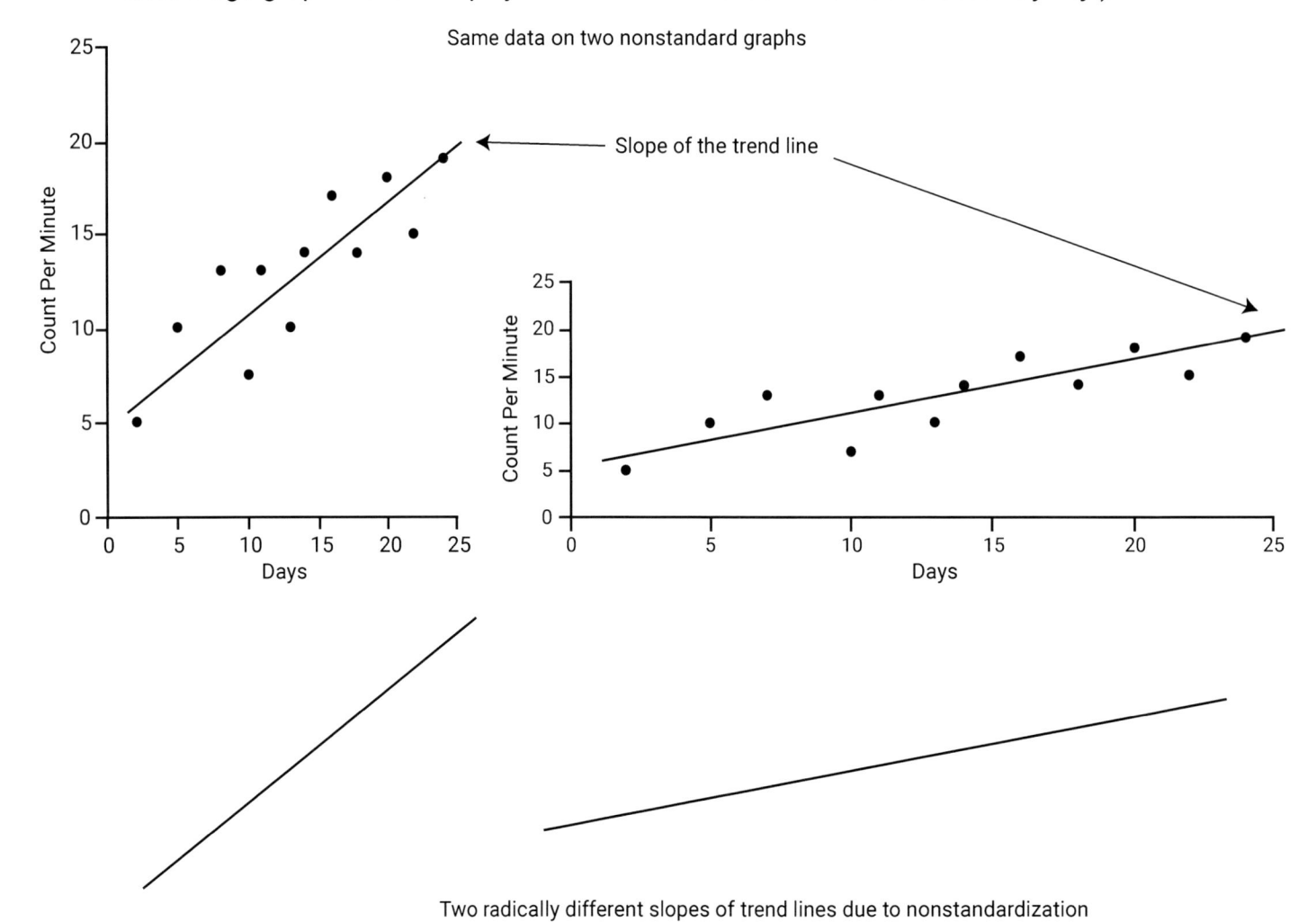

Figure 5. Graphs with the same data but different slopes due to changed axis sizes.

Look at the difference in the slopes. Ask yourself, do you think a person would evaluate how fast the data has changed based on the two slopes? Yes, yes they would. The slope in the first graph appears to rise more steeply than the second graph. Logic compels the graph reader to conclude the data changed more quickly in graph 1 than graph 2. The data haven't changed but we have two different conclusions!

Same data on two nonstandard graphs

Two radically different variability envelopes due to nonstandardization

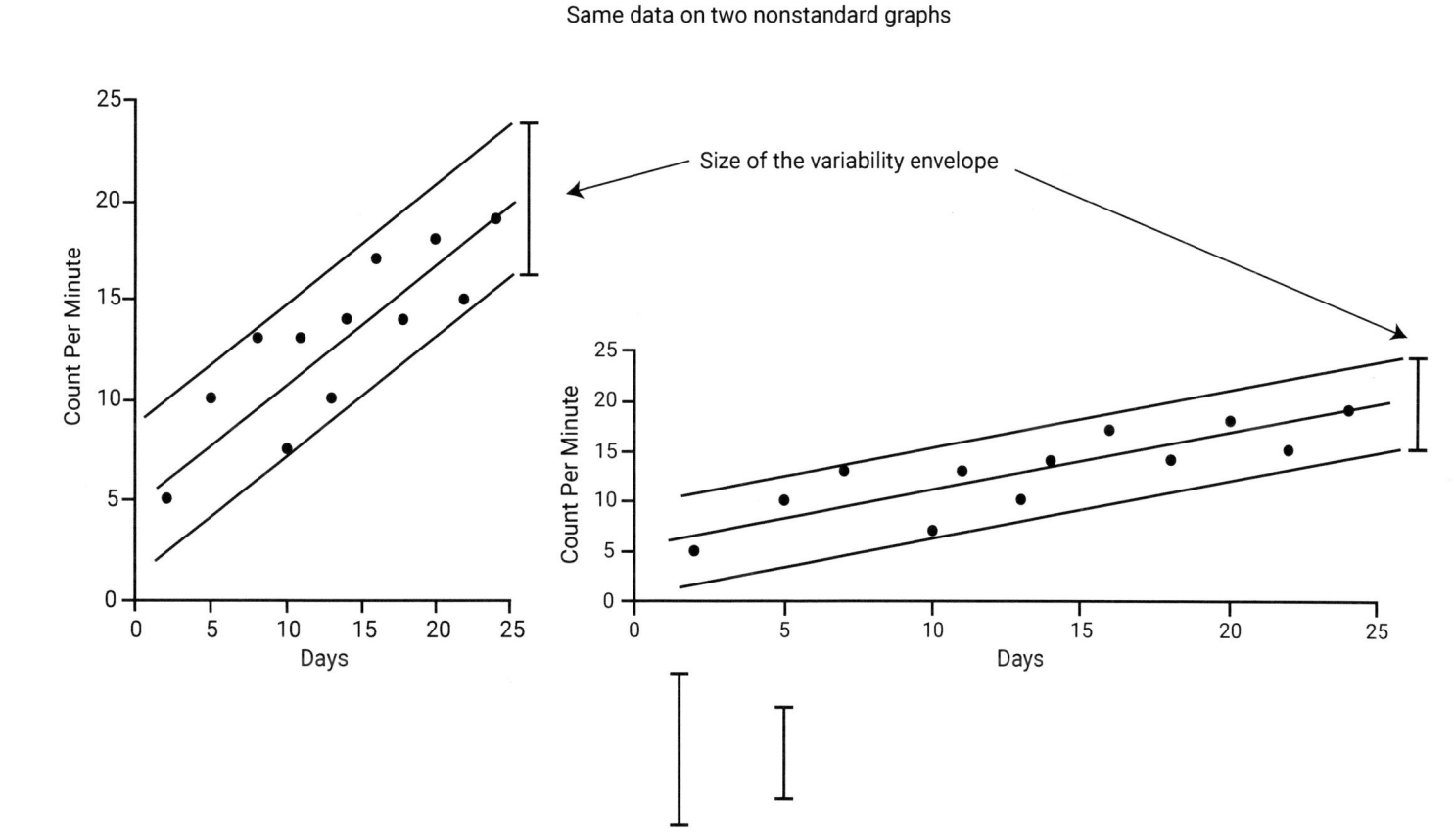

Figure 6. Graphs with the same data but different variability due to changed axis sizes.

Variability suffers the fate as slopes when nonstandardization rules the roost. Unlike slope that shows speed of data change, variability indicates how much control exists in a condition. For example, in a condition where a teacher implemented an intervention, a high degree of variability indicates weak control of the intervention (because the data bounce all around; the less regularity in the occurrence of behavior the less influence an intervention has exerted).

Take a look at Figure 6. Notice the great degree of variability in graph 1 and the smaller variability envelope in graph 2. The graph reader sees high variability in one graph but interprets the other graph's variability as moderate. I found a pic on the internet of some guy just exasperated (Figure 7). His emotions convey what I feel when I consider all the inconsistent information on nonstandard linear graphs out there.

Figure 7. Some random guy expressing frustration.

Conclusion

What do we think about nonstandardization? Not good but it does do something. A house made with nonstandard materials will stand but may have hidden, and potentially catastrophic failings. Apps made with nonstandard operating systems will have very limited appeal, market penetration does follow without everything working on the same platform.

How well should we trust nonstandard linear graphs? Certainly, the nonstandard linear graphs tells us something. But at a price. Like the examples mentioned previously, nonstandardization can contain concealed, nasty surprises. Should members of scientific communities like psychology and education continue to embrace and celebrate nonstandard linear graphs? Should high stakes decisions that affect the lives of school age children or adults with severe behavior problems continue to occur on nonstandard linear graphs? You decide graph maker and graph reader!

Chapter 1 : On Precision Teaching

When I first started learning about PT two attributes attracted my interest. One, the science involved. I learned about movement cycles, frequency, a Standard Celeration Chart, analyzing data, and decision making. But the mission of PT embodied by my mentor Dr. Steve Graf also pulled me in. Namely, the appeal to humanity and helping improve people's lives. As a young undergrad I came to the university idealistic and motivated to make a difference in the world. Learning about the science in PT showed me "how to." But concepts such as the big heart helped fill in the "why" and still energizes me to this day.

Entry: The Big Heart

Early in my career someone taught me about a Precision Teaching concept called "the big heart." Below see a rendition of what I learned.

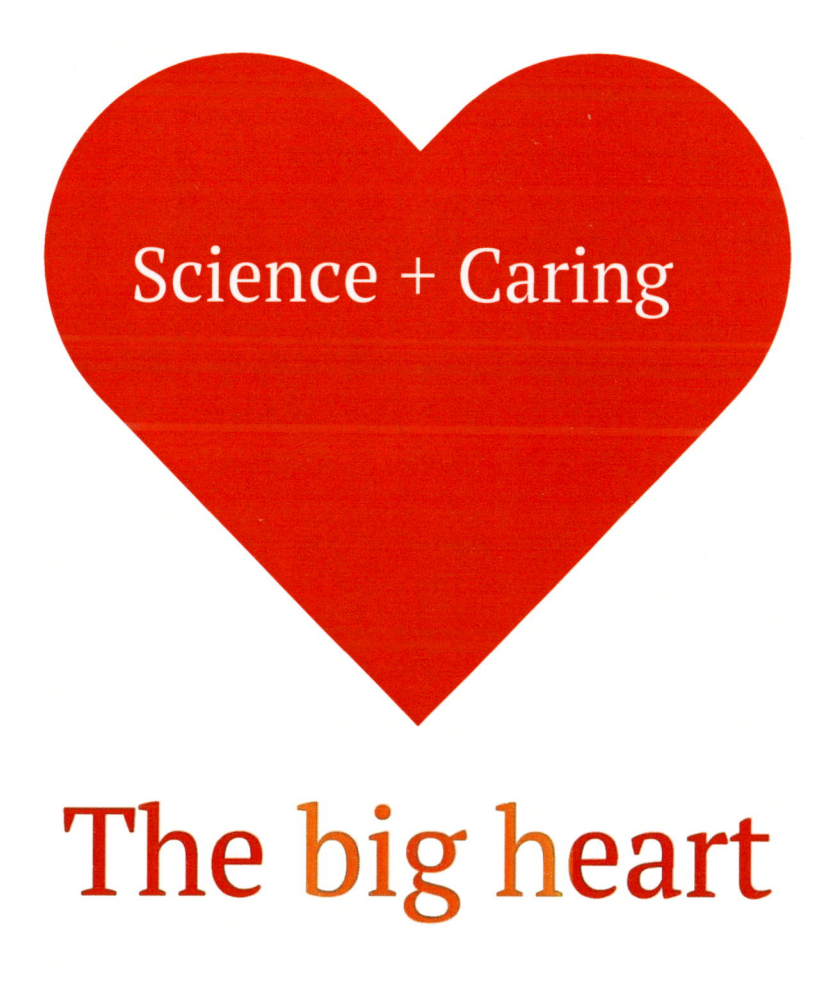

Figure 8. The big heart all Precision Teachers strive to employ.

I have sometimes seen the big heart as science + love. But either way we think about it, the big heart touches on a wonderful ideal.

Element #1 of the Big Heart - Science

With education, some people define it as an art or a social movement. For example, a blog I found explained science, education, and then art. The author concludes education functions more as an art. Science receives a less than a warm depiction. In the author's words:

"Our children are not laboratory rats and in the daily experience of education we only have a one time shot, we can never duplicate a day or an hour or even a minute of our experience with them. No day full of children can ever be experienced the same way twice. The results of our 'experiments' cannot be fed into a computer and statistically analyzed."

The author missed some fundamental aspects of science. First, we all live in nature. More to the point, we exist as part of nature. And nature has laws that govern everything from motion and biology, to matter and behavior.

Science seeks to uncover the deep truths of nature. For example, the science of behavior, behavior analysis, has discovered various laws that explain the occurrence of behavior. The law of reinforcement describes how behavior followed by a reinforcing event will result in an increased likelihood of the behavior occurring again in the future.

Example: Rick hasn't had a drink of water in 4 hours and sees a water fountain. Rick pushes the button on the fountain and water comes out. In the future when Rick hasn't drank water in a while (water deprivation), and in the presence of a water fountain, Rick will push the button on the water fountain to produce the consequence of water.

Side note, once in high school, some prankster lodged a small object in fountain and when I pushed the button the water shot out and drenched my face and clothes. Kind of embarrassing walking into Spanish class with water stain on my shirt and pants. Even to this day I check those fountains before drinking. High schoolers!

Because we humans now possess an understanding of some of the laws of nature, we can use that to benefit others. Some people, like the author in the previously mentioned blogpost miss fundamental aspects of science. When we conduct research in classroom with students we do so so that the information discovered can benefit other students and teachers.

Part of the big heart means we must use science and science's products to better our world. Engineering an effective learning environment for all students based on folk wisdom, common sense, or subjective preconceptions about education does not lend itself to reliable, valid, and meaningful information about learning and performance change.

Element #2 of the Big Heart - Caring

Education does form an official scientific discipline. And the practice of science has certain tenets. One of the tenet deals with the nature of scientific knowledge; information exists outside of humans' desires, values, and prejudices. In other words, what we may want to believe as true doesn't matter.

Gravity. We have so much information about gravity we call it a fact. But if we want to believe notions about gravity like Aristotle, that objects fall because they move towards their natural place, we find ourselves on the wrong side of scientific knowledge.

In education, we also have knowledge about many aspects of learning. And without getting into all them, the fact remains if we do not heed scientific knowledge we do so at the peril of our students. With our technological world the stakes for learning and achieving at the highest levels of competence has become a worldwide imperative. Therefore, the big heart needs science like never before.

But education deals with people. And as a science it fits in the category of "applied science." Working with people in applied fields like education (and medicine) comes with higher ideals. Namely, that of caring for our fellow persons.

We all want to live in a caring world. Caring covers the warmhearted, compassionate, thoughtful acts we do to improve our world. Not too long ago I visited a preschool classroom. I saw a scene unfold during snack time. The teacher passed out milk and straws to all the children. One little boy didn't get a straw for whatever reason. The teacher failed to see this boy desperately looking around for his straw. Tears started to well up in his eyes and he mumbled something quietly. Then a little girl sitting next to him gave up her straw and said, "You can have mine." I must admit that scene causes a little tear to well upon my eye. An act of kindness made all the world to the little boy who could now drink his milk with a straw.

With teachers, I always see similar caring acts on daily basis. Creating a list wouldn't do justice to the diversity of teacher kindnesses. But for all the caring teachers may do, hugging children and treating them with tenderness and attention will not teach them to read better. Science and the products of science reign supreme when it comes to knowing how to help students learn faster and more efficiently.

Compound #1 - Science + Caring = the big heart

Precision Teachers use the big heart because they have excellent scientific knowledge and embed it within a nurturing, considerate environment. Precision Teaching began in the 1960s and perhaps some of the cultural zeitgeist affected and shaped the practice of the first-generation Precision Teachers. I know from firsthand knowledge many of the practices from first gen PTers involved:

- Openness (e.g., "Chart Sharing" where people talk openly about data and celebrate student success)
- Fun and inclusion (e.g., making up songs about charting and singing them with the class)
- Student-centered compassion (e.g., "the learner knows best" which means understanding the data reflect the learners own unique responses to instruction)
- Gentleness and warmth (e.g., chart parenting - people spending a great deal of time teaching others how to apply Precision Teaching - for free and with nothing expected in return, aside from actually charting and doing PT)
- Deep concern (e.g., learning the science of measurement to ensure the most complete and accurate picture of the student's learning is evaluated).

As time moves forward the first generation PTers have instilled their values in the second and third generation Precision Teachers. The best of caring and science live on in each chart and with all the performers. The big heart epitomizes an important ideal for all of us to apply: Science + caring = the big heart

In a few places I tried to share information and knowledge about Precision Teaching. The concepts seem similar but have important differences. Precision Teaching provides a dynamic system that produces a significant amount of information. Outside of PT, its information and knowledge seem irrelevant to but a few. Yet many problems in psychology and education have a ready-made solution awaiting them in PT.

Entry: Information and knowledge

Francis Bacon said, "Knowledge is power." Has anyone ever said anything truer? Let's look at two concepts, information and knowledge. Information refers to ideas, operations, numbers, facts, groups of facts etc. (See: Kameenui & Simmons, 1990 *Designing instructional strategies: The prevention of academic learning problems*. They provide an excellent analysis of the differences between information and knowledge). From schools to the corporate world, when someone doesn't know something a teacher or corporate trainer provides instruction to help the person acquire the information.

If we examine all of the information a teacher hopes to impart, we can group it into a skill area. Skill areas might include reading, computer literacy, mathematics, leadership, or history. After taking in all of the information in a skill area knowledge emerges.

Knowledge, then, bestows one of the greatest powers a person, or people, can have. If a person can't read, they have very limited job options. Or if a person doesn't know about biology and germ theory, sicknesses and deaths will sharply rise. And if people don't know history, they have no way of learning from mistakes of the past (think about political scandals, wars, or people like Bernie Madoff who ran the most heinous Ponzi scheme ever).

PRCTA Cycle

PT offers a method for applying the science of measurement, data monitoring, and decision making to any targeted piece of information, skill, or behavior. The process vetted through research and many strikingly similar approaches incorporates the following method:

- *Pinpoint* behavior with the utmost precision

- *Record* pinpointed behavior with the most sensitive metrics available to humankind.

- *Change* the program or instruction if Standard Celeration Charted data and subsequent metrics indicate learning has not taken place or not occurred fast enough.

- *Try Again* if the learner has not made progress, use special procedures to help the learner succeed and reach their potential.

The above cycle yields precise, enlightening data (the kind of precise data that occurs in other natural science fields like Physics). When taken together as a body of information, the chart reader obtains hard won knowledge. PT helps generate such hallowed knowledge vital to performance change through metrics and analytics.

Metrics and Analytics

A metric refers to a standard of measurement. Metrics begin with counting, timing, or tracking data. The metric then sums the data or places it into a ratio. As an example, web metrics have a thing called a clickthrough rate or CTR. A CTR counts how many clicks a web ad receives and divides that number by how times a website shows the ad. Think about CTR the next time you click on an ad with your favorite celebrity drinking milk; big data has its eyes on you!

PT can handle any dimensional quantity but most practitioners focus on three big-time behavior metrics for directly measuring behavior: frequency or rate (the king of all metrics), duration, and latency.

As an example, a teacher might count the number of math problems answered in one minute. The count, say 18 correct digits written and 3 incorrect digits written over one minute, provides a frequency. The frequency comes to 18 correct and 3 incorrect digits written per minute.

If the teacher took each daily frequency and placed the data on a daily Standard Celeration Chart (SCC) a new metric emerges - celeration. Celeration tell us how fast the pinpointed behavior changes. In the figure below see how each frequency comes together to form a new metric.

Other metrics common to PT include the following: Accuracy pair, Accuracy ratio, Celeration, Bounce or Variability (Three total metrics - Total Bounce, Up Bounce, Down Bounce), Outliers, Improvement Index, Frequency Multipliers (aka Frequency jumps), Celeration Multipliers (aka Celeration turns), Bounce Change, and Improvement Index. change. All the previously mentioned metrics helps us see the targeted behavior in the right light. Namely, such precision metrics provide a level of information dramatically superior to typical nonstandard linear graphs and their reliance on using words instead of metrics (e.g., describing trend as moderately increasing, describing variability as highly variable). Would you rather have words or numbers to detail your data?

An analytic uses metrics to produce insight, prediction, and a deeper understanding of the data. In other words, the process of using data relationships to improve decision making and obtain new understanding of behavior falls in the domain of analytic.

An analytic in PT answers the questions, "Did an instructional program lead to better work productivity" or "What intervention program best helped my student learn to read?" Large scale analytics show what programs work best to rapidly teach student complex math and how many change interventions does it take to turn around struggling students.

Metrics and analytics lead to knowledge

The following graphic depicts a reality everyone must closely examine for developing true knowledge: the past, present, and future.

Figure 9: A street sign showing three time periods.

Time's arrow, or the arrow of time, came about in 1927 created by the British astronomer Arthur Eddington. Eddington put forth that everything travels one way. Therefore, making decisions directly relate to the quality of information one has. Precision metrics summarize, quantify, and qualify the past. The better the data, the more penetrating analysis one has in the present. And with such high value analytics at hand, projections and planning for the future promote sound judgement and quality navigation.

Poor decisions based on low resolution nonstandard linear graphs and crude metrics cost business organizations millions of dollars, waste time and resources, and result in the loss of a competitive advantage. When applied to learning at the school level, poor decisions can have truly devastating effects. Students do not learn to read well or at all, mathematics becomes a mystery instead of a joy, and science no longer inspires wonder but becomes a subject to avoid.

We decide and act. Basing judgements and analysis on high-quality data, as opposed to personal intuition and low-quality data, engenders superior decision making and performance excellence.

There exists a great deal of information on PT. The PRCTA cycle helps explain the measurement/decision making system. In this entry, I attempt to demonstrate one of the critical features of behavior charted on the SCC, celeration. So many metrics describe behavior change but most everyone first looks at the trend of data. On the SCC trend turns into celeration. Both the visualization and metric convey critically important information.

Entry: The power of celeration metrics

Many educational professionals have adopted a data-driven approach. "Data-driven" means what it implies, using data to inform instructional practices; not having Data from Star Trek drive you around like Miss Daisy. (*Author's note*: Some of my reference certainly seem dated and for people of a certain age. Forgive me younger readers for my dated references). Successful schools incorporate data-driven methods throughout their culture. Data-driven also requires practitioners engage in a cycle of assessment, analysis, and action. Does that cycle sound familiar?

Precision Teaching forms the ultimate system of assessment, analysis, and action with its PRCTA (Pinpoint-Record-Change-Try Again) cycle. A host of peer-reviewed articles and books have documented the success of the PRCTA cycle. While explaining the whole system necessitates an extensive treatise to fully explain the system, focusing in on core change measures does not.

The Secret Sauce

What distinguishes Precision Teaching from all other progress monitoring/data discovery programs lies in the Standard Celeration Chart (SCC) and its accompanying change measures (metrics). Unlike McDonald's and their Big Mac sauce and Coco-Cola's highly guarded formula for Coke, we will freely share with you the secret of success for best understanding behavioral change. Namely, the Standard Celeration Chart and its change measures. The infographic below shows three basic measures born from the SCC. Each measure does something you won't find anywhere else (especially with a nonstandard linear graph - that scoundrel of shifting axes will tell you something slightly different from other nonstandard linear graphs made by your friends and colleagues).

The Power of Basic Standard Celeration Measures

Do you use the best analytic tools for your decision making?
Check out the information for what you may have missed.

	What you see	What it tells you	Why you need it
Learning Speed	Celeration lines and standard weekly values	A celeration line with a value of **x2.0** shows a doubling of weekly performance or a 100% rate of growth	The speed of change applies directly to optimization (making the best use of performance data to optimize improvement). Low celeration of corrects demands a change to speed up learning
Learning Smoothness	Bounce envelope shown by top and bottom lines	A bounce envelope with a value of **x4.0** enfolds a data set and shows data varying or bouncing around up to 4 times	Bounce or variability shows the regularity and smoothness of learning. High bounce reveals erratic, sloppy, and unproductive performance change. Low or tight bounce demonstrates efficiency
Exceptionally Unusual Learning Instances	Outliers live outside of the bounce envelope	An outlier resting outside the bounce envelope by one course width (size of bounce envelope) has a probability of occurring **1 in a million**	Outliers are information gold mines. Positive outliers show conditions associated with terrific improvement. Negative outliers display grim circumstances adverse to healthy performance improvement

Other Advantages of Basic Standard Celeration Measures:

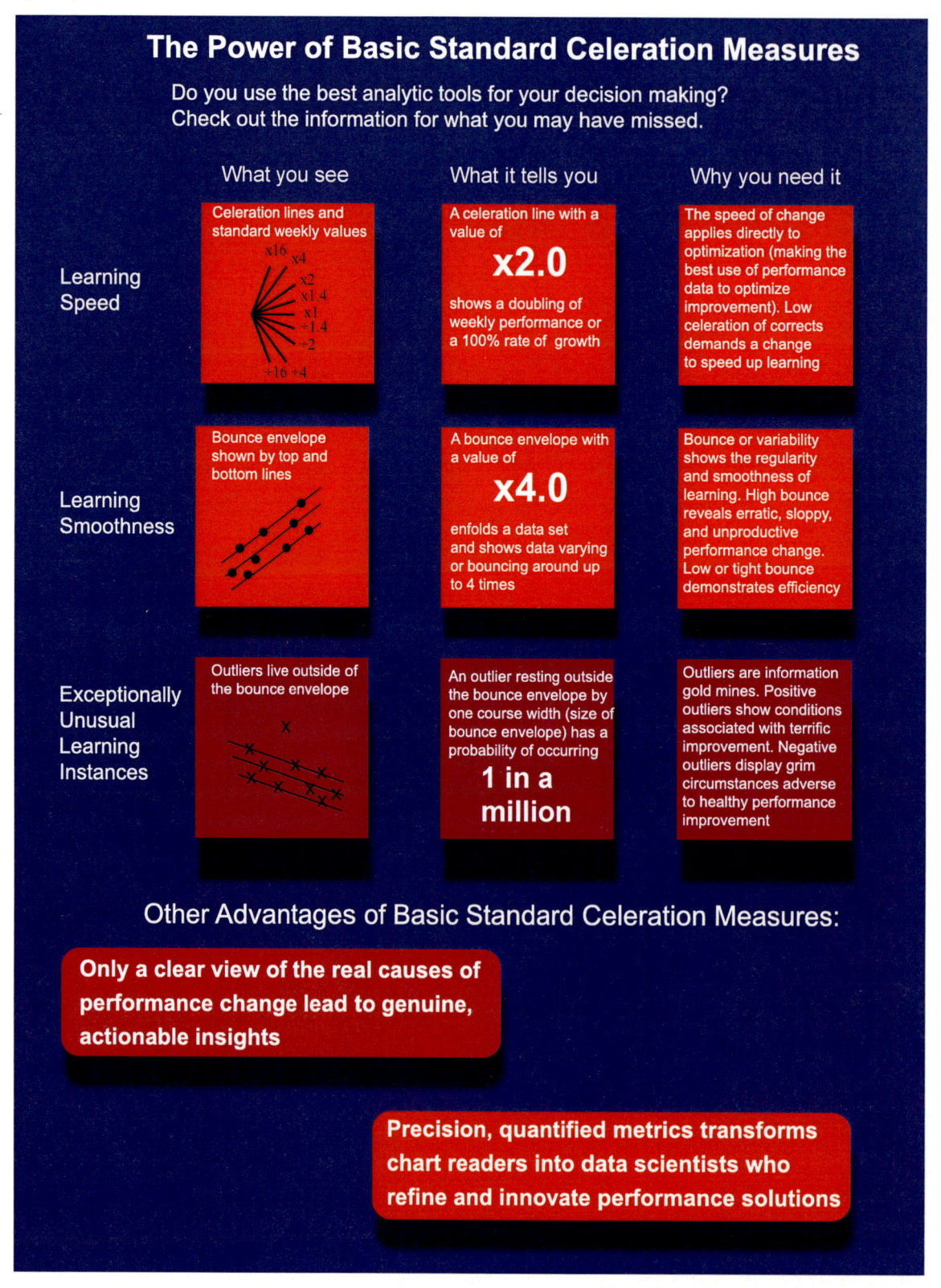

Only a clear view of the real causes of performance change lead to genuine, actionable insights

Precision, quantified metrics transforms chart readers into data scientists who refine and innovate performance solutions

Figure 10: An infographic showing three basic Standard Celeration change measures.

Simply put, better more informative metrics and a standard view of graphical features allow chart readers to fully see the data story. In future work we will closely look at each metric. Furthermore, we will examine how Standard Celeration Chart metrics explain individual performance data and help you make more informed decisions.

Learning speed

How fast does performance data change? A student learning how to tie her shoes could take one day, one week, one month, or one year. The speed of learning measured by celeration directly reflects upon the intervention used to teach shoe tying. Any change in a pinpoint comes from the power of an intervention (i.e., a special type of instruction, practice, or educational method). How useful/good would you rate an intervention that takes one week versus one month? Which interventions do students/clients/we deserve?

Measuring a performance for one day tells us how the person completed the task. But when we string those individual performances together across time, we call the change learning. Learning appears graphically on a daily SCC with a celeration line (Other SCCs exist so the following deals mainly with the daily SCC, not the weekly, monthly, or yearly). Each celeration line visually depicts the speed with its slope with a celeration value. The infographic in Figure 10 shows standard lines that have corresponding values, called a celeration fan. On the daily chart a x1.4 per week means the behavior grew or multiplied 1.4 times per week. A x1.4 per week value also means a 40% weekly change. A x2.0 per week represents a weekly doubling and a 100% growth rate.

On the other side of the celeration fan (Figure 1) behavior can decelerate and the value states how fast decay occurs. As an example, a ÷1.4 per week means a behavior divided 1.4 times, a 29% weekly change (e.g., starting a week at 14 under a ÷1.4 will yield 10 at the end of the week). Likewise, a ÷2.0 per week shows behavior halving each week, a 50% lessening.

How fast a behavior grows and how fast it decays allow us to optimize learning. Seeing a celeration line with a value of x1.1 per week would lead the chart reader to implement a change due to the slow 10% growth rate. Let's look at an example of a pinpoint (behavior) growing at the speed of a x1.1 per week. The Chart below shows the celeration of a student who started at 6 letter sounds correct per minute. Looking at the minimum aim for letter sounds, 100 letter sounds per minute, we see the typical paper daily SCC can't handle all the days necessary to show the change. All paper daily Standard Celeration Charts have 20 periods (140 days on the daily chart). I added 49 more days just to show how long it takes to get to the aim of 100, an astounding 27 weeks!

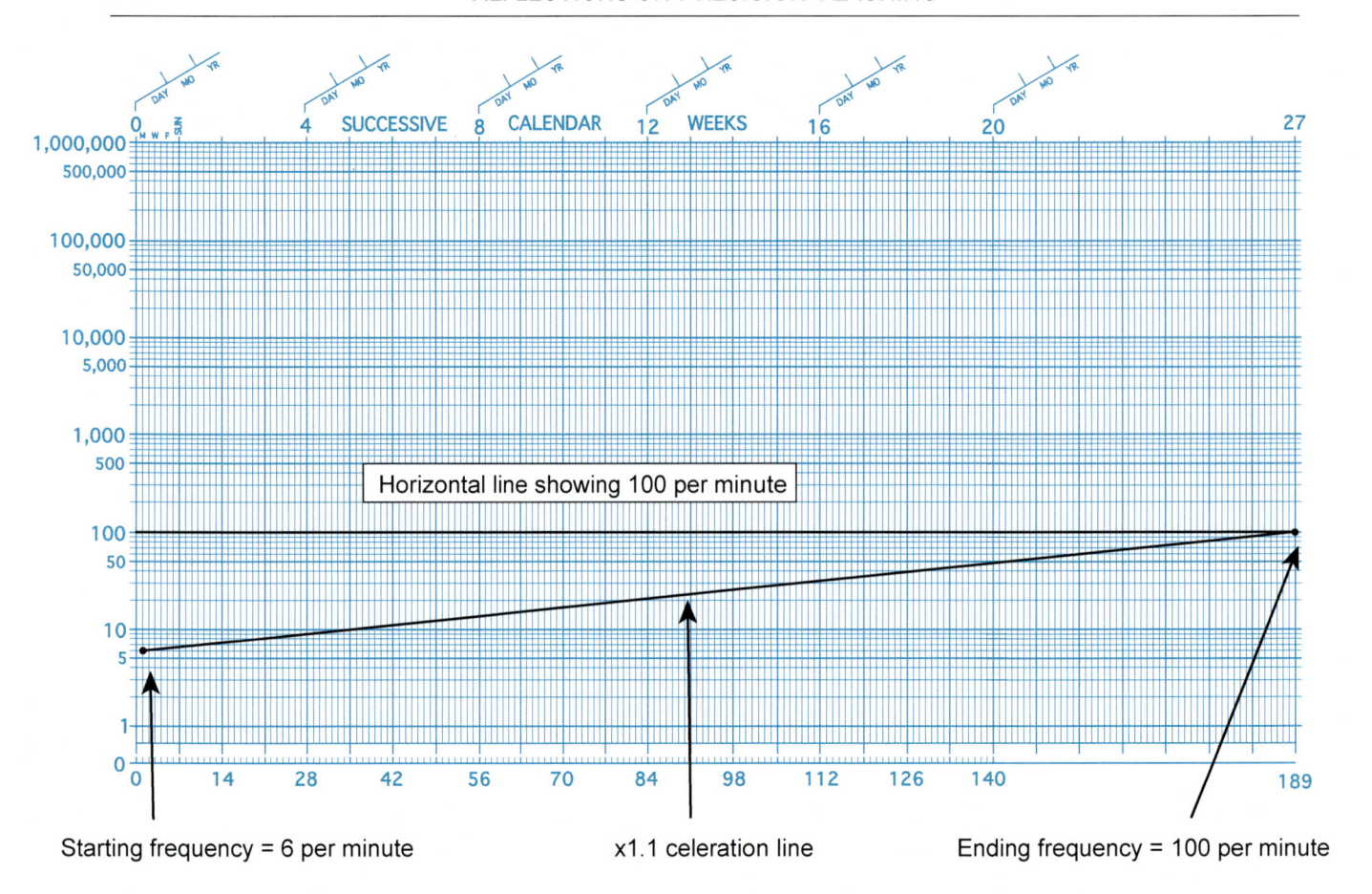

Figure 11: A Standard Celeration Chart showing the low growth rate of a x1.1 per week celeration.

Speed matters. We don't want any student having to suffer through almost 190 days of instruction or practice. Not using the SCC earns a decision maker (e.g., you, teacher, school psychologist) a stiff penalty - the lack of seeing the speed of learning with a celeration line and no quick, understandable metric.

The field of education has several happy declarations and platitudes that sound inspiring, "Aim for excellence," "We won't leave any child behind," and "Success, nothing less." No one argues with the sentiment of such statements. We all want to live in a better world and plant the seeds of a bright future for our children and the younger generation through educational distinction. For stellar outcomes, academic prosperity, and masterful skill development, however, we *must* pay heed to metrics like celeration. The faster someone learns, the more time they have to learn other skills. We should wield the power of celeration like a Jedi Knight's lightsaber helping others get better at whatever they endeavor to learn (*Author's note*: A Star Trek and a Star Wars reference in one blog. I must have had sci-fi on the brain).

Chapter 1 : On Precision Teaching

The more professionals I have spoken with, the more information I have gleaned from what people think about Precision Teaching (PT). I generally meet people who know little of PT. Or maybe the people heard about PT from a friend or colleague or had a lecture about the topic in graduate school. When I first entered the field, I felt great surprise by the lack of knowledge surrounding PT. As time moved forward, I learned that many people also have myths and misconceptions cultivated from poor source material. I tried to dispel just a few myths and misconceptions though many more exist than I could address in the following entry.

Entry: Precision Teaching: Misconceptions, Misunderstanding, and Myths

I began my college experience as a freshman psychology major at Youngstown State University (YSU) in 1985. As a first-year university student, I felt I really did not know much about anything. My goals centered on helping children and I had big dreams of becoming a clinical psychologist.

The psychology program at YSU had an eclectic mix of faculty. Some focused on social psychology and clinical psychology, while others taught general and educational psychology. The backgrounds of the faculty also varied with some espousing cognitive, Freudian, and behavioral theories.

In 1986 I had my date with destiny. A class called "Introduction to Learning" taught by Dr. Steve Graf, *Coach* as he would have people call him, would forever change my life. The class emphasized learning, but through the lens of something called "Precision Teaching."

Figure 12. A picture of Dr. Steve Graf and myself at my graduation party.

Now I find myself with a different job than my early dreams of clinical psychology. Yet, I did not lose my passion to help children and have channeled my efforts through research, outreach, and consultation. Thirty-four years later, I find myself following in the footsteps of my mentor, Steve Graf, still critically examining Precision Teaching and sharing its groundbreaking results with the world. Throughout my career, I have had interactions with thousands of students and professionals; occasionally, I hear a misconception of Precision Teaching.

I would like to share the top 3 PT Myths I have heard over the last 5 years:

Myth #1: Implementing Precision Teaching means 'going fast.'

"Going fast" stems from a concept called behavioral fluency. Behavioral fluency refers to the "fluid combination of accuracy plus speed that characterizes competent performance" (Binder, 1996, p. 164). As an example of behavioral fluency, a child would imitates one-step gross motor actions at 8 correct and 0 incorrect per 10 seconds. Another example involves a middle school keyboarder who types 60 words correct, with 0 incorrects, in 1 minute. In both instances, a person executes a behavior with high accuracy and speed. Research shows that when someone attains the level of behavioral fluency, several critical learning outcomes co-occur like retention, endurance, and maintenance (Johnson & Street, 2013).

Behavioral fluency has received a great deal of attention from behavior analysts because of its many positive effects. Recent studies demonstrate the wide-ranging effects such as nurses becoming fluent and generalizing their ability to perform venipuncture (Lydon et al., 2019), helping staff at residential homes learn and implement behavior support plans smoothly (Branch et al., 2018), and accurately, and enhancing 9 to 11-year-old students' grade level math (McTiernan et al., 2016).

"Going fast" or performing a behavior at a pace considered natural and automatic represents part of the behavioral fluency concept. However, Precision Teaching (PT) involves a four-step process: Pinpoint, Record, Change, Try Again. The following figure shows the four steps and briefly describes what each entails (Kubina, 2019).

Behavioral fluency emerged from the application of PT and its emphasis on the continuous recording of behavior in shorter time frames (e.g., one minute). Well over 40 peer-reviewed publications demonstrate the effects of behavioral fluency. Behavioral fluency studies began with PT and at times, some people equate the concept and measurement system as the same. Any behavior change agent can apply PT without invoking behavioral fluency or trying to get the client to "go fast."

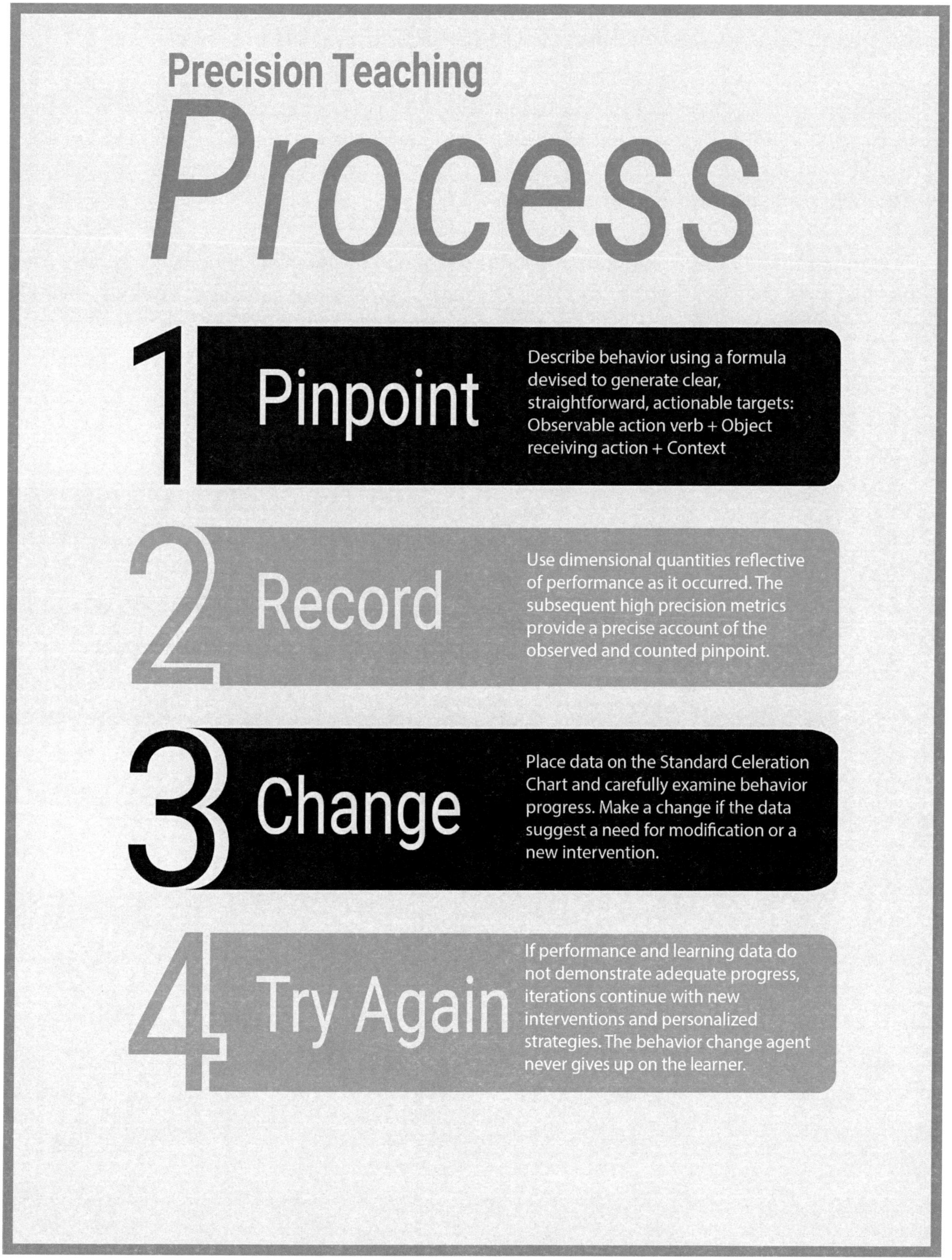

Precision Teaching Process

1. Pinpoint — Describe behavior using a formula devised to generate clear, straightforward, actionable targets: Observable action verb + Object receiving action + Context

2. Record — Use dimensional quantities reflective of performance as it occurred. The subsequent high precision metrics provide a precise account of the observed and counted pinpoint.

3. Change — Place data on the Standard Celeration Chart and carefully examine behavior progress. Make a change if the data suggest a need for modification or a new intervention.

4. Try Again — If performance and learning data do not demonstrate adequate progress, iterations continue with new interventions and personalized strategies. The behavior change agent never gives up on the learner.

Figure 13. The four-step process of Precision Teaching from The Precision Teaching Implementation Manual (2019).

Myth #2: I don't need to learn about Precision Teaching because the Behavior Analyst Certification Board (BACB) took it off the exam.

Certification occurs so that professionals possess a level of competency that allows them to effectively practice their craft in a targeted field. Just like Accountants can become Certified Public Accountants by passing the Uniform Certified Public Accountant Examination, behavior analysts can become Board Certified Behavior Analysts (or BCBAs) through supervised experience and passing an examination.

The establishment of the BACB marked a turning point for the field of behavior analysis, and the field grew at an astonishing rate. The Standard Celeration in Figure 3 displays the change of BCBA certifications depicting a 90 percent growth rate of BCBAs every five years! If the celeration remains true, by 2023 over 100,000 BCBAs will swell the ranks of certified behavior analysts.

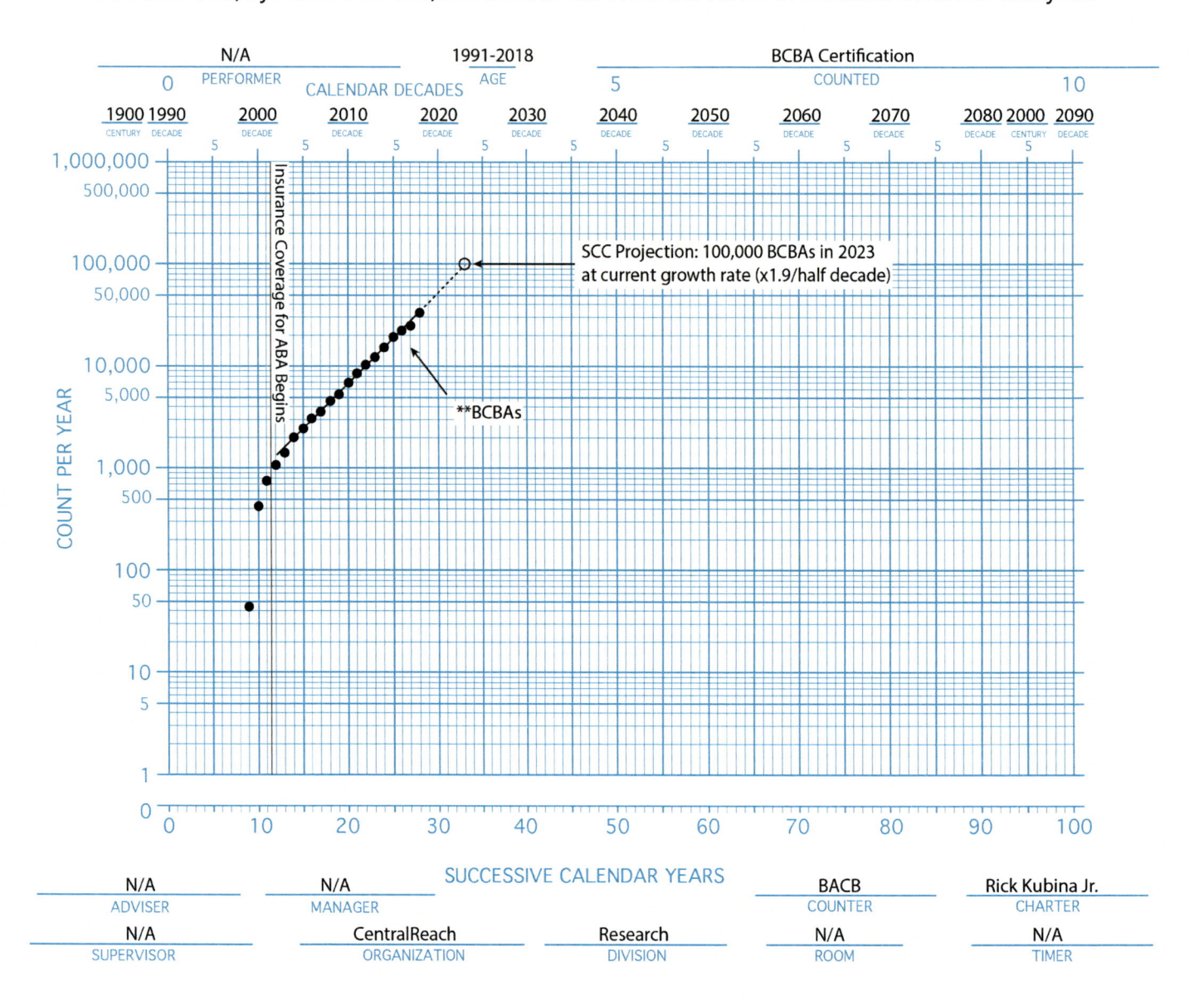

Figure 14. A Standard Celeration Chart showing BCBA growth across time.

According to its bylaws, the BACB "is to protect consumers of behavior analysis services worldwide by systematically establishing, promoting, and disseminating professional standards." Therefore, the board establishes what it deems appropriate for its standards. The standards then appear in a Task List forming the foundation of critical content and examinations of competence.

The process for determining what goes on the Task List and the exam involves a combination of surveying current practices from active professionals and a group of professionals from the BACB carefully examining survey data and discussing what best represents essential information for behavior analysts.

The fact that the BACB no longer requires knowledge of Precision Teaching or Standard Celeration Charting on an exam does not speak to the validity or utility of either. The decision reflects a continual revision process whereby the BACB continually strives to determine the best task list possible. Namely, one they feel best represents critical competencies for behavior analysts.

As a long time researcher and practitioner of behavior analysis and Precision Teaching, I believe all behavior analysts should incorporate PT in their practice because it provides a framework for labeling data; enhances data targets through "pinpoints;" creates a standard of universal measurement; quantifies data and research; and has countless other benefits for practitioners in the field.

The fact the BACB removed PT information in a behavioral competency examination should not dissuade exploration, study, and possible adoption of the system. Practicing and future behavior analysts should decide to learn about and use Precision Teaching based on the merits of what it has to offer in regarding to measurement and decision making.

Myth #3: Precision Teachers say everything needs to go on the Standard Celeration Chart.

Several aspects of Precision Teaching advance precision. Pinpointing behavior provides a precise label for behavioral detection and communication. Dimensional quantities like frequency (a.k.a. rate), duration, and latency each have precise values. But the Standard Celeration Chart (SCC) powers the Precision Teaching system and augments precision with a standard visual display.

Precision Teachers use the SCC with "time series data." Time series simply means data occurs through some unit of time. Hourly, daily, weekly, or monthly data fall under the domain of time series analyses. Some questions answered by time series analysis include: "Have my data changed across time? How much have my data changed across time? Will my data continue to change across time?"

The SCC has a ratio scale that best suits time series data. Ratio scales have the specific purpose of displaying how fast behavior changes and like the SCC, sometimes go by the moniker "rate of change chart."

Precision Teachers advocate the SCC when used with time series data. However, other visual displays can help behavior analysts and other behavior change agents understand their data.

Relational graphics. Relational graphics show a relation between two variables. For instance, a correlation between the number of cigarettes a person smokes each year and lung cancer. The data would not appear on a Standard Celeration Chart. Instead, the correlation would populate efficiently on a visual display that has dual equal interval vertical axes and a horizontal axis with time (Figure 4).

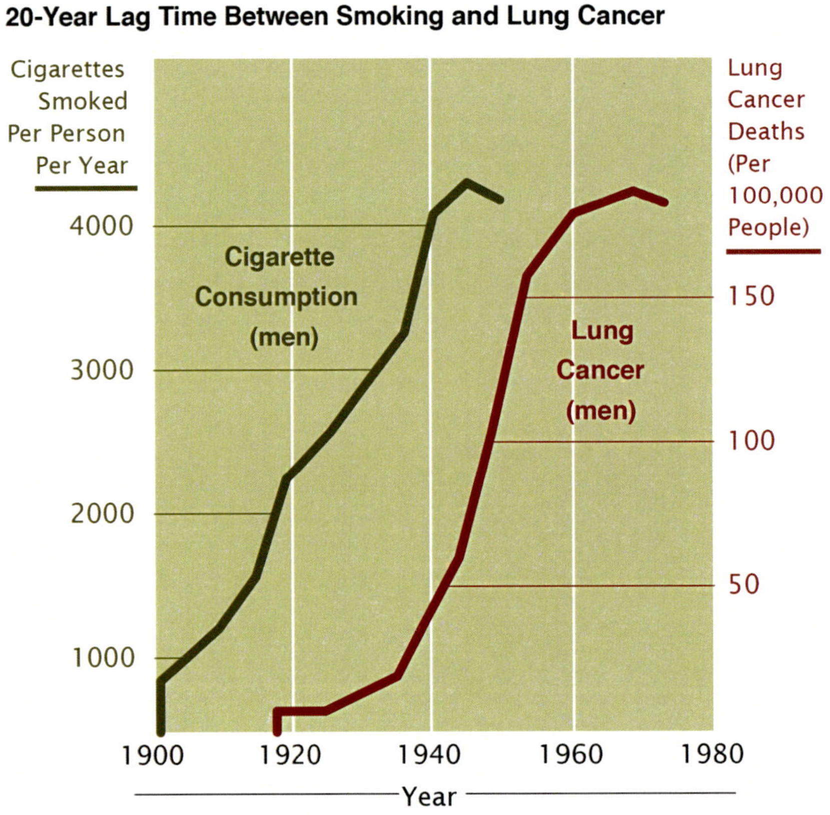

Figure 15. Correlating lung cancer and smoking. Source: https://commons.wikimedia.org/wiki/File:Cancer_smoking_lung_cancer_correlation_from_NIH.svg

A scatterplot offers a useful relational graphic used in behavior analysis. A 1985 article titled, "A scatter plot for identifying stimulus control of problem behavior" effectively demonstrated how a visual display other than time series graphics could provide insightful information.

The scatter plot shows the occurrence of "assaults" across hourly time intervals. If Joan had one assault in 30 minutes, the data appeared as a square. Instances of two or more assaults, a circle. The data in Figure 5 show a heavy concentration of assaults taking place between 1 and 4 PM on weekdays. It turned out the highest number of assaults tended to occur during prevocational and community living classes. The visual information allowed Touchette et al. to better configure Joan's schedule and modify activities, thereby reducing assaults and helping Joan live a better life.

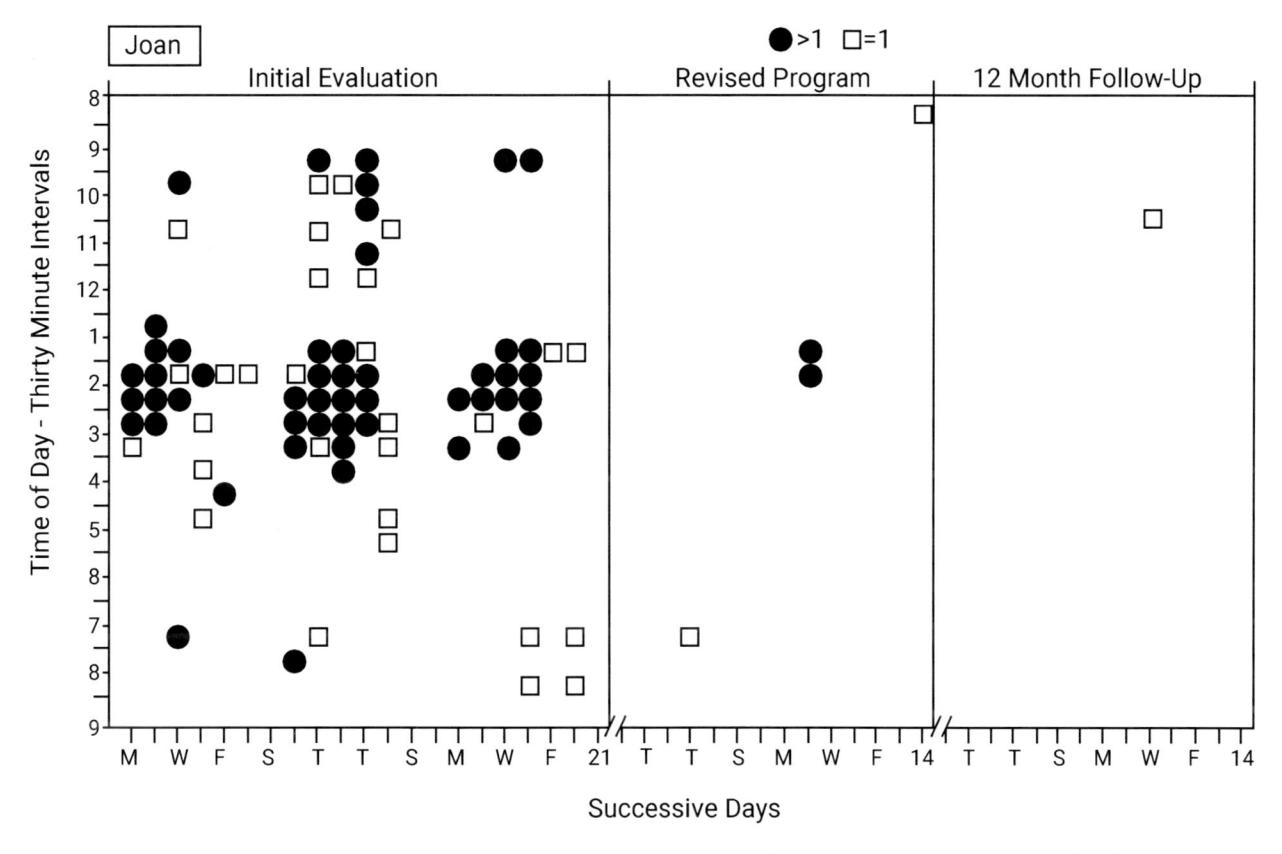

Figure 16. A scatter plot recreated from Touchette, MacDonald, and Langer (1985).

When it comes to behavior changing across time, Precision Teachers use a Standard Celeration Chart because of its physical properties that enhance data analysis and decision making.

Conclusion

Precision Teaching has a strong evidence base with thousands of articles in peer-reviewed journals in behavior analysis, education, social work, sports psychology, and a multitude of other fields. PT concerns itself with precision measurement, actionable insights, and high-quality decision making.

My hero worship comes through in this last entry. Ogden Lindsley founded Precision Teaching and had a profound influence on those who knew him. I count myself exceptionally fortunate to have had many conversations with Og. There are books and articles authored by Og, as well as videos of his presentations. If you get the chance, read and watch them!

Entry: An Ode to Og

Precision Teaching offers several important services for those interested in behavior change:

- A standard display system based on a ratio graph
- Standard, absolute, and universal measures of behaviors
- Reliable, straightforward, pinpoints of behavior (or behavioral targets)
- Easily understood metrics
- Insightful analytics
- A communication system that facilitates open collaboration and problem solving based on individualized data - visual patterns of data and quantified outcomes
- Rapid, meaningful, performance change

Where did Precision Teaching come from? From the brilliance of one person, the incomparable Ogden R. Lindsley (1922-2004) or Og as he would have you call him.

Figure 17: A picture of Og with my mentor Steve Graf and yours truly.

Before Og became the bow-tied, charming, creative force that brought the world amazing discoveries, he toiled away as an undergraduate and graduate student. But what a student! He earned his Bachelor's and Master's degree from Brown University and then went on to obtain his doctorate degree under none other than the most famous psychologist of the 20th century B. F. Skinner.

Ahead of his time

When people look back at visionaries and truly remarkable people, a common characteristic is they were ahead of their time. Og demonstrated again and again his technological contributions, ideas, practical applications, and foresight exceeded his contemporaries, and indeed the fields of psychology and education, by years. For instance, Og's Precision Teaching established daily progress monitoring. In Og's words:

"From our point of view, the only measure of a good teacher or good methods or good schools is the performance, the daily performance of the children. Most teachers will tell you, 'We do not have any measure of daily performance. It just would be impossible to measure the behavior of every child every day.' Many teachers have been told that the way to measure a child's performance is to give him a test. Tests are not measurements of child's performance —just a sample of it." (Lindsley, 1967, p. 9)

Og clearly differentiates testing from full-on performance monitoring. How do we know if behavior changes? Not from a test but from seeing the data each day. The variations (bounce) from one data point to the next in combination with a trend (celeration) paint the most accurate picture of behavior change we can hope to see.

Another forward-thinking concept from Og came to light when recognizing the dignity of all people. Back in the 1960s people with disabilities lived their lives in institutions or other sequestered places. But a label does not define a person. In 1964,

Og wrote a paper pointing out if students could not learn then we should seek answers by examining the instructional environment (Lindsley, 1964). Throughout the history of Precision Teaching, the emphasis on changing behavior or what teachers can do to arrange instructional conditions to help students succeed, not labels, became a central focus. In 1964 Og was taking on labels and helping people pay attention to the most important part of behavior change - behavior.

Og had many technological contributions. He gave the world the wrist counter, the "Lindsley operandum," (a way to keep track of human behavior from moment-to-moment), and of course the Standard Celeration Chart. I could go on demonstrating the professional impact Ogden Lindsley had on so many. But for me, I have tried to comport myself as scientist with respect to Og's model.

Chapter 2

The Keystone of Precision Teaching - Pinpointing

Having lived in Pennsylvania, The Keystone State, one inevitably learns about keystones. A keystone looks like a wedge-shaped stone found in the summit of an arch. Keystones hold all other stones in place. The influence and image of a keystone fittingly depicts the import of a pinpoint, the first step in the PT process. The pinpoint forms the central part of the PRCTA cycle. If one doesn't get the pinpoint right, the entire structure can collapse. This early entry shows my thinking of how pinpointing comprised such an important part of PT.

Entry: Classification in the sciences and PT

Classification is a practice to bring order to the vagaries of natural phenomena studied by all scientists. Classification refers to a process where an object, event, or idea is grouped and arranged by applying a logical or physical structure to the target phenomena. Well-known classifications occur throughout science. Examples include the famous Linnaean taxonomy, named after the Swedish botanist Carl Linnaeus, which classifies and orders life. Biological life, at its broadest, is the kingdom. Kingdoms are then further divided into phyla, phyla into classes, classes into orders, orders into families, families into genus, and genus into species. The broadly encompassing and unifying system for classification imposes order that is fundamental for scientists to study and understand life.

Other well-known classification systems are the geologic timescale with its classification and order of time and important events in the history of Earth (e.g., Cenozoic era > Paleogene period > Paleocene epoch). Astronomy has its stellar classification of stars, ordering stars according to their temperatures. And chemistry classifies elements with the periodic table originally developed by Dmitri Mendeleev. Classification systems move science forward. Precision Teaching is an applied science, like medicine, which also has different classification schemes aimed at bringing order to the main subject matter of education – behavior.

Precision Teaching orders behavior through different methods. First, all behavior we can name does not automatically qualify for analysis. Behavior must form a pinpoint which means it has to include a movement cycle (i.e., action verb + object like "turns page," "taps button" and "squeezes hand") and pass the "Deadman's test" or represent authentic, active behavior that a dead man could not perform (e.g., a deadman can sit in a chair - fail the deadman test, a dead man cannot chew food - pass the deadman test). Also, we need to add learning channels so we have a "pinpoint+" (said pinpoint plus).

Let's take the example of the verb "engages." When we say a student engages in reading, what does that really mean? Using movement cycles, a Precision Teaching might say, "reads word," "reads sentence," or "reads book." Both have an active present tense verb and an object that tells you how to count something. "Reads word" means a student reads one word and we record a count of one, assuming the student read it correctly. We could also count incorrects so if the student reads the word incorrectly we have a count of one incorrect.

The movement cycle (MC) changes into a pinpoint when we add context. "Reads word" + "from first grade must know list" is a pinpoint because we added context the MC. The context of a specified list, a first grade must know list, contextualizes the MC. Let's draw a comparison between "engages in reading" and "reads word from first grade must know list." Do you have any question, any question at all, what the second behavior looks like when compared to the first? "Engages in reading" seems like it communicates information but it does so only with each person making assumptions. In a science where precision reigns supreme, we never want to make assumptions when defining the object under observation. Ever!!! I added three exclamation marks just so you know I am serious.

Could you tell the difference between a sighted and visually impaired student with "engages in reading?" Precision Teaching further classifies behavior concerning learning channels. If we say child A used the learning channel set "see-say" and child B "touch-say" can you guess which one is sighted and which one is visually impaired? Of course you can. Can you guess which one is sighted and which one is visually impaired if I used "engages in reading" to describe both? Precision Teaching is an applied science that classifies behavior like no other field in education or psychology. Because Precision Teaching is meant to augment other curricula or learning methods, it can be used in conjunction with whatever the person is measuring. But it all starts with the pinpoint.

I found myself writing about pinpoints a great deal after publishing *The Precision Teaching Book* in 2012. And I learned that while the concepts seem straightforward, it requires skill to come up with good pinpoints. I also learned the tremendous value of pinpoints. Pinpoints transform the way anyone looks at behavior. Plus, pinpoints appreciably enhance the detection of behavior and the subsequent count. I wrote the present book in 2020 and what I have learned in the eight years since writing the following blog has convinced me that every professional who works with another person and desires behavior change, must use pinpoints as the first step.

Entry: Pinpoint detection

Let's say you want behavior change. The change can involve absolutely anything. Eating fewer double stuffed Oreo's, reducing/eliminating swearing when watching your sporting events in public, saying more kind words to children you babysit, or <insert your behavior change target>. Before we can address what you would do to make your goal a reality, an absolutely critical task to complete involves first identifying the behavior. Why so important?

Detecting pinpoints

In Precision Teaching the term pinpoint refers to a phrase describing directly observable, measurable, active behavior. The pinpoint means people will have great precision when detecting whether a behavior occurs or does not. If people can't figure out, or have poor reliability determining, the presence or absence of a pinpoint, a real problem exists. How can anyone ever conclude an intervention worked if problems exist with pinpoint detection? And for that matter, how do we know if a problem even exists if we have trouble identifying the targeted behavior (i.e., pinpoint) in the first place?

Figure 18 shows the possible outcomes of pinpoint detection (*Author's note*: Signal detection theory inspired the figure and I used their framework as a model to help me better understand behavioral detection). A pinpoint can occur, and an observer can detect it. In such a case we have proper discovery, a legitimate hit. Likewise, a pinpoint did not occur, and the observer did mark an occurrence.

	Record pinpoint occurred	Record pinpoint did not occur
Pinpoint occurred	**Proper detection of pinpoint's occurrence**	**False Negative**
Pinpoint did not occur	**False Positive**	**Proper detection of pinpoint's nonoccurrence**

Figure 18: A matrix showing the possible outcomes when detecting a pinpoint.

In both of the previous scenarios things can go wrong. If a pinpoint occurs and the observer does not record an instance of occurrence, then we have a false negative. False negatives lead an observer to conclude the presence of behavior where none exists. For instance, a teacher monitors a student's cheating behavior during class. The teacher perceives the presence of cheating when in fact it did not occur or appeared much less frequently than observed.

Another pinpoint detection problem takes place when an observer does not notice the presence of a pinpoint but the pinpoint did manifest itself. Using the previous example, a teacher does not observe a student cheating but the cheating pinpoint did take place. The teacher would falsely infer no problem with cheating exists when it does.

What to do

- The best way to address pinpoint (behavior) detection starts with generating a solid pinpoint. I showed a video of a young girl writing answers to basic multiplication problems (i.e., one digit times one digit) to students in a class I teach. Next, I asked them to tell me what they saw. The pinpoint list they generated follows below:
- A student is writing answers to math problems.
- She answers problems by writing the answer with a marker.
- Writing answers for multiplication probes.
- Using a writing device to produce answers to a non-completed math equations.
- Writing answers.
- Writing math facts
- Answering multiplication problems with a marker.
- Student will answer math fact problems, specifically multiplication, when seeing the problem.
- Determining the correct answer to simple multiplication problems.
- Written answers for written math stimuli.
- Multiplying digits and writing the answer to the problem.
- Applying the multiplication algorithm to multiplication facts.

As you can see from the list, a great deal of variability exists in the labels of the behavior. And with great variability comes potential for great problems discerning the presence or absence of behavior. Which label should we pick?

Pinpoint+

A supreme standard of behavior classification exists in Precision Teaching. Namely, a pinpoint captures the essence of behavior. In the science of behavior, behavior has a definition that revolves around movement. The founder of the science behavior, B. F. Skinner used the following classic definition for behavior: "Behavior is what an organism is doing; or more accurately what it is observed by another organism to be doing" (Skinner, 1938, p. 6). Contemporary definitions of behavior follow suit: "Behavior is anything an animal (including the human animal) does" (Malott & Shane, 2014, p. 6). "Behavior is that portion of an organism's interaction with its environment that involves movement of some part of the organism" (Johnston & Pennypacker, 2009, p. 31). Therefore, good comments of behavioral detection will involve movement.

In Precision Teaching, the term movement cycle refers to a short phrase containing a directly observable action and an object receiving the action. Examples include hits ball, slaps hand, bites food, waves hand, and writes word. All the previous movement cycles directly, and unambiguously, lead to sharp detection of behavior.

When we add context to a movement cycle, we have just produced a pinpoint. Context means the circumstances that form the setting for the behavior. In the previous movement cycles, see how adding context makes them even more conspicuously evident:

- Hits ball with a bat
- Slaps hand when giving a high five
- Bites food during lunch
- Waves hand when saying goodbye
- Writes word in notebook

A third element to describe behavior appears in the form of a learning channel. A learning channel refers to the linked unit of a sensory *In* (any of the senses - smell, taste, see etc.) and a behavioral *Out* involved in performing a behavior. For instance, seeing a math problem and writing answers would form a see-write learning channel set. Hearing a song playing on the radio and singing along with it falls under the hear-say learning channel set.

Behavior is fluid and complex. By using a pinpoint plus a learning channel, detecting behavior significantly improves. And when behavior detection improves, the data gain reliability and foster insight.

My thoughts on pinpointing grew across the years and with practice I became skilled at creating pinpoints. Still, that didn't mean I wouldn't come across behaviors that vexed me. And full disclosure, I still have some behaviors that await solid pinpoint designations. But I have the privilege of working with many good colleagues and they figure things out where I have not. The beauty of science! In this entry I discuss pinpoints and share a breakthrough some colleagues made as a result of learning pinpoints.

Entry: Agents of precision

Creating good pinpoints can sometimes make for a daunting task. Pinpointing might take time, involve checking the dictionary, and sometimes having a healthy debate with colleagues about word choices. But everyone can learn the steps for creating a good pinpoint:

1. Action verb (make it present tense by adding an "s")
2. Object that receives the action of the verb
3. Context of action + object

Check out the picture sequence in Figure 19 and think about how you would label the behavior.

Figure 19. A behavior in need of a pinpoint

I like to ask people what they see and how would they label the behavior. The answers vary considerably similarly to when I have done so in the past:

- Throwing a paper airplane
- Grasping a paper airplane and throwing it
- Launching a paper plane
- He is throwing an object

All those previous answers do describe behavior. But how do we count "Throwing a paper airplane?" When does the behavior start and stop with the verb "throwing?" Grasping a paper airplane and throwing it" actually involves counting two behaviors: grasping and throwing. And can a person throw a paper airplane without grasping it? Therefore, we don't really need the added baggage of a second behavior.

What about "launching a paper plane?" The second definition of launch reads "start or set in motion." That might work but the verb launch lacks precision. How exactly did the person launch the plane? Launching does not necessarily mean throwing. And the last classification, "he is throwing an object" has two problems. First, the statement describes the person actively behaving, not the best label for determining when the behavior ends. Second, the object receiving the action, "object," does not have the same precision as "paper airplane." People can easily identify "paper airplane" over the more general term "object."

Pinpointing behavior

Let's plug in the behavior to our pinpointing formula.

1. Action verb (make it present tense by adding an "s") - Throws

Definition of "throw" works well: propel (something) with force through the air by a movement of the arm and hand

2. Object that receives the action of the verb - Paper airplane

Paper airplane serves our purpose best because it receives the action of throw. We make it singular because a count of one equals "throws airplane." If we said "throws airplanes" we have a much harder time counting one instance of the behavior.

3. Context of action + object - In hallway

Looking at Figure 19, we see the context for our count. If we wanted to count "throws airplane" somewhere else, like "during class," we could. The context alters our evaluation of the pinpoint. We would consider "throws paper airplane in the hallway" a leisure skill and consider it an acceleration target. "Throws paper airplane during class" makes for a deceleration target, something we wouldn't like to see. Our final pinpoint then becomes "throws paper airplane in the hallway." Success!

Challenging pinpoints

The more a person pinpoints the greater likelihood of running into a difficult behavior. One of the more challenging pinpoints I have encountered came in the form of "eye contact." People have difficulty counting eye contact because it forms a noun and does not contain movement. In other words, it does not pass the "dead man's test."

Some teachers have used the pinpoint "moves eyes toward speaker." A dead man cannot move his eyes towards a speaker. But the "moves eyes" pinpoint better captures instances where someone looks at another. Let's say I called your name. We could count "moves eyes toward speaker." But eye contact lasts longer than a glance. Teachers oftentimes want a sustained gaze. What pinpoint to use?

Recently I had visitors from across the pond. Two fellow colleagues, Jen Shahin and Erin Baker, worked with us on the challenge of coming up with a pinpoint for eye contact. Success!

Both Jen and Erin puzzled through many different action verbs and objects receiving the action. They came up with "aims gaze at speaker for 3 seconds." An absolutely wonderful pinpoint that passes the dead man's test and makes for an easily countable behavior.

I always take great joy in finally cracking the nut of a tough pinpoint. Perhaps that sounds nerdish, but I live in the world of behavior change. Coming up with an easy to count pinpoint demands careful work. Agents of precision will always endeavor to create pinpoints with the most clear, observable action verbs, accurately named objects, and unambiguous contexts.

Part of the versatility PT enjoys stems from its purpose, an elegant measurement and decision making system. Practitioners and self-improvement enthusiasts can use any method or curriculum with PT. I tend to practice in the field of behavior analysis. Thus, many different curricula benefit from the addition of PT. Not too long ago, some colleagues asked me how a popular curriculum like PEAK Relational Training System would benefit from PT. The entire PT answer would take quite a while to write. But I did tackle one small part of PT, pinpointing, and demonstrated how it could impact PEAK.

Entry: Pinpointing and PEAK

The grand science of behavior, behavior analysis, has made remarkable strides helping people live better lives. The founder of contemporary behavior analysis, B. F. Skinner, often wrote how science can improve human behavior and society at large. For example, one of his papers described problems with the American educational system and potential solutions. "We could solve our major problems in education if students learned more during each day in school. That does not mean a longer day or year or more homework. It simply means using time more efficiently" (Skinner, 1984, p. 950). Behavior analysis has demonstrated through applied experimental research how it can measurably enhance educational performance and learning.

Students with Disabilities on the Rise

Many demographic studies show certain disabilities categories have increased dramatically over the years. None has shown such rapid growth as students with autism spectrum disorders (ASD). The most recent prevalence data from the Centers for Disease Control and Prevention place autism as occurring in 1 out of 59 children, up 15% from 2014.

Children with ASD present a number of behavior, social, and cognitive challenges. And unfortunately, a recent systematic review and meta-analysis of the long-term overall outcome of ASD in adolescence and adulthood presented disappointing results (Steinhausen, Jensen, & Lauritsen, 2016). Only 19.7% of the participants in the studies had a good outcome, with "Normal or near-normal social life and functioning satisfactorily at school or work." The vast majority (i.e., 47.7%) of participants had poor ("Severely handicapped, but some potential for social progress") or very poor outcomes ("Unable to lead any kind of independent existence").

Applied behavior analysis has answered the call for producing superior outcomes for students with autism. Not only does the science of behavior boast many experimental studies that show how to change behavior and effect learning, but many more programs and curricula have started to come to market. The PEAK Relational Training System (or PEAK) represents one very popular and promising curriculum available to behavior analysts.

PEAK

PEAK has received increasing attention in the behavior analytic research and practice as a comprehensive treatment model for improving language skills and "learning to learn." PEAK offers four modules (i.e., Direct Training, Generalization, Equivalence, and Transformation) with each containing a series of programs. PEAK also boasts several established and emerging research studies demonstrating efficacy.

A program like PEAK has many strengths and great versatility. PEAK offers an assessment, a curriculum (i.e., four modules or books), data recording sheets, instructions for error corrections, and goal criteria for individual programs. However, PEAK users could benefit from a measurement system such as Precision Teaching.

Precision Teaching has four steps: Pinpoint, Record, Change, and Try Again. Each step has a specific purpose. Namely, elevating the detection (Pinpoint), counting, (Record), decision making (Change), and recursive problem solving (Try Again). All the steps come together and present critical information in the form of carefully measured behavioral data. The data then allow the behavior analyst to understand progress in a very precise manner.

Pinpointing has specific appeal to behavior analysts as a way to establish a highly detectable, countable, and actionable behavioral target. The following section describes how to create a pinpoint for PEAK. For further reading on pinpoints, read our blogs here or here.

Creating a Pinpoint+

The specific program "Hands Still" will serve as an example of how pinpointing can augment PEAK. Hands Still (PEAK Direct Training Module 1B) specifies its goal as a situation where a person (e.g., behavior analyst, teacher, parent) asks another person (e.g., child, student) to keep their hands still. The program sheet describes the materials needed for the teaching interaction, instructions for the caregiver or teacher, and typical stimuli helpful for the session.

Pinpointing derives its form from the goal, materials, or stimuli suggested for the program, and the directions for the person who will implement Hands Still. The working model for the pinpoints+ specifies the following information necessary for translation.

- Action verb (what will the child do)
- Objection receiving the action (what object will receive the action or active verb)
- Context (details further contextualizing the movement cycle)
- Learning channel (the sensory Inputs and the physical Outputs specifying stimulus control)

    a. What action verb would capture Hands Still? Having one's hands still suggests the absence of behavior. Pinpointing reminds the creator to view all behavior as active and seek out an active verb. "Places" offers a good choice for an action verb. Places means to "put in a particular position."

Places what? The action verb needs an object. Place "hands" completes the movement cycle. At its core, the movement cycle "places hands" allows a behavior analyst to count the behavior with precision. "Places hands" has a clear beginning, the child placing their hands, and an equally obvious ending, the child moving their hands from the placed position.

Adding context to "places hands" further enhances the countability of the targeted behavior. As indicated earlier, context can cover where the behavior occurs, when it occurs, with whom it occurs, or with what it occurs with.

The instructions in Hands Still specify that the behavior analyst will tell the child "Hands still." Then the child must emit the behavior. Therefore, places hands could become:

- Places hands on table when told to do so (where and when)
- Places hands in lap when told to do so (where and when)
- Places hands in pocket when told to do so (where and when)With added context, the behavior analysts and RBTs using PEAK can count the behavior with high precision. Furthermore, the behavior analysts can accurately deliver reinforcement for a specific topography. Targeting "places hands on table" makes clear what to reinforce and what to expect will happen more often in the future. "Places hands in pocket" or "places hand

in lap" did not receive reinforcement and therefore will not come under control of the verbal stimulus "hands still" unless specifically singled out.

Also, the child just placing their hands on the table without the instruction from the behavior analyst or RBT would not receive reinforcement. The selected context helps clarify when the reinforcement event will happen.

The plus (+) in the pinpoint+ refers to the learning channel: a pinpoint plus a learning channel, thus the pinpoint+. The Sensory In involved with the verbal stimulus "Hands still" would come from the following options: Free, touch, taste, sniff, see, hear, feel. With the behavior analyst saying "Hands still," the child would "hear" the command.

The Out or Output classifying the movement cycle component for the pinpoint+ could fall under any of the following: Aim, do, draw, emote, mark, match, say, select, tap, free, write. "Places hands" best fits the "do" output. "Do" classifies bodily movements as "do" something.

"Hear-do" forms the input-output for stimuli and behavioral classification. A child who learns something under the hear-do learning channel set has a very specific behavior established. The more discrepant the channel set from the original, the less likely the behavior will occur. For instance, see-do means the child saw a visual stimulus and did something (e.g., saw another child blow bubbles with their straw and imitated the behavior, see-do). A child who heard a verbal stimulus and did something would not likely perform a see-do classified behavior due to the specificity of reinforcement. As an example, a child learns one-step motor imitation, PEAK Direct Training Module 4B. The pinpoint+ for the behavior: See-do imitates one step action as demonstrated by teacher. Subsequently telling the child to perform the behavior (e.g., "Touch your arm") operates under different learning channels: Hear-do touches arm when told by teacher. Bringing it all together, a pinpoint+ for Hands Still could appear as "Hear-do places hand on table when told to do so."

The clarity, exactitude, and precision of using a pinpoint+ for the "Hands Still" program confer significant advantages. Detecting and counting the behavior occur with higher accuracy due to the sharpness of the target. And the focus of reinforcement also improves as the pinpoint+ distinctly communicates to the behavior analyst when to apply the reinforcing event.

PEAK users would also experience the value of enhanced tracking and problem solving. Enhanced tracking occurs because each pinpoint+ spells out exactly what the child has learned. Learning to place hands on a table when told to do so means the child has learned one behavior successfully. Then, learning to place hands in pocket might not only happen faster but would represent a second behavior brought under stimulus control.

Conclusion

Precision Teaching has four steps, all of which would help PEAK users precisely measure performance and learning changes for selected programs. Pinpoints advance superior outcomes in several ways. Perhaps most important, behavior analysts have a precision target advancing behavioral detection and communication among team members. PEAK presents a compelling option for improving language and other important skills for learning, problem solving, and communication. The addition of pinpointing and Precision Teaching may foster even greater applied and experimental discoveries.

Chapter 3

Counting Behavior

Another process essential to PT involves counting. One might think such a simple topic would not warrant extensive deliberation. But in education and psychology some practitioners and researchers apply poor measurement practices. The previous chapter discussed how pinpoints bring clarity to behavioral detection. So too does the choice of observation and subsequent unit for counting the behavior. The following chapter contains only three entries, but each touches upon a worthy aspect of counting. The next entry features one of my first attempts to showcase the importance of counts and their units.

Entry: Counting and timing behavior

In the applied science we call medicine, a patient visits a doctor due to some condition adversely affecting health. The applied medical model involves the doctor obtaining information to identify the problem (e.g., virus, unregulated cell growth, parasites, deteriorating muscle). After determining the cause of the health condition, the doctor prescribes an intervention aimed at curing or fixing the problem.

The doctor exercises considerable discretion specifying the amount of an intervention. If the doctor recommended radiation therapy to kill cancer cells, the dosage is measured in rads or grays, both units describing the absorbed radiation dose. When a doctor suggests using pharmaceuticals, dosages are mainly calculated with the metric system such as liters and grams. Indeed, accurately calculating doses is a key portion for many health care workers such as the National Council Licensure Examination for Registered Nurses. Dosages within medicine are scrutinized so intensely due to the outcomes. Too little of a dosage and the intervention fails. Too much of a dosage and the patient suffers harmful effects. Just the right amount of the dose, called a therapeutic or curative dose, results in highest probability of overcoming the original problem.

As an applied science, education (as a whole) missed the mark when it comes to applying precision in the process of describing the presenting problem, determining proper "dosages" or the amount of an intervention to implement, and evaluating subsequent intervention effects on learner behavior. Descriptions used to first identify the problem range from unobservable or ambiguous non-behaviors to real, measurable behaviors. Dosage, or the amount of how much of an intervention a learner should receive is manifested through indirect measures like converted scores or with dimensionless units like percentage. The resulting effects on behavior make it exceptionally difficult to confidently understand what exactly changed and how well the learner profited from the intervention. Through the act of counting behaviors in time, the field of education has at its disposal a standard, absolute, universal unit of measurement (i.e., frequency) that enables education to function as other applied sciences like medicine, which employ sensitive measures in treatment and evaluation of their subject matter. The nucleus of a science of education is frequency, found by counting and timing behavior.

Counting behaviors in a time interval provides a world class dimensional quantity called frequency. All behaviors have a frequency. Therefore, frequency can serve people interested in behavior change better than almost any measure. Unfortunately in education very few people use frequency and instead use dimensionless quantities such as percent to monitor behavior across time. But when frequencies move, they transform into another useful behavioral unit, celeration. Readers may detect my affinity with frequency in the next entry.

Entry: Moving frequencies

Do you realize that every person you ever met does things measured by frequency? In fact, every person that has ever lived and ever will walk planet Earth will behave, act, and move measured by frequency. Frequency forms a fundamental dimension of all behavior. And as universal measure of behavior, we can value frequency as one of our most precious assets.

Frequency, as used in the natural sciences, means count over time or count/time. Every behavior we value or despise has a frequency. Take playing the piano for example. A novice trying to improve piano playing has a moderate frequency of incorrect keys tapped and the low frequency of correct keys tapped. Improvement comes with practice. Practice, well good practice, means the frequencies move in desired directions: the frequency of incorrect keys tapped decelerates while the frequency of correct keys tapped accelerates.

What about social behaviors? When we have conversations occasionally another person interrupts us. Conversational interruptions occur at a frequency. The frequency of 1 to 2 interruptions per five-minute conversation will seem normal and bother the speaker actively involved in a discussion. However, 3 to 5 interruptions per five-minute conversation breaks the "acceptable threshold" and moves into mildly to moderately annoying territory. A person with a frequency of 6 to 10 interruptions per five-minute conversation would appear as discourteous; we will avoid or limit our conversations with such a serial interrupter.

In the discipline of education and psychology, frequencies for different behaviors need established. Then when a teacher or psychologist wishes to grow or decay certain behaviors, different interventions are applied to move the behavioral frequencies in the desired directions. Everything we consider good-bad, normal-abnormal, correct-incorrect has a frequency.

If we look at our laws and what we consider crime, almost any breach of the law, a frequency of 1 in a lifetime, can be considered bad. Once we have a frequency determined for a behavior, the trick is to figure out how to move those frequencies upward (i.e. acceleration), downward (i.e. deceleration), or in some cases, maintain the present level of frequencies.

Frequency offers the most versatile and sensitive of measures. When we place it on a ratio chart, like a Standard Celeration Chart, we have a visual record of a person's behavior. As we apply different interventions, the subsequent frequencies will move upward, downward, or maintain (the direction is called celeration – steeper the slope the faster the rate of change) and vary between one another (we call the varying movement bounce – the higher bounce the more irregular and less control exerted on the behavior).

Look at the following segment of frequencies taken from a student teacher working with kindergartener building frequency (practicing) with letter sounds. What do you notice about the direction (celeration) of corrects and incorrects? What other critical information is revealed by an intensive focus on frequency?

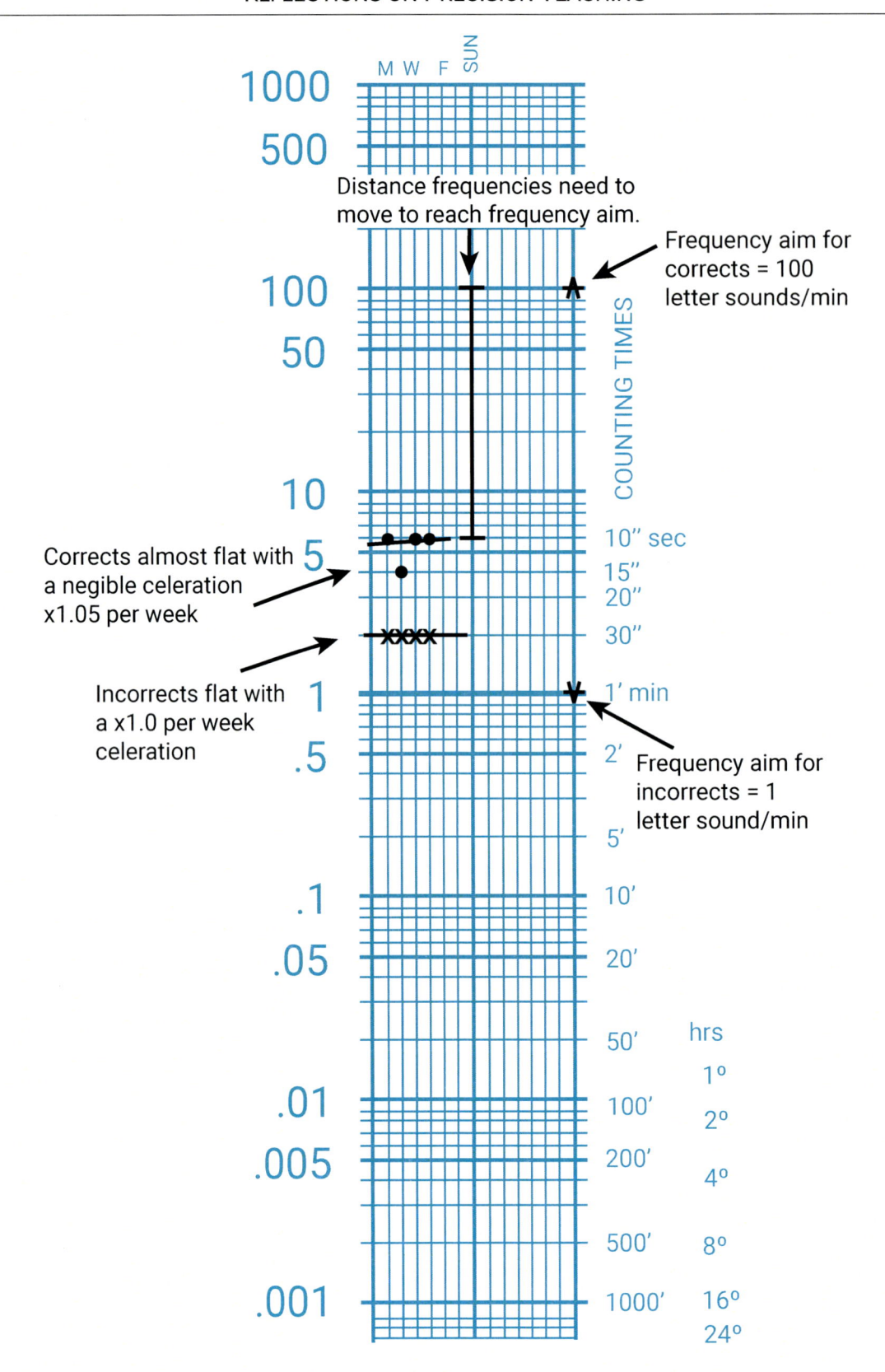

Figure 20. An SCC segment showing reading frequencies across time.

Corrects grow at a painfully slow rate, x1.05 per week. Anything x1.0 stays the same, so x1.05 is insignificant growth. For incorrects, the student continues to make 2 incorrects per

54 | RICK KUBINA

minute on each of the four different assessments. Look at how far the student must move their frequencies to hit the aim for corrects. They have a lot of work ahead of them; we know this because the distance from the goal (100 correct per minute) and present frequency of 6 immediately jump out at us visually. If we used percent correct, we would not have such an eye-opening experience.

Frequencies, strung together, tell us that the student needs help with an intervention. Their corrects have not grown fast enough and her incorrects remain stable at 2 per minute. Each frequency gives us information on the day's performance. But examining frequencies (or performances) across time they tells us about learning. Precision Teachers use the word celeration to quantify learning; no one else has it!

Frequencies do not move on their own, that is why we have the institution of education. A teacher must implement some type of intervention so the performance frequencies will grow or decay depending on the goal of the program. With a science-based approach to education, we have a literature base that demonstrates what works and what type of learner would benefit from a particular invention. Solid instructional programs will work for the vast majority of learners, thus the emphasis on discovering interventions through a systematic, scientific approach. In the end, each learner is an individual. Discovering what interventions best allow each student to reach their potential are truly moving frequencies.

Precision Teaching has its own set of special jargon just like any other science. The concepts that underlie the terms have both technical and practical significance. The "record ceiling" represent one such important term. A record ceiling displays the upper limit or ceiling one may have when counting a behavior. Any record ceiling will immediately show the chart viewer the restriction. In some cases, the situation dictates placing a ceiling on counting. Other times people may choose to impose ceiling for convenience. No matter the reason the record ceiling shows everyone the counting restriction.

Entry: The 'record ceiling'

In 1981 an important paper appeared in *The Behavior Analyst* titled: Current measurement in applied behavior analysis. The paper reviewed the practice of using discontinuous time-based measures to count and record behavior.

Interval recording represents a prime example of a discontinuous time-based method for behavioral observation. Let's take the example of "momentary time sampling" or MTS. To use MTS, an observer looks to see if the behavior occurs during a specified moment or a pre-selected interval of time (Cooper, Heron & Heward, 2020). Thus the name, momentary time sample.

Some people choose to use interval recording methods like MTS to count behavior. Making the decision to measure only a sample of the full range of behavior creates an artificial ceiling. In Precision Teaching we call all practices in which we have an upper limit on what we can record a "record ceiling."

The term record ceiling functionally defines its use. Namely, making a record of an observation that has a ceiling or the greatest possible count. Thus, on the Standard Celeration Chart the record ceiling tells chart readers for the particular data point a ceiling occurred with the number of behavioral records observed.

On the chart cross section we can now see the two frequencies and the destination of the record ceiling. The record ceiling draws out attention to something different about the observation. By displaying the record ceiling chart readers have additional information guiding their analysis. The data can only go as high as the record ceiling.

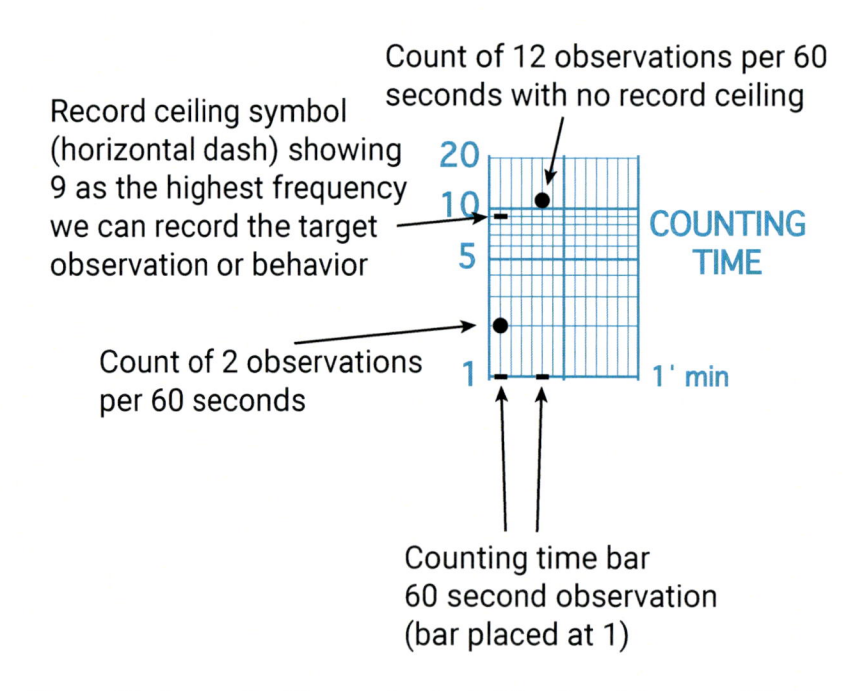

Figure 21. A record ceiling contrasted with a time (aka record floor).

Record ceilings can arise from places other than discontinuous time measures. For example, teachers may decide to provide a limited set of response items to a student. Let's say the teacher gave a spelling test that had 10 spelling words. Ten serves as the maximal value.

Another symbol used in Precision Teaching looks like the record ceiling but serves a different purpose. The time bar, a dash, looks the same as a record ceiling. However, the time bar typically shows up below the data unless the count comes to 1 (data would rest on the time) or 0 (data would appear below the time bar at a divide by 2 distance). Record ceilings, like the time bar, give the chart reader more information. And any extra details help the performer and educational team fully analyze the data and facilitate decision making.

Counting behavior dictates how one might represent the behavior in terms of a unit. Counting all observed behavior in an interval of time forms frequency or rate. But many people outside of Precision Teaching just take the count and transform it to a percent which loses any dimensions of the count, such as time (an essential dimension in frequency). But some people have gone way overboard and vilify all instances of percent. Percent certainly has limitations and in some instances, forms a poor choice to represent counts of behavior. However, situations exist in which percent may serve a useful purpose.

Entry: Stop hating on percent

I recently attended a conference where one of the speakers apologized for sharing a finding with percent. I will admit that apology surprised me.

Should we apologize for the product generated by multiplication? Do we say "sorry" when we receive the quotient from a division problem? It seems odd if not somewhat amusing to express regret for math. But here we had a professional doing just that.

Percent

Percent simply refers to a notation for hundredths. A percentage applies to the number obtained by finding the percent of another number.

Example 1: I did a random sample and counted 2 people out of 100 have red hair. Therefore, 2% of the people in my sample have red hair.

Example 2: First grader, Sarah, spelled 8 words correctly out of 10. Sarah spelled 80% correct words on her spelling test.

Example 3. For the "Biggest loser contest" at work, Mike weighed 220 pounds and lost 20 pounds (final weight 200). Amy weighed 115 pounds and lost 15 pounds (final weight 100 pounds). Mike had a 9% reduction in total weight. However, Amy had a 13% weight reduction and won the contest.

Information

The percentages in the examples above give useful information. No reason at all to apologize for using them. Then why all the fuss? Wait, did I just use "fuss?" (Rick's mental note, update references and never use "fuss" again).

Saying 2% of a sample has red hair quickly communicates a relationship. Namely, 2% tells us we have a small number of people with red hair. Likewise, Sarah spelling 80% of her words correctly also offers useful information. The percent value quickly and simply conveys size or scale.

A further advantage occurs when examining the Biggest Loser Contest (example 3). If the contest just looked at the largest amount of weight lost, Mike would have won. But Mike weighed more to start with. Amy losing 13% percent of her weight compared to Mike's 9% means when comparing relative weight loss, Amy did better.

As we have seen, no reason to become upset at the percentages. They do what they do. But at times, using percentages can pose problems in certain situations.

The Problem with Percentages for Time-Series Behavior

In Education and Psychology, many practitioners measure time-series behavior. Time-series analyses involve carefully measuring behavior over a period of time.

Example 1: First grader Sarah spelled 8 words correctly out of 10 (80%) on Monday. Tuesday through Friday Sarah had the following percentages: 80%, 70%, 90%, 90%.

Example 2: Fred and Jill want to stop smoking. Fred recorded the following percentage decreases using a nicotine patch: Monday 10% less cigs smoked, Tuesday 12% less cigs smoked, Wednesday 13% less cigs smoked. Jill used the cold turkey method (which involved lots of encouragement from her friends). Her reduction for Monday, Tuesday, and Wednesday respectively: 6%, 6%, 8%.

With time-series behavior, professionals (e.g., teachers, school psychologists, behavior analysts, psychologists) need the most precise information they can bring to bear to understand the effects of intervention on behavior. Adding information to Sarah's spelling performance demonstrates a problem. Look at her data in time:

Monday: 8 correct, 2 incorrect in 40 seconds

Tuesday: 8 correct, 2 incorrect in 42 seconds

Wednesday: 7 correct, 3 incorrect in 39 seconds

Thursday: 9 correct, 1 incorrect in 55 seconds

Friday: 9 correct, 1 incorrect in 56 seconds

While Sarah improved her words spelled correctly, she did so at the expense of time. It took Sarah much longer to spell more words correctly. Percent completely ignores the time element.

If time matters, and it should to everyone serious about behavior change, disregarding how long it takes to perform a behavior will lead to less effective interpretation and subsequent decisions.

What about Fred and Jill? Again, we have a problem. Percent only tells us the size or scale of each measure. We don't know the relative difference between how many cigarettes Fred and Jill smoked. If Fred had a pack-a-week problem whereas Jill smoked a pack a day, Jill's relative change could dwarf Fred's. Therefore, how can we know if the nicotine patch or the cold turkey method work better without more precise numbers?

As a general rule, professionals concerned with the most accurate numerical representation of a person's behavior should not use percentage for time-series behavior.

Conclusion

Percent has its place in the world of math and can help people understand some phenomena with a number. Yet in other situations, such as an intensive analysis of time-series behavior, percent can hide important features of behavior change. Know when and when not to use percent. As the famous Psychologists Alfred Adler said, "Mathematics is pure language - the language of science." Let's make sure we always speak as clearly as possible!

CHAPTER 4

Linear Graphs versus Standard Celeration Charts?

W<small>HEN I PRACTICED</small> special education, Direct Instruction, behavior analysis, and Precision Teaching in traumatic brain injury post-acute rehabilitation centers, I cut my teeth as a practitioner. I tried many interventions in the literature and created new ones. Though it all, I used the SCC and it became my guiding light and seemingly a talisman. This may sound immodest, but I applied my craft adroitly and succeeded where many of my fellow clinicians failed. I certainly possessed no more intelligence than they. But I had knowledge of powerful instructional arrangements (i.e., Direct Instruction) and principles of learning and powerful behavior change procedures (i.e., behavior analysis), moderated by the world's best measurement and decision making system, Precision Teaching. Along the way I found myself trying to convince my colleagues they needed to use the SCC. I have carried on and implored others to elevate their visual and quantitative perspective of behavior and decision making ability by adopting the SCC. The following entries showcase both my early and more advanced efforts at logic and persuasion.

Entry: Four warning signs of a poorly constructed line graph

The amount of statistical graphics generated worldwide staggers the mind. In his breakout book *The Visual Display of Quantitative Information* (1983), Tufte reported between 900 billion and 2 trillion images of statistical graphics appear in print each year. Tufte reported the information in 1983, imagine the number in 2015! (*Author's note*: Now imagine that number in 2020!)

A large majority of statistical graphics fall under the category of a "line graph." Line graphs, or linear graphs, represent the most popular type of graphs encountered in print and visual media. Line graphs show time series data. Namely, data that occur across a unit of time.

Many disciplines of science, and even popular culture, make use of line graphs to show data advancing across time. For example, a 2008 Gallup poll examined the self-reported alcoholic beverages of choice for 30 to 49-year-olds. As the line graph below shows, beer still reigns king. Wine has made some significant inroads through time but still remains in the backseat. And liquor preferences have demonstrated a stable trend since 1993.

Do you most often drink liquor, wine, or beer?

Based on U.S. adults who drink alcoholic beverages

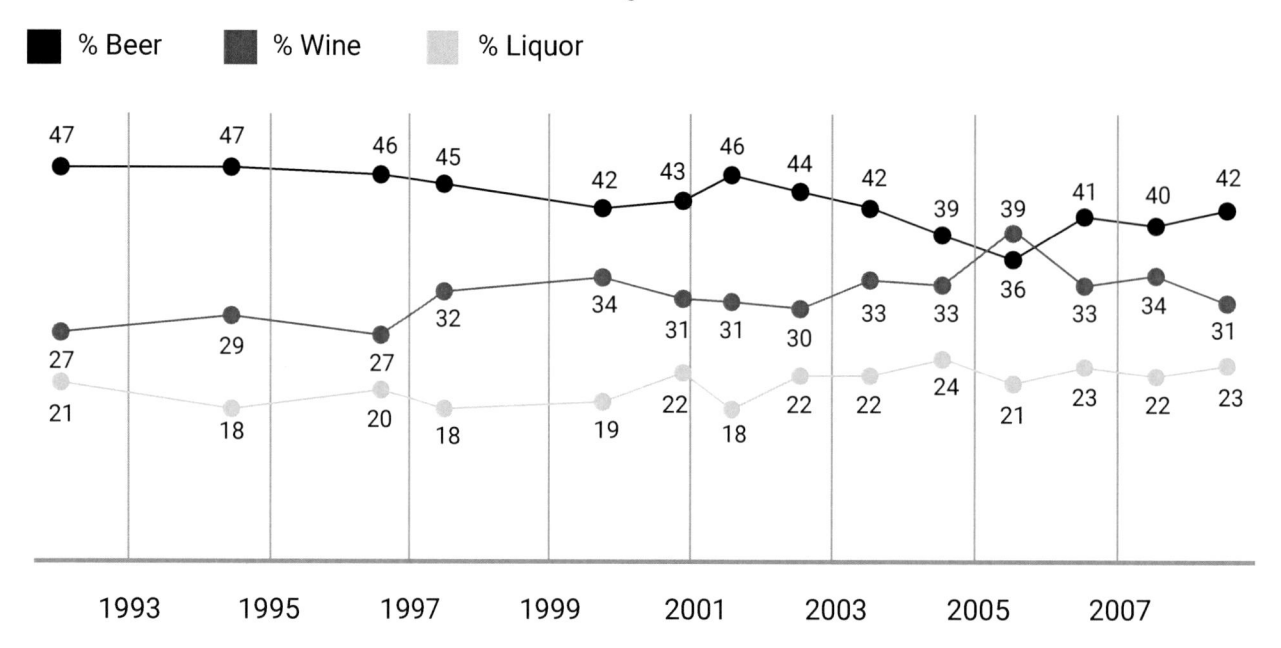

■ % Beer   ■ % Wine   ▢ % Liquor

```
47   47   46  45        43   46  44   42              41   40  42
              42                          39   39
                                                  36        33  34
          32       34                33   33                    31
27   29       27        31   31  30
         18                                       21   23   22  23
21                 20        22      22   22  24
              18       19        18
```

1993   1995   1997   1999   2001   2003   2005   2007

Figure 22. A recreation of a Gallup Poll linear graph showing beer, wine, and liquor preferences of 30- to 49-year-olds across time.

Teachers, school psychologists, speech and language pathologists, behavior analysts, and a host of other people in education rely on line graphs to make important decisions. Decision making fueled by line graphs can range from moving a student on in a curriculum sequence to aiding the determination of whether a student qualifies for important services (e.g., special education).

Yet both practitioners and consumers of visualization must remain vigilant when viewing graphs. Making a significant educational decision (and don't they all qualify as worthy of attention?) based on a line graph of poor scientific quality seems particularly troubling.

With the proliferation of graphing websites (e.g., http://www.onlinecharttool.com/) and programs such as Microsoft Excel, anyone with access to a computer can produce a line graph. The days have long passed when a drafter would create a line graph following specific rules with exacting detail.

Rules, indeed standards, for producing a line graph have existed for years. As an example, the Joint Committee on Standards for Graphic Presentation shared a set of rules to help guide anyone construct a proper line graph in 1915. And in 1938 the American Society of Mechanical Engineers shared principles of graphic presentation so line graphs (1) truthfully represent the facts, (2) have a design that attracts and holds the graph viewer's attention, and (3) possesses clarity facilitating easy decoding of the information.

CHAPTER 4 : LINEAR GRAPHS VERSUS STANDARD CELERATION CHARTS?

The standards shared in 1915 and 1938 still apply to today. Knowing some of the fundamental design rules to line graphs helps guard against the uncritical acceptance of graphs with misleading or deceptive information.

> **Rule #1:** The proportional construction rule refers to the physical proportion of the vertical to the horizontal axis. Published recommendations suggest a ratio of vertical to horizontal axis ranges of 5/8 to 2/3, with a maximum of 3/4 (American National Standards Institute & American Society of Mechanical Engineers, 1960, 1979; Bowen, 1992; Cooper et al., 2020; Johnston & Pennypacker, 1980; Schmid, 1992).

Notice the two graphs below that violate the proportional construction rule. As a result, the slope of the line and the variability of the data will change. In one case the data become exaggerated (the first stretched out vertical axis on the left) and in the other compressed (the compacted vertical axis on the right).

Proportional construction rule violations

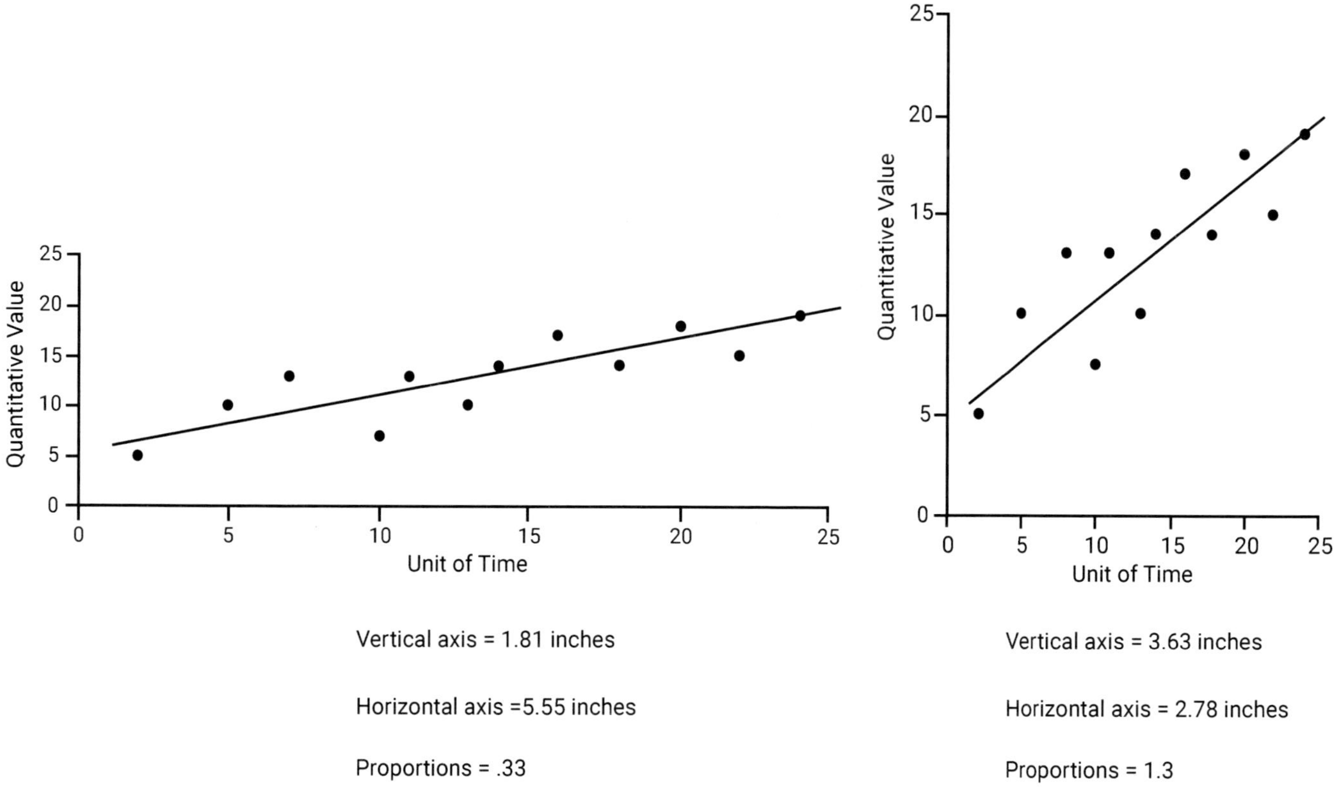

Vertical axis = 1.81 inches

Horizontal axis = 5.55 inches

Proportions = .33

Vertical axis = 3.63 inches

Horizontal axis = 2.78 inches

Proportions = 1.3

*Recommendation for the proportional construction rule span 5/8 to 3/4 (vertical to horizontal axis). The proportional construction rule also provides recommendations for aspect ratios. The aspect ratio for a graph come from a calculation of height to width. The proportional construction coverts to decimal form, .63 to .75 (the decimal equivalents of 5/8 and 3/4 respectively).

Figure 23. Two line graphs violating the proportional construction rule.

If you see graphs that disregard the proportional construction rule, and sadly you will see many, exercise caution in interpreting the claims. Visual analysis relies on well-formed graphs with the correct proportion of the vertical to the horizontal axis. As Schmid (1992) reminds us "...grid proportions are of pronounced significance as the determinants of the visual impression conveyed" (p. 28).

> Rule #2: Label and scale the horizontal axis with a unit of time. Time-series line graphs must have a unit of time on the horizontal axis (Robbins, 2005). Examples of units of time range from seconds and hours to days and years. Unfortunately, many people use "sessions" on the horizontal axis. American Society of Mechanical Engineers, 1960, 1979; Bowen, 1992; Cooper et al., 2020; Johnston & Pennypacker, 1980; Schmid, 1992).

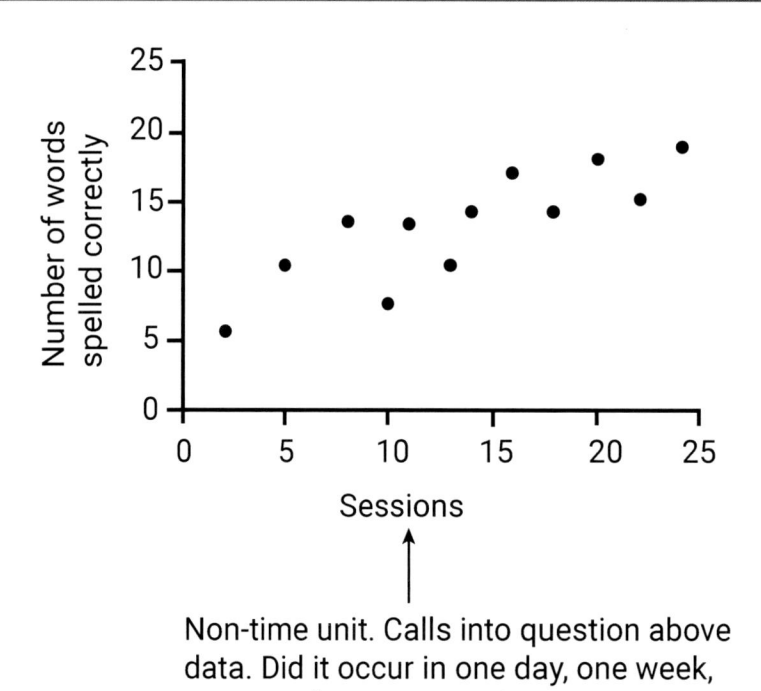

Non-time unit. Calls into question above data. Did it occur in one day, one week, one month, or one year?

Figure 24. Graph with a non-time unit session.

How long did an intervention take? With sessions we have no idea. Do the data ascend or descend because the session length increased or decreased? In other words, did the timing length increase or decrease resulting in more or less data simply due to the artifact in the length of the observation/recording time? Graph readers have absolutely no idea of what went on during a recorded "session." And if someone writes an article and keeps track of time but uses sessions as a label, then the person committed a labeling error by not using an accepted unit of time.

The National Institute of Standards and Technology (2014) defines time units as minutes, hours, days, weeks, and years based on the second; sessions doesn't represent a unit of time. Remain wary of line graphs labeled with the non-time unit sessions; sessions offer no advantages for visually analyzing behavior and instead impede the accurate and efficient portrayal of behavioral data.

> Rule #3. Tick marks have labels. To decode information, a core feature of a line graph entails the labeling of ticks. The horizontal axis for a time series graph will display some unit of time. The vertical axis must have a quantitative value showing the measure of interest. Yet graphs appear in print and on websites without containing one or both axes' tick marks with labels.

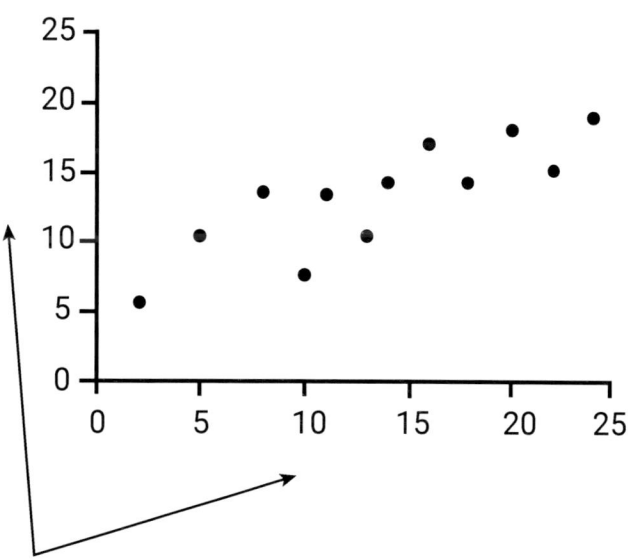

A graph construction sin. Who knows what the heck the data means even with a graph title. Sadly these types of graphs appear not only in media but also professional journals.

Figure 25. A line graph missing scale labels.

Can you figure out what happened in the graph above? No one can, except for maybe the author who created the now information-veiled line graph. Whether scale labels don't show up due to someone forgetting or willfully ignoring the quality feature standards of the line graph, the result has the same effect. Namely, effective graphic presentation of valuable information diminishes significantly. Side note: Other problems include line graphs with no tick marks or quantitative values that do not properly align to the tick mark. Tick marks also matter!

> Rule #4. Data points clearly visible. Rule #4 seems a no-brainer; difficulty seeing the data means graph readers have struggle to detect trends and emerging patterns. The figure below shows very small data points to illustrate the point.

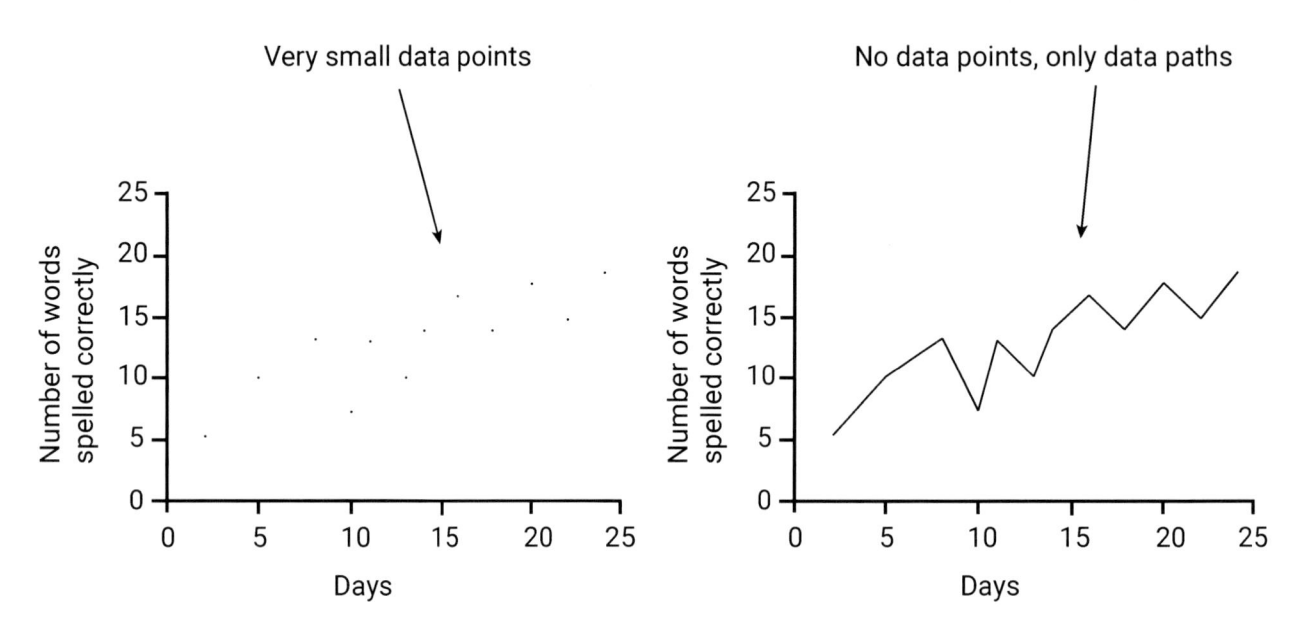

Figure 26. A line graph with hard to see data points.

Conclusion

Poorly constructed line graphs (i.e., failing to follow the rules above) signal potential hazards. Line graphs require adherence to construction features for showing data with clarity, legibility, and graphic integrity. Line graphs with design flaws do not inspire confidence and can negatively affect students whose academic and cognitive growth rely on effective decision making. Finding a graph lacking one or more quality features should alert the graph reader to potential inaccuracies or exaggerations in the stated conclusions. Sadly, ill-conceived linear graphs exist in almost every journal and poorly constructed graphs have become the norm. Don't take my word for it, open your favorite journal and look!

Linear graphs take data and display them based on design principles. Namely, linear graphs have the purpose of showing sheer amounts of change. Sheer amounts of change mean how much more or less of a quantity changes across time. A deceptive effect can occur when comparing two sets of data. Because the linear graph has its main charge to show how much quantities change, significant growth patterns become obscured. The effect will always happen because linear graphs do not show proportional change; instead they show absolute amount of change.

Many times in practice, professionals such as teachers or behavior analysts have different quantities on linear graphs and miss important behavioral patterns. Analysis and decision making proceed without realizing or considering a lower magnitude quantity that may reveal a dramatic change. I have always thought students or clients served by professionals deserve better from the instruments used to reflect behavior change. The following entry displays the effect and hopefully encourages others to see how a ratio graph will help more people than a linear graph.

Entry: Quick fact: Linear graphs can fool you

Linear graphs do a number of things to data that can have negative effects on interpretative behavior. For example, linear graphs will always show changes between different magnitudes in a manner that can mislead the chart viewer. Take the data set below:

Accel data	Decel data
123	3
129	5
122	4
131	6
125	3
127	5
132	7
126	4

Table 1: Data showing two sets of data at different magnitudes.

What do those data look like on a linear graph? The two data paths show that both appear to have a flat trend. The upper series, which has a higher magnitude than the lower series, looks almost the same in terms of growth, very little.

Trend lines for nonstandard linear graph

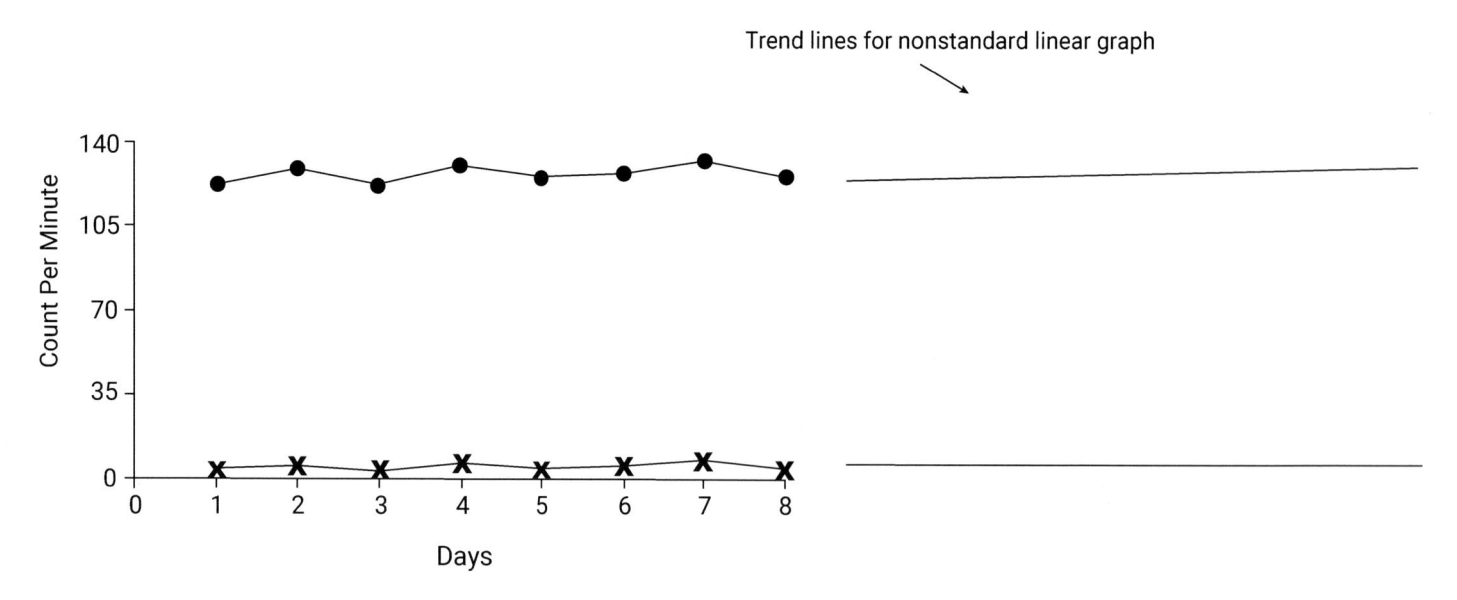

Figure 27. A linear graph showing the change between two sets of data with different magnitudes.

But when we chart the data on a Standard Celeration Chart (SCC) we have a very different picture. Well, as Emeril Lagasse would say, "Bam!" (*Author's note*: Not sure how well that catchphrase has aged!)

Standard Celeration Chart segment

Trend lines for data SCC segment compared against trend lines for nonstandard linear graph (Figure 27)

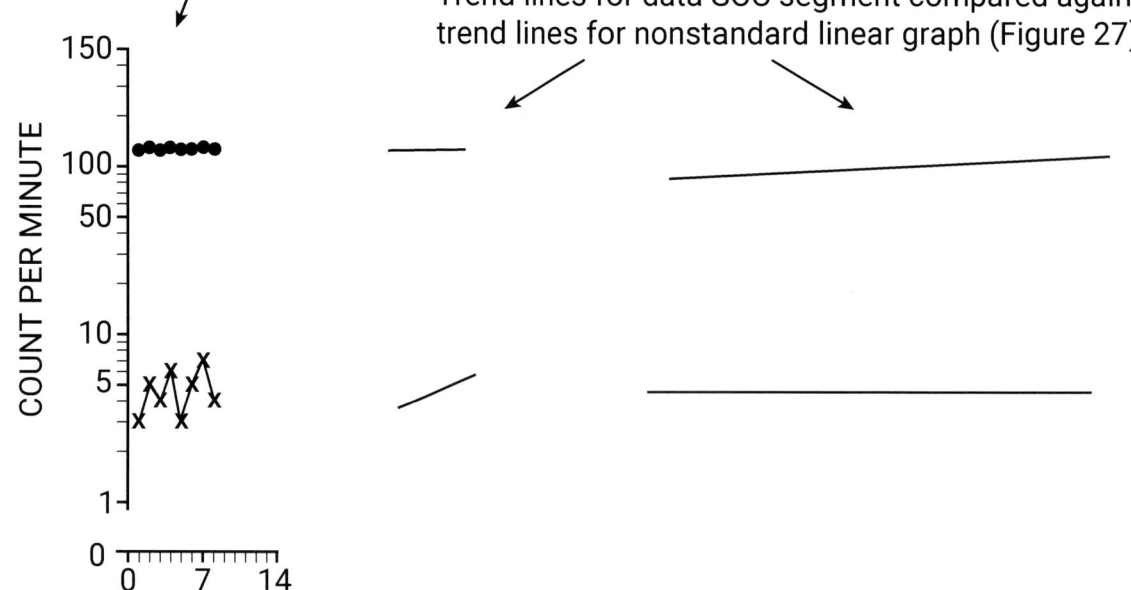

Figure 28. A Standard Celeration Chart showing the change between two sets of data with different magnitudes.

The SCC differs from a linear graph in that it shows ratio changes rather than absolute amounts of changes. The result of such an important feature demonstrates that ratio changes better represent relative differences between data at different magnitudes.

A change from 1 to 2 represents a x2 change, a 100% increase. Going from 10 to 20 also has the same ratio, a x2 change or a 100% increase. Therefore, when placing data on the SCC it will evenhandedly show changes between different magnitudes. Linear charts do not. Though linear charts will show changes of absolute amount.

This ends your quick fact!

In the following blog, I finally began to express a distinction I learned about graphing that I never could quite articulate in the past. In the Precision Teaching community, many have compared linear graphs to Standard Celeration Charts with the latter the hero and the former the bad troublemaker. Generally speaking, many of the points made struck me as sensible and still do to this day. But casting all linear graphs as awful felt wrong. And now, I can pinpoint my feelings, and the following blog did so. Linear graphs do show data differently than SCCs and showing those differences helps contrast the two visual displays. But the *nonstandard* nature of linear graphs makes them untenable. Nonstandardization brings forth many unappealing outcomes ranging from persistent confusion and misinterpretation to flagrant exaggeration and outright fraud. In the following entry, I point out some differences from linear graphs and ratio graphs and start to bring forward the problems of nonstandardization.

Entry: Why NSLGs stink

Have you seen an NSLG lately? No doubt you have if you interact with any kind of information or persuasion-based media. An NSLG refers to a **N**on**S**tandard **L**inear **G**raph, and it stinks. Let's look at little more closely at what we mean by an NSLG. Then we can address why we think they stink.

Why we use/need graphs

So many kinds of data graphics exist that it would take a very large book to properly describe them all (and those books do exist). One class of graphic displays we see quite often falls under the category of "time series."

A time series graphic shows data changing across an interval of time. How many pounds did a person lose across days? What number of speeding tickets did police issue during holiday weekends? How many hurricanes took place each month last year? The data on a time series graphic, frequently displayed on a "line chart," tells a story of change.

Two main characters in the data story include "trend" and "variability." Sometimes the weird actor, "outlier" joins the cast. Trend refers to how a measured quantity increases, decreases, or stays the same. Variability displays the stability, irregularity, or volatility of the measured change. An outlier refers to exceptional performance of the positive ("Wow look how awesome she did!") or of the negative type ("Ugh, what the heck happened there!").

A nonstandard linear chart from Gallup (of the famous Gallup poll) website serves up a nice example of a time series graph. United States Presidential job approval statistics began in the late 1930s and have become an important piece of information. The approval rating acts as a barometer of public support for the President of the United States. The nonstandard linear graph below shows the job approval rating of George W. Bush. The graph has the percentage of approval rating on the vertical axis and the time displayed in months/years on the horizontal axis.

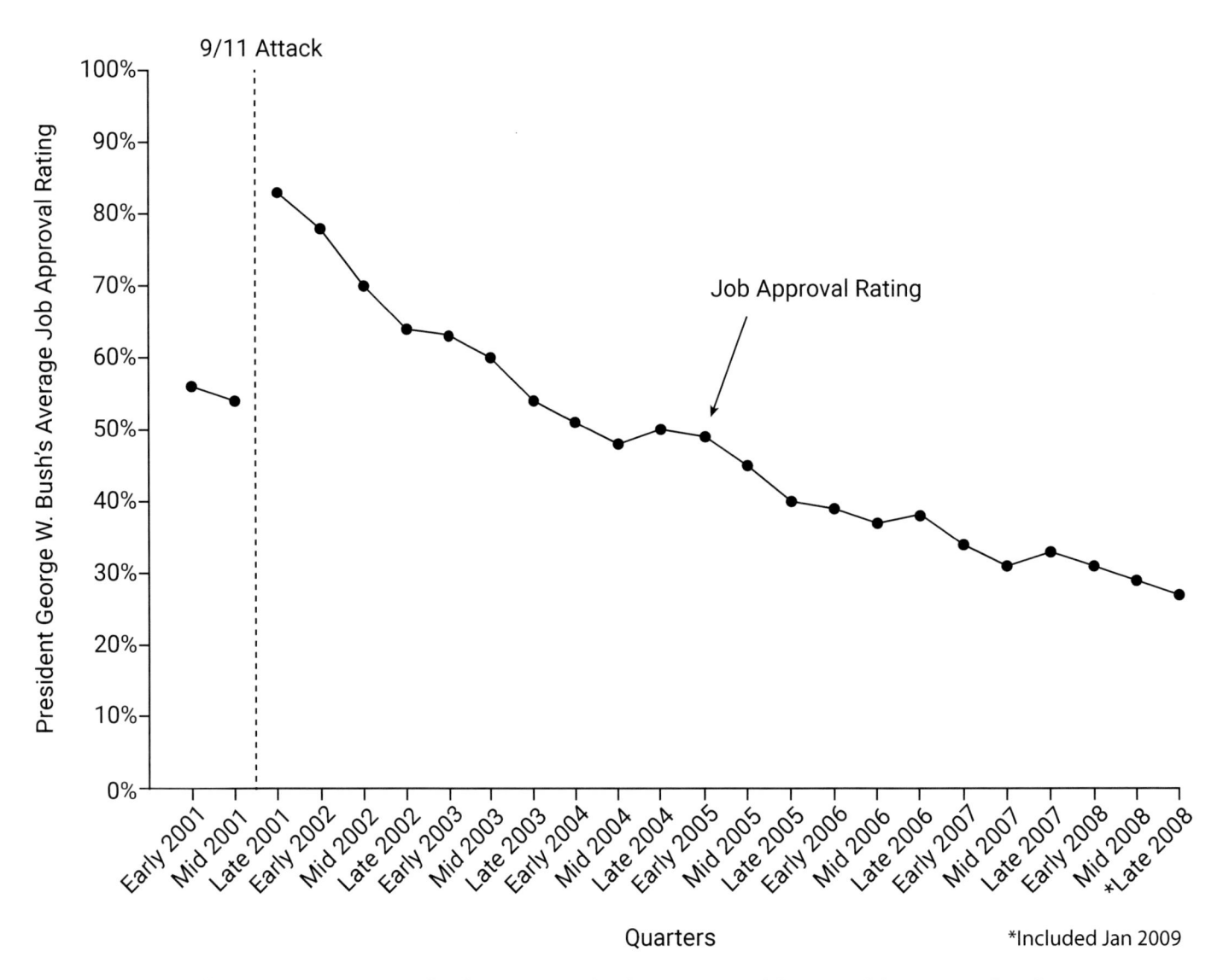

Figure 29: A nonstandard linear graph showing President Bush's approval ratings.
Source: http://www.gallup.com/poll/103798/bushs-yearly-approval-average-fourth-worst-gallup-annals.aspx

What story of change does the line graph tell? The spike in 2001 comes after 9-11. Following the monstrous terror act, America united behind their President. As time went on, the trend of the data tells a story of a country whose approval rating for the President declined across the years. *Why* it happened requires more information on the graph and a deep analysis, and such information forms another story.

With an immediate examination of the line graph, any chart reader can discern important information with the quick and enlightening power of the time series graph. Look at the table below and compare the effect of looking at numbers to looking at a line graph.

Quarter	# of Polls used in Avg	Approve	Disapprove
Early 2001	38	56%	25%
Mid 2001	39	54%	33%
Late 2001	68	83%	11%
Early 2002	58	78%	16%
Mid 2002	66	70%	23%
Late 2002	69	64%	29%
Early 2003	98	63%	31%
Mid 2003	55	60%	33%
Late 2003	73	54%	40%
Early 2004	65	51%	34%
Mid 2004	66	48%	48%
Late 2004	71	50%	46%
Early 2005	53	49%	46%
Mid 2005	41	45%	50%
Late 2005	60	40%	55%
Early 2006	58	39%	56%
Mid 2006	58	37%	57%
Late 2006	74	38%	57%
Early 2007	64	34%	61%
Mid 2007	42	31%	63%
Late 2007	45	33%	61%
Early 2008	50	31%	63%
Mid 2008	46	29%	66%
Late 2008*	67	27%	68%
Average		49%	45%

*Included Jan 2009

Table 2: A table with President Bush's approval and disapproval ratings.
Source: http://partisanid.blogspot.com/2013/07/title.html

Making judgements with numbers alone does not inform the reader as well as the graphic form of the data. Numbers matter, but visualization displays interesting information and subtle and not so subtle patterns lost to a numerical table or number alone.

Line graphs imperative

The world needs time series visual displays, and you see them everywhere. Line graphs show change across time, and preferably through an "in your face" manner. People use the knowledge to make important, high stake decisions (decisions not well answered by numbers or just a statistic).

As an example, teachers measure student performance in reading and then graphically display the data on a line chart. If the student's data across time shows the student has not learned fast enough, the teacher will make a change. If the student continues to exhibit no change or a lack of significant change, the teacher will take more measures to provide help. A worst-case scenario occurs when the student doesn't improve even through the teacher has tried a number of interventions. The student may then receive a referral to specialist (e.g., reading specialist, special education teacher, school psychologist).

What if the graph the teacher used didn't tell the data story correctly? In other words, the graph could indicate a lack of progress when the student has a learned at an acceptable rate (we call the previous situation a false negative). The graph makes obvious the false negative below.

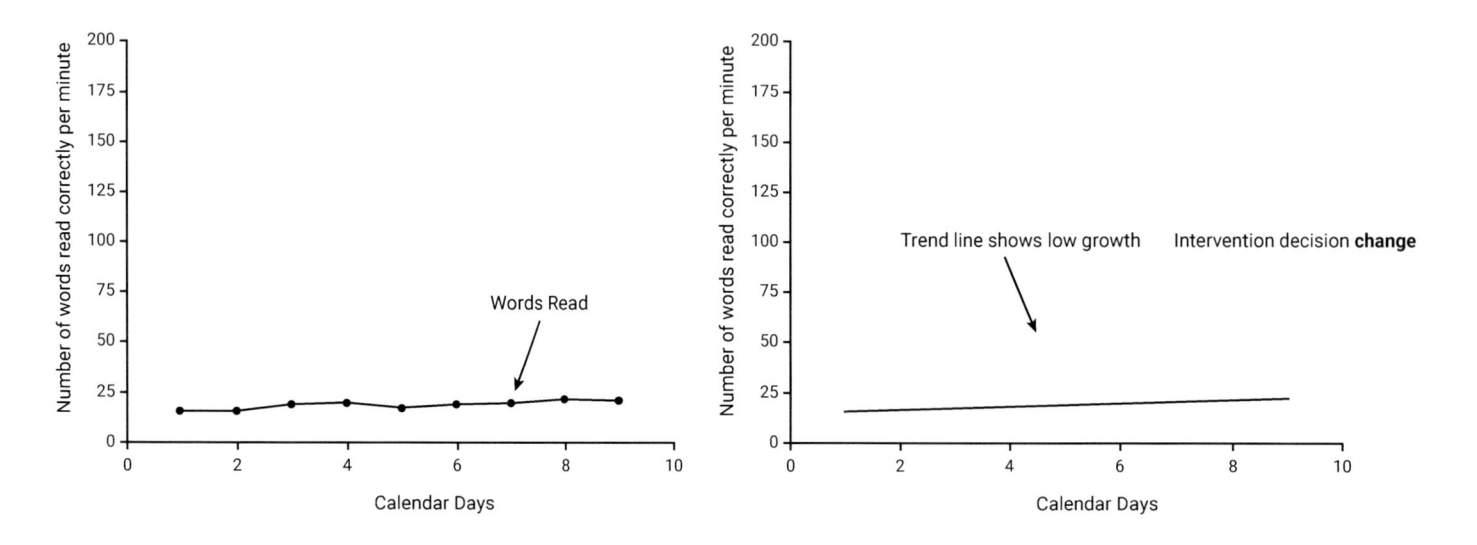

Figure 30: A graph showing data on a NSLG with a very low growth rate.

On the other hand, a graph could show the student making very rapid growth when the student made progress at a lower rate of change (a false positive). In other cases, the false positive could show a rapid rate of growth when the student has made very little growth.

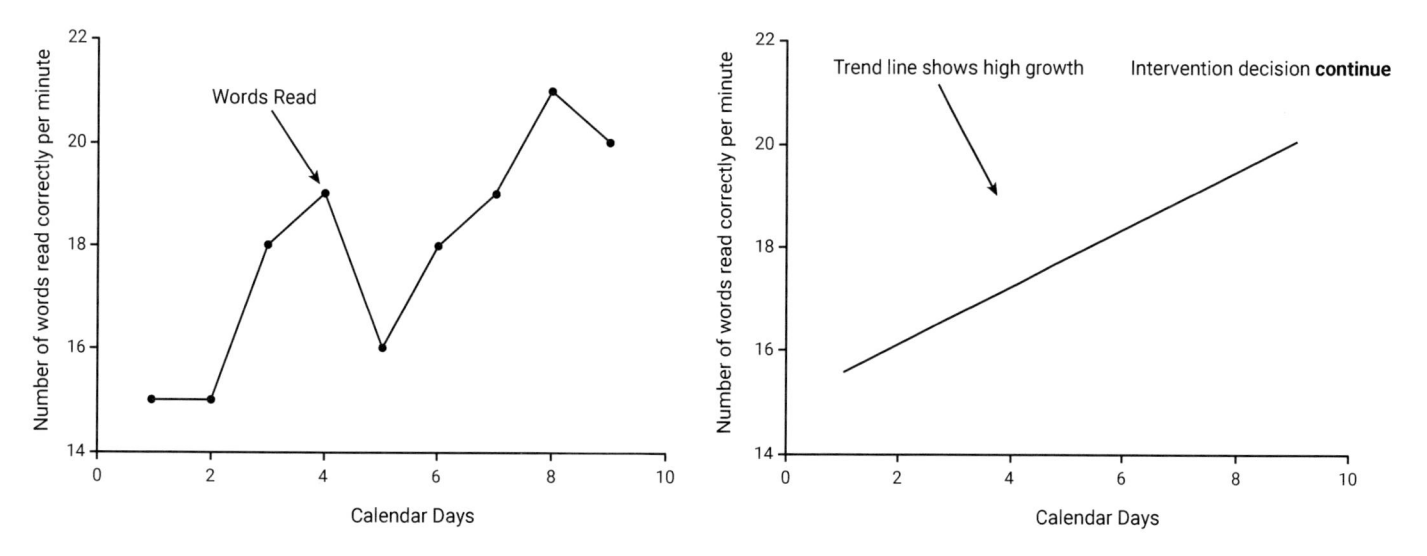

Figure 31: A graph showing data on a NSLG with a very high growth rate.

False positives and false negatives give us a headache

As a savvy graph reader, you have probably deduced why the line graphs above provided false impressions. With the one graph the vertical axis had a scaling of 0 to 200. With the second line graph the vertical axis started at 14 and ended at 22. Do you claim shenanigans? If yes, welcome to the world of NSLGs!

Why do so many people scale the graph to whatever number they feel like? Because they can. Because we don't have rules to say otherwise. Because NSLGs, by their very nature, thrive in a miasma of nonstandardization.

People make decisions from line graphs that range from low stakes (e.g., how many wins have I had in my Pokémon card game league) to high stakes (e.g., will a student enter special education). All information has value (Rick lost his Pikachu card to Phil last week because he didn't pay attention to his graph).

You may have time series data. And if placed on a line graph then the data rise to a level of importance. What display you pick to view your data will make a world of difference. If you choose a NSLG you may fall prey to many of its weaknesses. As we move forward, we will lay out in painstaking detail all the many limitations, and sometime outright deceptions, NSLGs contain. But we do not mean to imply all NSLGs are evil. NSLGs have value if they meet the following criteria and move closer to a standard:

1. Follow proper construction rules
2. Graph readers need to see/focus in on absolute change
3. The nonstandardized graph does not distort the data and tell a different story to the graph reader

The problem we have with NSGLs, and why they stink (most of the time); graph makers frequently violate one or all the NSLG usage guidelines. For example:

Problem with rule #1. A crack team of data scientists from Penn State, Pitt, and Vanderbilt recently conducted an expansive study of NSLGs (time series line graphs) in 11 journals (Kubina, Kostewicz, Brennan, & King, 2017). After closely examining 4,313 NSLGs the researchers discovered many graphs contained construction and labeling errors. For example, graph makers violated the proportional construction rule 85% of the time. Furthermore, for multiple graphs within the same figure, 69% of the reviewed graphs did not scale the vertical axis to the same terminal value (meaning comparisons of trend and variability between graphs falls out of whack - kind of like comparing a race where people run different lengths). Many other problems came to light which we won't go into here. But the analysis of the study makes sense of a perverse graphing policy - when everyone practices nonstandardization, no one is wrong.

Problem with rule #2. We want to view absolute change when we *only* care about the sheer amount of differences in quantities and nothing more. Let's compare two companies.

Company A		Company B	
1st quarter revenue	2nd quarter revenue	1st quarter revenue	2nd quarter revenue
$100,000	$200,000	$19,500,000	$20,000,000
Absolute amount increase from Q1 to Q2		Absolute amount increase from Q1 to Q2	
	$100,000		$500,000

Table 3. Revenue from two different companies.

The table above shows Company A had $20,000,000.00 revenue in the second quarter. When compared against the first quarter revenue, we see a $100,000 increase. Company B posted $20,000,000.00 in second quarter revenue. Again, comparing against the first quarter we observe an increase for company B but for $500,000.00. We can clearly compare the results of both companies and conclude Company B did better than Company A in absolute amount of revenue (Company A had a $100,000.00 increase and Company B $500,000.00 gain).

Can we then conclude we should invest our money in the stock of Company B instead of Company A because Company B made had significantly more revenue than Company A (to the tune of $500,000 more)? If we let absolute amount guide our decision making, we will invest in Company B.

But relative change gives us different information from absolute amount of change. Absolute amount of change looks at sheer differences while relative change focuses on relative differences. With the additional information in the table below we see the percentage of increases for revenue for Company A and B. When we compare first quarter (Q1) and second quarter (Q2) changes we now see very clearly Company A has an insane 100% growth rate and Company B grew by a minuscule 2.6%. In light of relative change, which would you now invest in?

Company A		Company B	
1st quarter revenue	2nd quarter revenue	1st quarter revenue	2nd quarter revenue
$100,000	$200,000	$19,500,000	$20,000,000
Relative change increase from Q1 to Q2		*Relative change increase from Q1 to Q2*	
100% growth or x2 (doubling)		**2.6% growth or x1.026 (slight change)**	

Table 4. Revenue from two different companies examined with relative change.

In business, science, and life we better judge the significance of differences with relative change. Relative change always shows how much one quantity changes relative to another; critical information because we can now judge the changes against one another. Take a moment and look at scientific journals for psychology and education, guess what kind of time series graphs you find? Almost all nonstandard linear graphs presenting us with the crude gift of absolute amount of change.

Problem with rule #3. As shown above in the two animated figures, we have two stories based on the scaling of the vertical axis. One shows a slow increase while the other shows a rapid increase. The same data telling two vastly different stories should cause us to pause and say, "What the H E double hockey sticks???"

What to do

Related idea: I find it disconcerting when people try to dismiss correlations by uttering the phrase "Correlation does not imply causation." True, but a correlation by itself provides information in exact concordance with its design. Likewise, a linear graph will visually depicts the information in direct relation to graph construction and the linear graph's mission - showing absolute amounts of change.

No need to get angry at a correlation. Therefore, let's not hate on linear graphs. But we must recognize numerous problems associated with nonstandardization. We must further acknowledge the various limitations of a linear graph. For example, linear graphs focus only on absolute amount of change when we need to see the world of behavior through the lens of relative change. Linear graphs have their place in the world, but so many of them distort the present information due to nonstandardization and its insidious effects. We can do better.

Let's embrace the distinguished features of the Standard Celeration Chart. The ordered, rational geometry of celeration lines, bounce, and clearly detectable outliers means chart readers make better, faster decisions. And superior decisions lead to superior outcomes.

My time as an experimenter, teacher, and advocate of Precision Teaching and Standard Celeration Charting has led to a wealth of encounters. My experiences fell in different categories: pleasant interactions, acceptance and gratitude of new knowledge, skepticism, and confrontations (on occasion aggressive) and rejections of information. I have heard all of the standard and novel reasons to reject the SCC and its utility. One frequent condemnation of the SCC surrounds math, and the complaint takes some form of, "Oh, people can never understand that complicated chart. There is too much math for people to use it." Interestingly I don't hear the previous objections very often when people compare purchasing big ticket items such as loans or cars.

While I could take a chapter explaining the illogical arguments in such statements, the truth about linear graphs and the SCC lies in a universal fact; both constituent instruments transform numbers so we can apply quantitative reasoning to the content. In other words, graphs and charts provide a simple device for understanding processes that all have inherently complex math underlying their visual representation. I tried to share some of that math and make a case for the SCC's superior functionality and effectiveness in the following entry.

Entry: Counts and visual displays

The following figure shows counts of behavior and portrays those counts graphically in sets. The counts can represent any learner behavior the teacher may wish to measure (e.g., interrupting a conversation, volunteering to do a classroom chore, the number of toys put back in a toy box, writing antonyms, or factoring trinomials). The dots represent the physical amount for each count (e.g., for 2, the two dots show 2 written antonyms, or two competed chores).

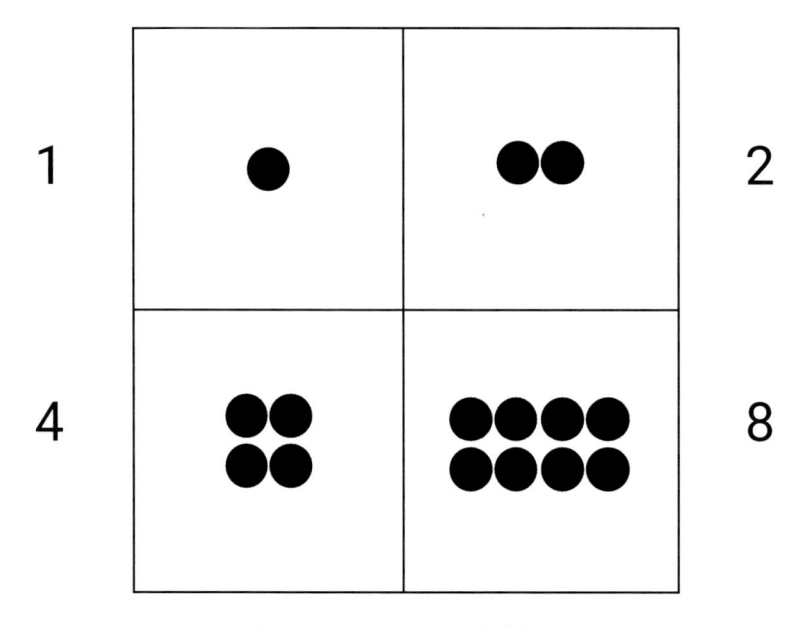

Figure 32. Counts of objects.

When displayed on charts, the counts in the Figure 32 transform into an ordered arrangement of data. The resulting visual pattern provides information to the chart reader beyond just examining numbers or counts alone. When displayed on an arithmetically scaled line chart, Figure 33, the differences between 1 and 2, 2 and 4, and 4 and 8 all have differences in the amount of space given to represent the change. The change from one to two has the smallest space because it has the least amount of total change. Conversely, going from 4 to 8 we see the largest amount of space showing the greatest amount of total change. With arithmetically scaled charts (also called linear graphs) the relationships between quantities will always appear as shown in this example because the architecture of the graphic has the specific design for showing the absolute amount change. Arithmetically scaled line charts exist to show how much more (amount) or less (amount) a quantity changes. Teachers who use these charts place all their analytical ability on knowing only whether an intervention produced a greater or lesser amount of the targeted behavior.

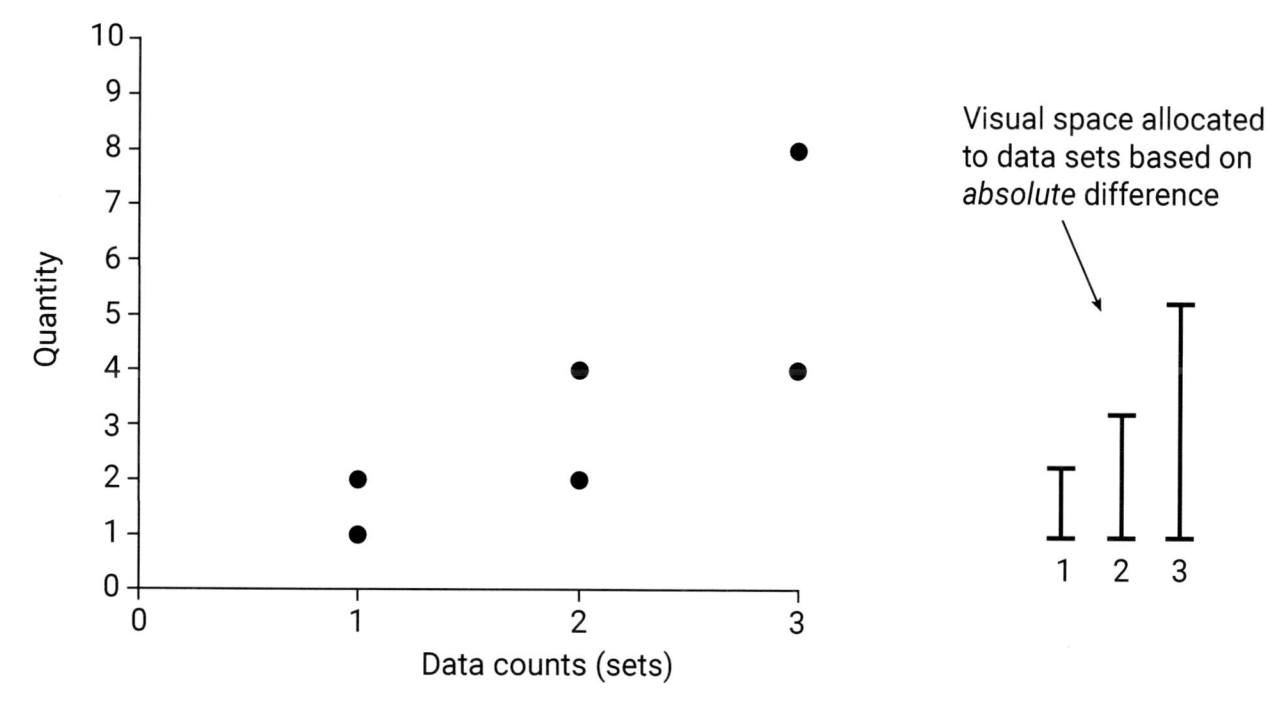

Figure 33. Display of the counts on an arithmetically scaled or linear graph.

The displays on ratio charts, or charts with semilogarithmic or multiply/divide scales, illustrate the proportionality between 1 and 2, 2 and 4, and 4 and 8. The amount of space appears equal on the cross section for the charted data with all three data sets because all have a proportional change of x2.0, or a doubling. Ratio charts focus the eye of the chart reader on relative and proportional effects. The objective of the resulting visual pattern between the two types of time series graphics, arithmetically scaled (linear graphs) and ratio charts, seems at odds. How can a substantially larger amount of change not always convey greater significance when compared to a smaller absolute amount of change? The example in the differences between a cross-section of an arithmetically scaled (above) and a ratio scaled or ratio line chart (below) help to answer the question.

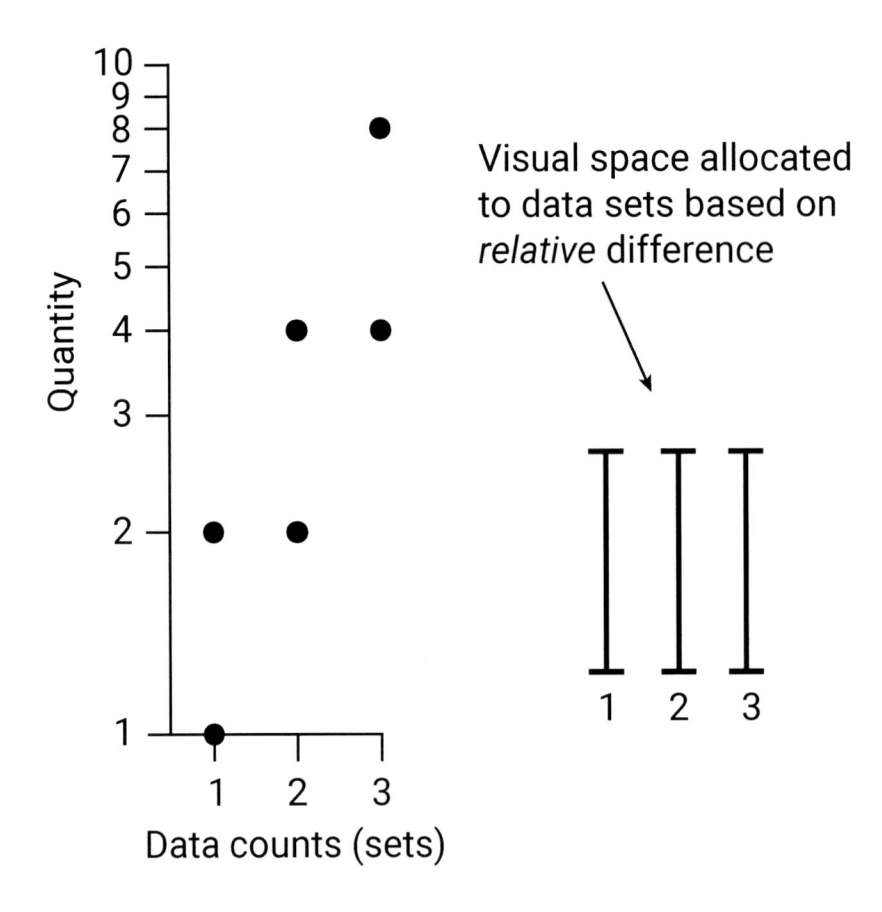

Figure 34. Display of the counts on a ratio graph.

It follows that analysis of visual data occurs as a principle result of the dimensions inherent in the graphical display. All the arithmetically scaled and ratio charts will have critical features that impose order to the data set such as scales, data labels, and an aspect ratio. The resulting data picture significantly affects the chart readers analysis, interpretation, judgement, and subsequent decision making. Decisions based on only what provides more or fewer amounts (Figure 33), provide very different information from a visual display (Figure 34) showing how things change in comparison to one another (relative change). Contrasting the two visual displays gets to the heart of how we determine significance of changing quantities.

4 to 8 is +4 while 1 to 2 is +1. If we only care about which provides more, then we value 4 to 8 change more than 1 to 2 change. But 1 to 2 change = 100% change and 4 to 8 = 100% change. On arithmetically scaled line charts, visually people see the 1 to 2 change the same as a 7 to 8 change (both show +1) but 1 to 2 = 100% change while 7 to 8 = 14% change. In the add world, and with arithmetically scaled line charts, we value the change of 1 to 2 as much as we value the change of 7 to 8. We should get very excited, however, at the 1 to 2 change, and not so much with 7 to 8 change when we look at the data in the multiply world and on ratio line charts. And if you don't think relative change has more value than absolute change, answer this question: if you invested your money which return rate would you rather have: a 100% return rate or a 14% return rate?

People always, always answer that question the same way: they say they want a 100% return rate over the 14% return rate. How do we calculate return rates? We must use the first number, where we start from, to the second number. Yes, if you said to me "Rick do you want $1,000 or $10 I will say "I want $1,000." But if you say to me, "Well you have to give me $10,000 if you want $1,000" I might not have $10,000. But I do have $100 so I can get the $10 deal (both of these figures, the $1000 and $10 come from a 10% calculation). When the fields of education and psychology place so much stock in only absolute amount of changes, epitomized by arithmetically scaled line charts, we fail to appreciate that true significance of changes and only look for what produces the biggest changes ignoring the facts of percentage changes.

The technical features (i.e., showing relative and proportional change) of a ratio chart, or what people in the past have called a semilogarithmically scaled chart, make one wonder why it has never taken hold in scientific disciplines like education and psychology. According to Schmid and Schmid (1979, p.99), "The semilogarithmic chart is unequaled for many purposes, especially in portraying proportional and percentage relationships. In comparison with the arithmetic line chart, it possesses most of the advantages without the disadvantages. This type of chart not only correctly represents relative changes, but also indicates absolute amounts." In their book, Engineering graphics, Giesecke et al. (2001, p.846) reinforce Schmid and Schmid and other authors when they write, "Semilog charts have the same advantages as rectangular coordinate line charts (arithmetic charts)... When rectangular coordinate line charts give a false impression of the trend of a curve, the semilog charts will be more effective in revealing with the rate of change is increasing, decreasing, or constant."

Consider the ratio chart. And if you consider the ratio chart, consider one of its most sophisticated forms, the Standard Celeration Chart. You will see the significance of data change in a whole new light.

So far in my lifetime I have engaged in three debates pitting linear graphs against Standard Celeration Charts. One debate had a decent sized crowd while the other two had less than 10 people attend each event. In one of those smaller debates I had a fellow debater who made one point that had me thinking quickly to counter the claim. I spent more time after the debate fleshing out my thoughts. The point made sounded logical on its face, but after reflection the pronouncement had no merit. The following entry conveys my logic.

Entry: Nonstandard linear graphs or Standard Celeration Charts?

Recently I engaged in a debate concerning whether to use a nonstandard linear graph (NSLG) or a Standard Celeration Chart (SCC) for time series behavior. I took the side of the SCC. A point of contention arose when one of my fellow debaters claimed the SCC took longer to explain to teachers. Therefore, the debate argued teachers should use linear graphs as the analytical instrument of choice.

I responded that generally it takes me about three hours to get people familiar with the SCC so they understand and can use its basic capabilities. (*Author's note*: I had this debate prior to the expansiveness of a digital SCC when the paper SCC held dominance as the preferred choice). The other person noted it takes very little time to familiarize people with linear graphs, therefore, we should use the linear (my colleague meant NSLG but didn't say that) instead of the SCC.

The logic train seemed straightforward:

1. Nonstandard linear graphs appear easier to understand than the Standard Celeration Chart.
2. Teachers do not have a lot of time to learn a new graph or chart.
3. We should use linear graphs because teachers can pick them up quickly and don't have the time to learn something more involved.

I don't know what people thought in audience, but I saw a few head nods at my fellow debater's assertion. Due to the format of the discussion I had little time to rebut the proposition. But I can now!

Ease of understanding versus complexity

My debating colleague had a point. Nonstandard linear graphs take less time to explain to teachers probably because they already have extensive experience with the visual display. We see linear graphs everywhere! Newspaper stories, popular magazine articles, scientific journals, even in sarcastic political commentaries.

Regardless of the "familiarity argument" (i.e., more people have used the linear graph and know it better), when we dissect the faulty syllogism from above, we run into a serious problem. Why should familiarity or how long it takes to explain a chart guide our decision for adoption? Or for that matter, how does the complexity of a graph signal a superior choice?

Let's insert some different targets in the above logic and see if how we appraise my colleague's point.

1. Calculators take less time to understand than computer driven statistical programs (e.g., Excel).
2. Teachers do not have a lot of time to learn a new statistical program.
3. We should use the calculators to solve advanced statistical problems because teachers can learn it quickly and don't have the time to learn something more complicated.

Perhaps you agree the complexity of a chart or how long it takes to learn it should drive the decision to adopt a visual display. If not, what should guide our decision making? What the chart can actually do!

The SCC provides different information from the linear graph. Many sources explain in great detail why we should prefer a ratio (also referred to as semilogarithmic or semilog) chart to a linear graph (e.g., advantages in finance, education, science). The following table came from an article written by a chartered financial analyst (CFA). The CFA argued for a "semilog" scale instead of a linear scale. I summarized the author's arguments with the arguments covered investing.

Reason for Ratio Scale	Advantage
Ratio scales have more use than linear scales due to an important aspect of investing - emotionality.	Investors can better gauge changes and reduce their emotional swings when examine their investments in relative terms.
Investors care more about gains and losses in relative, not absolute terms.	A stock that gains ¢50 will matter little for a $500 stock but would make for a dramatic gain for a ¢20 stock.
*Linear scales work almost as good as good as ratio scales, but only in the short term.	Investor's emotionality doesn't change much for short term moves. Also, the difference between both scales "is barely visible for the very-short-term chart, so the difference in usefulness is also barely seen."
Investor perceive prices in relative, not absolute terms.	Stocks that move by $0.01 or 0.1% have an almost imperceptible effect (expect in the case of penny stock that has a value of $0.01!).

*Author took issue with a claim from "Stockcharts" which claimed linear scales work better the ratio scales.

Table 5. A summarization from a CFA explaining why ratio charts work better than linear graphs for investing. Source: http://www.sunshineprofits.com/gold-silver/questions-and-answers/which-scale-is-better-linear-scale-or-logarythmic-scale/

And then we have the whole matter of why a standard view provides a 10x or better advantage over nonstandard graphs.

The next time someone tells you we should select the nonstandard linear graph over the Standard Celeration Chart because teachers (or parents, students, or whoever) understand it better, remember the problem with such logic. A magnifying glass takes way less time to learn when compared to a microscope, but which resolving power would you rather have to see the world with clarity?

I wrote the following entry back in 2012. It became clear to me that certain truths existed. First, in education, psychology, and behavior analysis, many professionals use time series displays to understand how behavior changes. Second, the vast majority of those professionals almost exclusively use nonstandard linear graphs (NSLG). And those NSLG have many problems that the professionals most likely do not yet realize. Some problems with nonstandardization and construction errors make the graphical output suspect at best and misleading at worst. Third, the sciences of education, psychology, and behavior analysis immediately divest themselves of all problems associated with NSLGs by adopting the Standard Celeration Chart.

Entry: The king of all time-series visual displays

How do we know if the behavior we measured changed across time? We display it visually. We have two broad choices for time-series visual graphics: arithmetically scaled and ratio scaled line charts. Each chart displays the behavior and can tell us if the change stays the same, goes up, and goes down. Beyond that we will find major differences.

Before I get into major differences let us do an analogy. Pretend you have a child who needs medical treatment. You go to a doctor who offers a diagnosis of the problem with two levels of information. Version one diagnostics has very basic information and uses qualitative (i.e., words) descriptors. For example, the doctor says your child's pulse is very fast. Your child also has a high temperature. Furthermore, your child has abnormally high respirations. That's all the information you get. Version two diagnostics has descriptive and wonderfully quantitative (i.e., numbers) information. The doctor says your child's pulse is very fast at 110 beats per minute. Your child also has a high temperature, 101.9 degrees. Furthermore, your child has abnormally high respirations, 27 breathes per minute. Which version of information do you want the doctor to use to figure out what is going on with your child? Is there any parent on Earth that would pick version one diagnostics? No parent would want the doctor to use less information.

Let us now bring this analogy closer to home. Suppose you have a child who needs educational, behavioral, or psychological treatment. You go to a teacher, behavior analyst, or psychologist who offers a diagnosis of the problem with two levels of information. Version one diagnostics has very basic information and uses qualitative (i.e., words) descriptors. For example, the teacher/behavior analyst/psychologist says your child's reading behavior is very poor. Your child also makes many mispronunciations. Furthermore, your child recalls very little information after reading a passage. That's all the information you get.

Version two diagnostics has orders of magnitude more descriptive and quantitative (i.e., numbers) information. The teacher/behavior analyst/psychologist says your child reads text at 57 correct words per minute. Your child also mispronounces words at a rate of 8 word per minute. Furthermore, your child can only retell 2 thought units per minute after reading a passage for two minutes. Which version of information do you want the teacher/behavior analyst/psychologist to use to figure out what is going on with your child? Guess which version our education system, discipline of behavior analysis and psychology use? If you guessed the more basic, version one form of diagnostic information you have answered correctly.

Why do we find ourselves in this sad state of affairs? I will attempt to answer that complicated question in time. But in the present, I tell anyone who will listen to me we must, *must* use the version two level of diagnostics. Namely, let's use a visual display that provides numbers and understandable comparisons of the data, the Standard Celeration Chart. Let's avoid the most basic, and prone to provide misleading rate-of-change information, visual graphic nonstandard arithmetically scaled chart. (Author's note: I used "arithmetically scaled chart" earlier in my writings as a direct influence from Calvin Schmid, an unsung visual graphics/data scientist hero. I have since changed to using the term linear graph, or nonstandard linear graph which occurs most often).

What version does almost every single teacher, behavior analyst, and psychologist use: the nonstandard arithmetically scaled line chart. For example, I just completed an extensive survey of behavior journals and found out of 2039 graphs 99.997 were of the arithmetically scaled variety. But you don't have to take my word for it, open any journal and see for yourself (of course don't pick the Journal of Precision Teaching and Celeration because that only has SCCs). (Author's note: Sadly we said goodbye the journal around 2011).

Below please see a table adapted from *The Precision Teaching Book* (Kubina & Yurich, 2012). After reading the table, which visual graphic provides the most information? Which visual graphic will make the most difference for teachers, behavior analysts, and psychologists?

Technical Features	Nonstandard Linear Graph	Standard Celeration Chart
Absolute amount of change	Yes	Yes
Relative change	No	Yes
Proportional change	No	Yes
Rates of change	No	Yes
Clearly comparing and depicting the change between two or more quantities on the same chart (with one having large quantities and the other small quantities)	No	Yes
Produces straight lines when percentage rate of growth is constant	No	Yes
Forecasting or projecting future trends with a straight line (growth or decay assumes ratio growth)	No	Yes
Variability normalized	No	Yes

Technical Features	Nonstandard Linear Graph	Standard Celeration Chart
Standardized with a 34 degree angle (x2 or doubling) moving from bottom left to top right corner	No	Yes
Standard measurement scale for classifying and categorizing all behavior pinpoints	No	Yes
Consistent user interface	No	Yes
Standard chart symbols (conventions) for displaying data, time, and information	No	Yes
Accommodates charting of all observable human behavior, from 1 per day to 1000 per minute	No	Yes
Quantify performance change with frequency multiplier	No	Yes
Quantify learning change with celeration multiplier	No	Yes
Total variability or bounce around celeration quantified, up bounce and down bounce quantified	No	Yes
Advanced celeration analysis	No	Yes

Table 6. A table adapted from *The Precision Teaching Book* listing advantages of the nonstandard linear graph and SCC.

The measurement and visual display landscape of education, behavior analysis, and psychology needs to change because every single person who scrutinizes data deserves the best, most ethical intervention possible. The visual display filters and tells the chart reader what has happened, and it does so through the lens of the selected visual display (e.g., nonstandard arithmetically scaled chart, Standard Celeration Chart). As a rational, concerned consumer or deliverer of educational, behavioral, or psychological services, let's work to make the SCC the preferred visual display system for time-series data. Our connection to the data, and the people whose behavior we measure, will dramatically improve. In the end, education, behavior analysis, and psychology operate on the principle of helping people grow. Shouldn't we use the most informative visual display possible to analyze, interpret, and communicate data?

Chapter 5

Inside the SCC

Precision Teaching has many books that address the technical features of the chart. Many of those books appear in Table 7. A lot happens inside the chart. Readers will notice two of the books I wrote appear in the table below. I took great pains in those books to describe different visualizations and explain change metrics inherent in the SCC. When I blogged, I also found myself addressing essential facets of the SCC. Some of the topics bordered on the very technical while others extolled the worth of specific SCC properties like celeration.

Book and Edition	Brief Description
Graf, S., Auman, J., & Lindsley, O. (2007). The one year standard celeration chart. Graf Implements.	An innovation of standard celeration charting. Discusses many components analyzing behavior on an SCC but also introduces the one year SCC.
Graf, S., & Lindsley, O. (2002). Standard celeration charting 2002. Graf Implements.	Steve Graf and Ogden Lindsley offer a very fine description of the SCC and many important chart concepts. The book uses Information Mapping and real world data to illustrate fundamental chart features.
Haring, N. G., White, M. S., & Neely, M. D. (2019). Precision Teaching — A practical science of education. Sloan.	The PT book has two main chapters on describing important components of the SCC and how to make decisions. The other chapters focus on different PT concepts but use the SCC to illustrate the content.
Koorland, M. A., & Martin, M. B. (1975). Elementary principles and procedures of the standard behavior chart (3rd ed.). Odyssey Learning Center.	The third edition appeared in 1975 and had as its stated goal to "simplify and further illustrate the principles and procedures of the Standard Behavior Chart as first presented in the *Handbook of the Standard Behavior Chart*."
Kubina, R. M. (2019). The Precision Teaching Implementation Manual. Greatness Achieved.	The PT Implementation Manual has several chapters devoted to explaining how to analyze SCC data in different configuration (i.e., within and between conditions).
Kubina, R. M., & Yurich, K. K. L. (2012). The Precision Teaching Book. Greatness Achieved.	The PT Book shows how to use the Finder and other means to analyze and interpret SCC data. A problem solving chapter also demonstrates how to use the chart to help move progress forward.

Book and Edition	Brief Description
Pennypacker, H. S., Koenig, C. H., & Lindsley, O. R. (1972). Handbook of the Standard Celeration Chart. Precision Media.	The classic 1972 handbook has everything a charter could want in terms of technical features of the SCC. The first edition came during a time of great expansion for PT and has some of the best descriptions of chart concepts and data features.
Pennypacker, H. S., Gutierrez, A., & Lindsley, O. R. (2003). Handbook of the Standard Celeration Chart (Deluxe ed.). Cambridge Center for Behavioral Studies.	The deluxe edition is also the second edition to the previous handbook. There are some interesting changes and clarifications on some concepts. Owning both editions will serve as a good addition to any professional library.
White, O. R., & Haring, N. G. (1980). Exceptional teaching (2nd ed.). Merrill.	Owen's 1980 PT classic has a great many practical examples along with SCC concepts. Exceptional teaching showcases how to adapt SCC into teaching and helping people achieve efficient and effective learning.

Table 7. A list of several books that explain the Standard Celeration Chart.

The following blog represents my efforts to share important technical features of the SCC, which have a target audience of Precision Teachers. I wrote other more general blogs aimed at convincing non-Precision Teachers they should pay attention to, and adopt, the SCC. Well, more than pay attention to it; adopt and use it! I wrote the following entry on charting zero for my Precision Teaching peers. Like any science, people who practice PT do not all agree on everything! I tried to use logic to persuade my colleagues that the convention Ogden Lindsley adopted should apply to our entire field. Not everyone charts zero the same way. I hope my blog changed some people's thoughts on the matter.

Entry: Charting zero

A recent post to the SClistserv (which you should join if you haven't already) asks how the frequency multiplier works in the case of 0 or a no count frequency. The answer reinforces many of the four reasons I have advanced in the discussion of which convention Precision Teachers should adopt to represent 0 on the chart. The convention I advocate: place acceleration (•) or deceleration (X) data at a x2 (times 2) distance below time bar (Graf & Lindsley, 2002). The reasons for adopting the convention follow:

1. Graphical communication of 0 observed or detected instances of the pinpoint clearly represented by using same symbol for acceleration and deceleration behavior.
2. Allows measurement of "change measures" such as celeration, bounce, frequency multipliers, celeration multipliers, and Accuracy Improvement Measure (AIM). (Author's note: I have since referred to AIM as the improvement index, a PT term introduced in the past).

3. Facilitates consistent, accurate measurement of "change measures" such as celeration, bounce, frequency multipliers, celeration multipliers, and Accuracy Improvement Measure (AIM).
4. Going from or to 0 (zero) is a big deal.

Let's look closely at each reason.

1. Better graphical communication with the 'Zero at a x2 distance below time bar.'

Look at the figure below. Precision Teaching has conventions for acceleration and deceleration data that everyone agrees on. A dot for acceleration data and an X for deceleration data. Looking at the two charted data sets (Figure 35) we have one set with congruence and equality, all the symbols represent acceleration data (the four dots going from 0, 1, 2, to 3). But with the ? symbol, we now have incongruence. Three symbols represent acceleration data and another symbol that requires explanation.

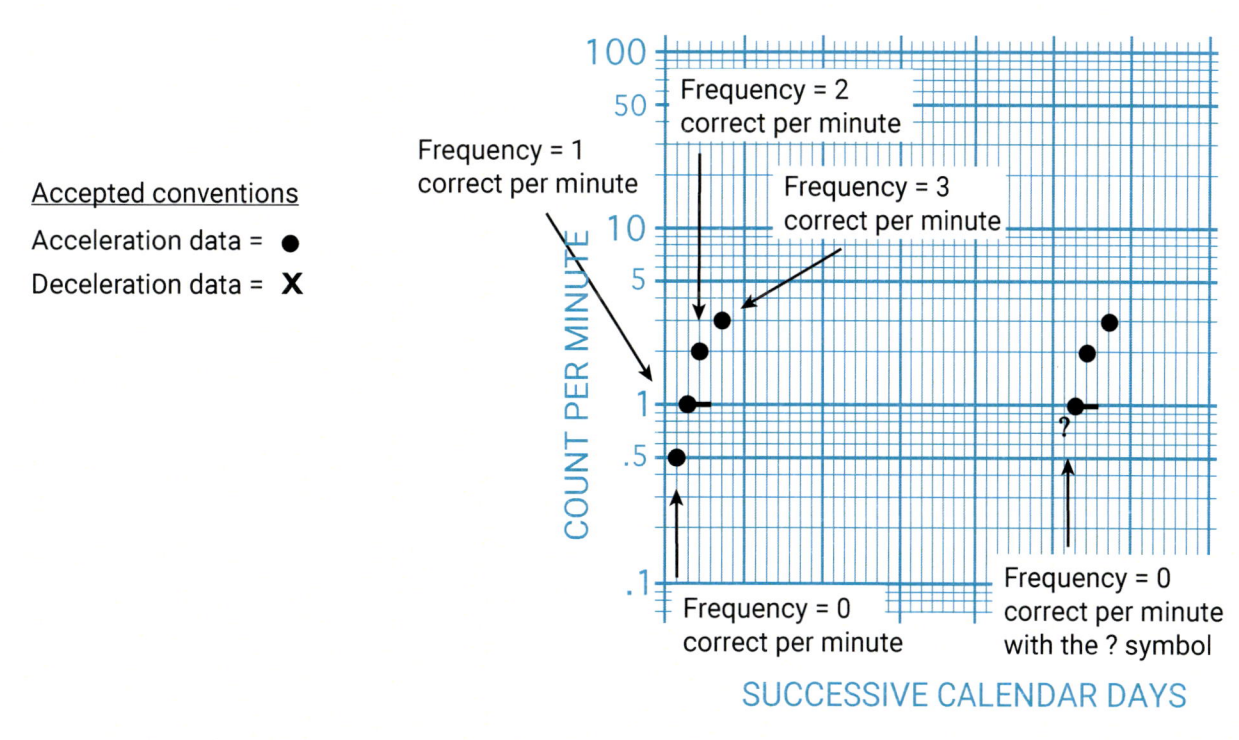

Figure 35. Standard conventions used on the Standard Celeration Chart.

Try the following exercise with the basic lesson we learned from Sesame Street:

●   ●   ●   ?

One of these things is not like the others,
    One of these things just doesn't belong,
    Can you tell which thing is not like the others,
    By the time I finish my song?

How can the wisdom of Sesame Street possibly lead us astray?

2. Allows measurement of Precision Teaching change measures.

In the measurement world of Precision Teaching, change measures (e.g., celeration, bounce, frequency multiplier) function as proverbial yardsticks providing numbers that express the magnitude of change. Furthermore, the significance of the measured data also falls in the domain of the quantified change measure. Many people immediately abandon typical equal interval graphs once they embrace PT change measures and have a quantifiable value with which to understand the world. Take celeration, a line that states how much a range of frequencies grew across a time period. For example, a series of acceleration data that grew at x2.0 per week may mean the measured quantities changed from 10 to 20 (or 5 to 10 or 100 to 200) across the week. A significant amount of growth!

Some change measures like the frequency multiplier require measuring from one data point to the next. Without a proper 0 convention some people will ignore the change measure or measure it incorrectly (using a second data point that is a value other than 0).

3. Consistent, accurate measurement of Precision Teaching change measures.

As previously mentioned, when people use the ? convention, we have trouble with things like frequency multipliers. Going from dot to dot or X from X makes sense but not from ? to dot or X. Therefore, some people who use the ? symbol do not calculate frequency multipliers correctly.

Look at Figure 36. If we use a Finder, we can quickly work out the multiplier. As an example, a 1-minute counting time has 0 corrects. The next frequency has 2 corrects. Moving from 1 to 2 we see the distance at x2.0. The frequency multiplier says the second frequency jumped up x2.0 or doubled from the first frequency.

CHAPTER 5 : INSIDE THE SCC

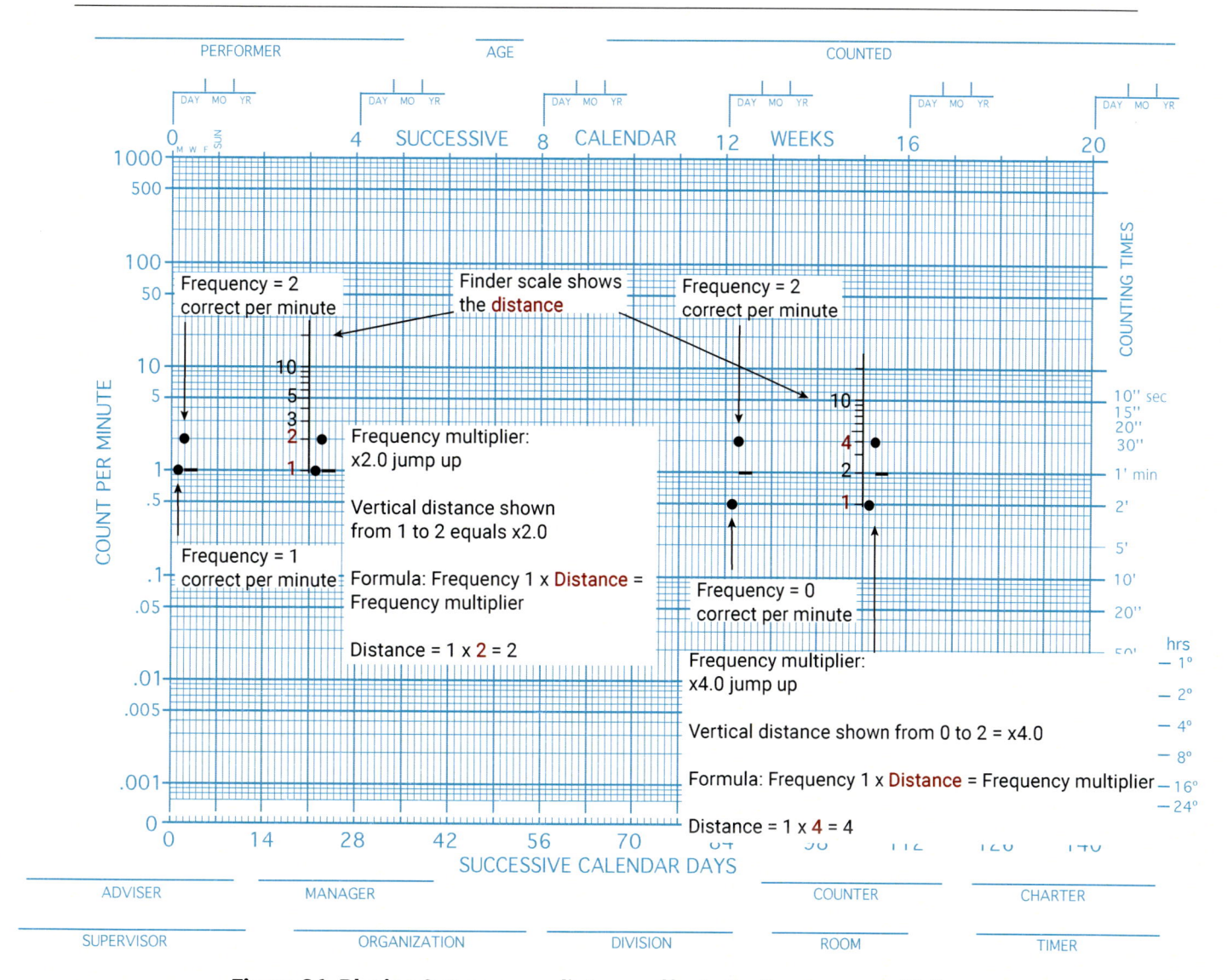

Figure 36. Placing 0 at a proper distance affects the frequency multiplier.

Placing the 0 at a x 2.0 distance below the time bar with Finder has the dot on the .5 line. Measuring to the 2 yields a x4.0 frequency multiplier. The behavior has quadrupled or jumped up 4 times. The Finder shows the distance with which we can calculate the frequency multiplier. Technical note, if we used the scale of the chart and not the Finder we use division. Namely, we divide the larger number by the smaller. So 2 ÷ 1 = 2. And 2 ÷ .5 = 4 (for the second set of data look closely at where the dots line up on the SCC, the top dot lies on the 2 line and the bottom dot representing 0 lies on the .5 line).

At this point you might ask how does a behavior going from 0 to 2 equal a x4.0 change? 0 x 2 = 0 not 4. The previous math doesn't lie, but on the Standard Celeration Chart 0 does not exist. Therefore, we use a special convention to handle a zero count frequency. By adopting the "Zero at a x2 distance below time bar" the 0 will assume a value that we can then calculate. So zero for the 1 minute time bar means 0 takes on the value of .5. If we had a time bar at 30 seconds, the time bar would rest on the 2 frequency line. Zero for a time bar on the 2 frequency line would then be placed on the 1 frequency line (i.e., Zero at a x2 distance below 30 second time bar means 2 ÷ 2 = 1).

Why a x2.0 distance below the time bar? The answer brings us to the next point:

4. Going from or to 0 (zero) is a big deal.

Consider we have a child that can say 1 letter sound correctly. Going from 1 to 2 letter sounds demonstrates a frequency multiplier of x 2, a big deal! But from 0 to 2 we have a frequency multiplier of x4.0. Why the difference curious people want to know? Well, going from 1 to 2 means the behavior just doubled, a large feat of behavior change. However, going from 0 to 2 means we had the absence of behavior to the presence of behavior, an even bigger deal! A child that can't say any letter sounds then says 2 letter sounds? Whoa!

The genesis of behavior, or going from nothing to something, should garner our appreciation and awe. In fact, Ogden Lindsley (the founder of Precision Teaching) mused that we might have zero placed at a x3.0 distance below the time bar because he found such a change astonishing.

What about the other direction? We can go from nothing to something but what about going from something to nothing? A student that calls out in class has a behavior that represents a deceleration target. A teacher that sees a student go from 2 to 1 talk outs has witnessed a ÷2.0 jump down in frequency. But what about the student that goes from 2 to no count frequency of 0? A jump down of ÷4.0! In Og's words: "Performance lives in the multiply world – grows and decays by multiplying and dividing. When performance drops from 1 to zero it drops out of the multiply world where it can be reinforced and accelerated" (Lindsley, August 16, 2000).

If we care about reinforcing behavior, then it must come into existence for us to apply reinforcement to it. On the hand, if we want a behavior not to come into contact with reinforcement, we must move it out of existence. Both achievements require remarkable effort and we must recognize those instances as an empirical marvel.

The convention for zero (0): "Zero at a x2 distance below time bar." Let's use it!

∽

Learning the technical language of a discipline takes time and effort. The terms sometimes do not seem obvious or intuitive. Precision Teaching adopted Plain English to avoid some of the pitfalls that come with overly complicated jargon. Still, every discipline grows, and some terms can change through refinement or substitution. For years people in the PT community used the term "phase change" to apply to a change in an intervention. The phase change does not technically pertain to intervention changes such as the introduction or withdrawal of a variable. I had fun in the following entry contrasting the traditional term phase change and the better alternative, condition change. Fun because I love science and contributing to the technical grandeur of Precision Teaching.

Entry: Condition change or phase change?

When applying the scientific method, people manipulate or observe "variables." A variable refers to any factor a scientist can control, change, or measure in an experiment.

Examples of variables: a drug designed to cure strep throat, an exercise method geared towards helping people lose weight, a reinforcement program used to improve students' homework completion.

When a scientist applies a variable, the graphed data reflect the degree of change. A graph showing the data from an experiment will show different variables as "conditions." Conditions show the presence or absence of variables.

Rod doesn't like to sit still

Let's imagine we conducted an applied experiment with first grader Rod. Rod has a shock of red and an infectious personality. The kind of kid we all love to hangout with. In class, Rod frequently stands up, stretches, or runs in place during circle time. Rod's behavior distracts the other students (though some laugh) and causes the teacher Ms. Shubin to stop her instruction and prompt Rod to sit back down.

Ms. Shubin wants a change so she can teach Rod and the other students better during circle time. She decides to do an applied experiment. She has pinpointed Rod's undesirable behavior as "free-do raises body from the mat." Ms. Shubin wants to decelerate Rod's behavior so she uses an X on the chart.

The Standard Celeration Chart exquisitely shows behavior change through time. In fact, Ms. Shubin believes no better chart exists for times series behavior (Who could disagree with her; Good call Ms. Shubin).

Notice the first condition in which Ms. Shubin counts, times, and records the pinpoint - baseline. Baseline does not mean Rod doesn't do anything. Baseline indicates no special experimental arrangements have occurred with any of the recorded behavior. The baseline condition occurs twice as shown in Figure 37.

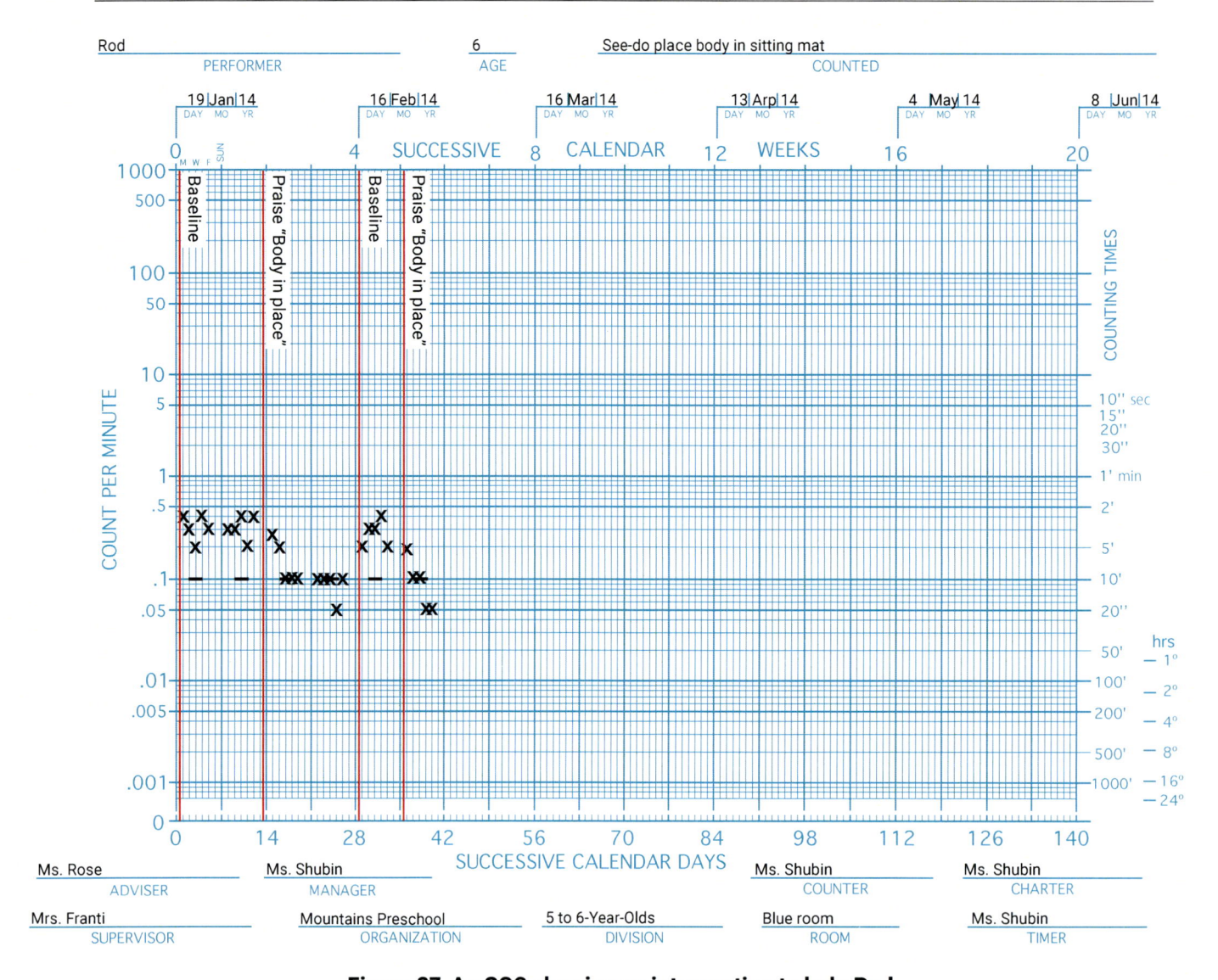

Figure 37. An SCC showing an intervention to help Rod.

Ms. Shubin has implemented an intervention where she periodically praises Rod for times she observes him with his body placed on the mat. The intervention for praising Rod qualifies as a condition. Notice in the figure below the two instances in time during which Ms. Shubin runs the intervention condition.

The applied study Ms. Shubin has run alternated two conditions: baseline and the intervention "Praise Body in place."

Phases differ from conditions

Figure 38 shows four phases. A phase refers to a period of time. We can see in the first phase Rod did his thing during baseline. Then in the second phase Ms. Shubin brought her A-game and ran a nice intervention. During the third phase Rod went back to baseline where no teacher intervention occurred. The fourth phase ushered in the intervention for a second time.

Phases differ from conditions. With phases we have periods of time. With conditions we have variables. Therefore, when doing a study, we want to see what conditions the experimenter applies across time. Figure 38 shows the Condition Labels and the Condition Lines.

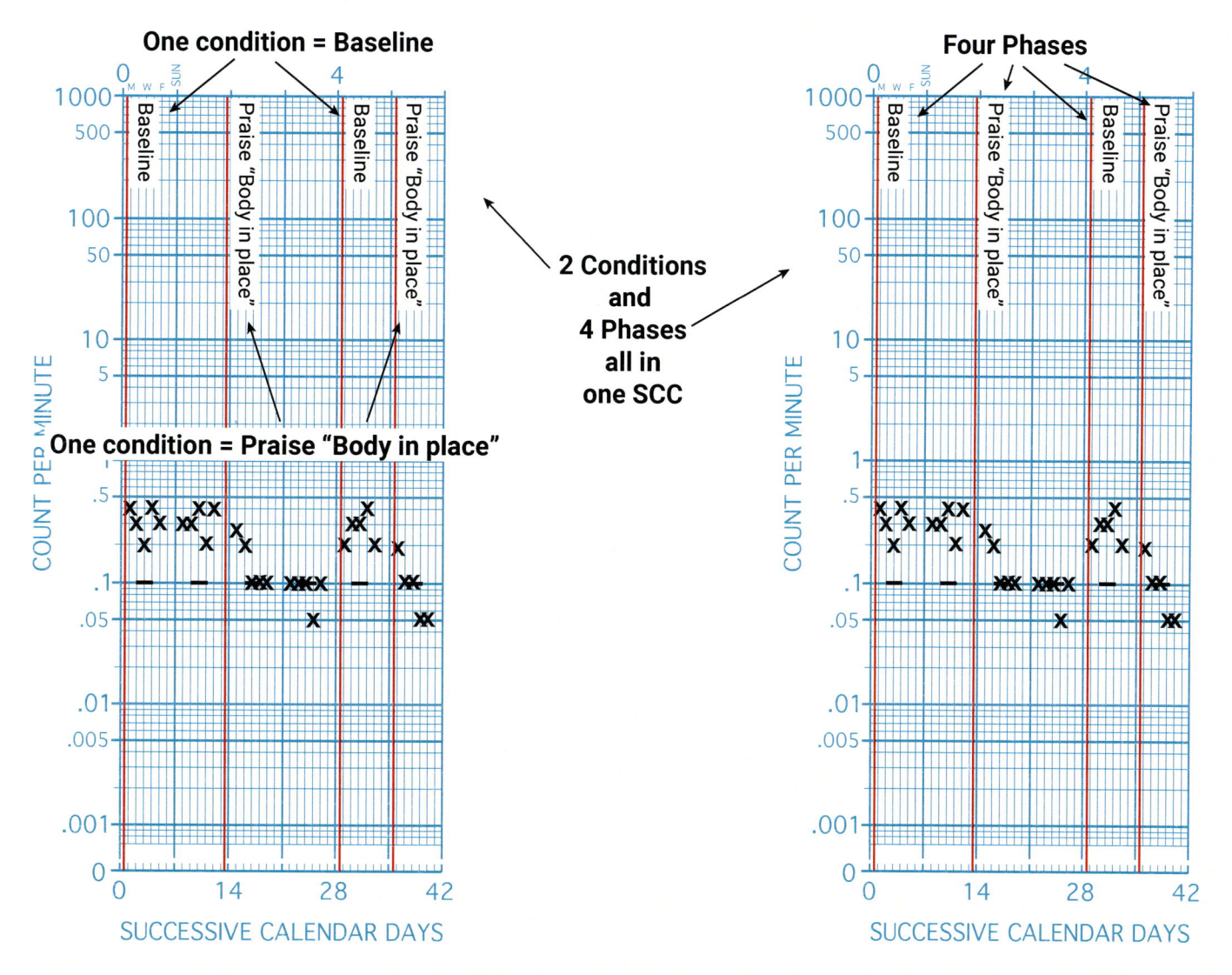

Figure 38. A close look at phases and conditions.

Condition labels tell us what has happened to the data under the label. When a new condition arrives, a condition line tells us if we have a major change in effect.

People use the term phase change line and condition change line synonymously. Should they? If we strive for technical adequacy, we should answer the previous question with a polite "no." A phase change would mean we have switched to a new period of time, but a condition change line provides more information telling all chart readers a new condition has begun. Furthermore, the condition label informs the chart reader as to exactly what transpired. So we would not classify the use of the term phase change as wrong. Instead we should encourage "condition change" because it more aptly describes and informs the chart reader as to what has happened. Unless we really just wanted to refer to the passage of time with new phases.

Condition change lines and condition labels, let's use them!

∞

Celeration constitutes one of the powerful effects of charting frequencies across time. I tried to do two things in a few of my blogs. One, explain the concept of celeration. And two, describe the importance of having such a unit of measure. The Standard *Celeration* Chart and the Standard *Celeration* Society share a middle name due to the high regard the Precision Teaching community has for celeration. I have found using different examples and analogies useful in explaining terms. The following entry marks one of my early blogging attempts to provide a fair account of the value of celeration.

Entry: Celeration – Why growth rates matter

A headline read "Economy adds 103,000 jobs, but it's not enough." The news story indicated the United States added 103,000 jobs in September 2011, but the addition of jobs fell short of a meaningful gain. Think about that for a moment. Does 103,000 new jobs seem like a big number?

If you gave me $103,000 dollars that would make a huge difference in my life. $103,000 is a three-order magnitude change from the 1 dollar in my pocket. My purchasing power would really change.

If the platelet count in my blood dropped by 103,000 that count indicate a viral infection, sepsis, or a cancer like leukemia. I would have great concern with 103,000 less platelets traveling around the Rick Kubina blood stream.

For a smaller town like State College (where The Pennsylvania State University resides), if 103,000 people immediately moved in, we would have a severe problem. The community falls on the smaller side and would have immense difficulty integrating those numbers on a long-term basis. (Note: They do okay on football Saturdays, however!) Everything would change regarding traffic patterns, food availability, health care services, and safety – everything.

Why then, does the absolute amount of change, +103,000 jobs, appear so gloomy? I have just demonstrated the importance of big number changes. It all comes down to absolute and relative change. Absolute changes only deal with how much more or less a person has. The reason absolute number change becomes a problem begins by examining the source of change.

If I had a net worth of $100 and received +$103,000, the change would equal 1,029,900% change, a huge difference! But if I had made it really big and had the 2012 net worth of Bill Gates, $61,000,000,000 (61 billion) receiving $103,000 more means my net worth changed 0.00017%, less than a 10,000th of a change. Think about it in these terms; if I had a $100,000 and someone gave me ¢16 (16 cents), that would represent a very, very small change.

As for platelets count, a normal or healthy count ranges from 150,000 to 400,000 platelets per microliter or mcL. Going from 200,000 mcL to 97,000 mcL (-103,000) means I should see a doctor and have some tests run. The same holds true if I gained too many platelets. A low number of platelets signals excessive bleeding for a person should they receive a cut. But with an exorbitant number of platelets a person can develop blood clots and experience troubling health outcomes like a stroke.

Rates of change matter. Rates of change tell us if a person may have a life ending disease and whether a nation has an unhealthy unemployment rate. So many decisions rely on the information provided by rates of change. How fast did something change and by how much. But what about education and psychology? How often do researchers and practitioners reply on rates of changes? Open any journal and look at the graphs or experimenters and you will have your answer. Most people only care about how much something has changed, not how much and how fast.

Precision Teachers have long relied on rates of change. On the Standard Celeration Chart, Precision Teaching offers a rate of change measure called celeration. Celeration has units over time (count/time) per time unit (i.e., count/time over time). Celeration visually portrays how a measured behavior changes: acceleration, deceleration, or no change over time. Each celeration has a value. The value states how fast and how much the measured behavior changes. Take the example in Figure 39, a cross section of a daily Standard Celeration Chart (or an SCC segment).

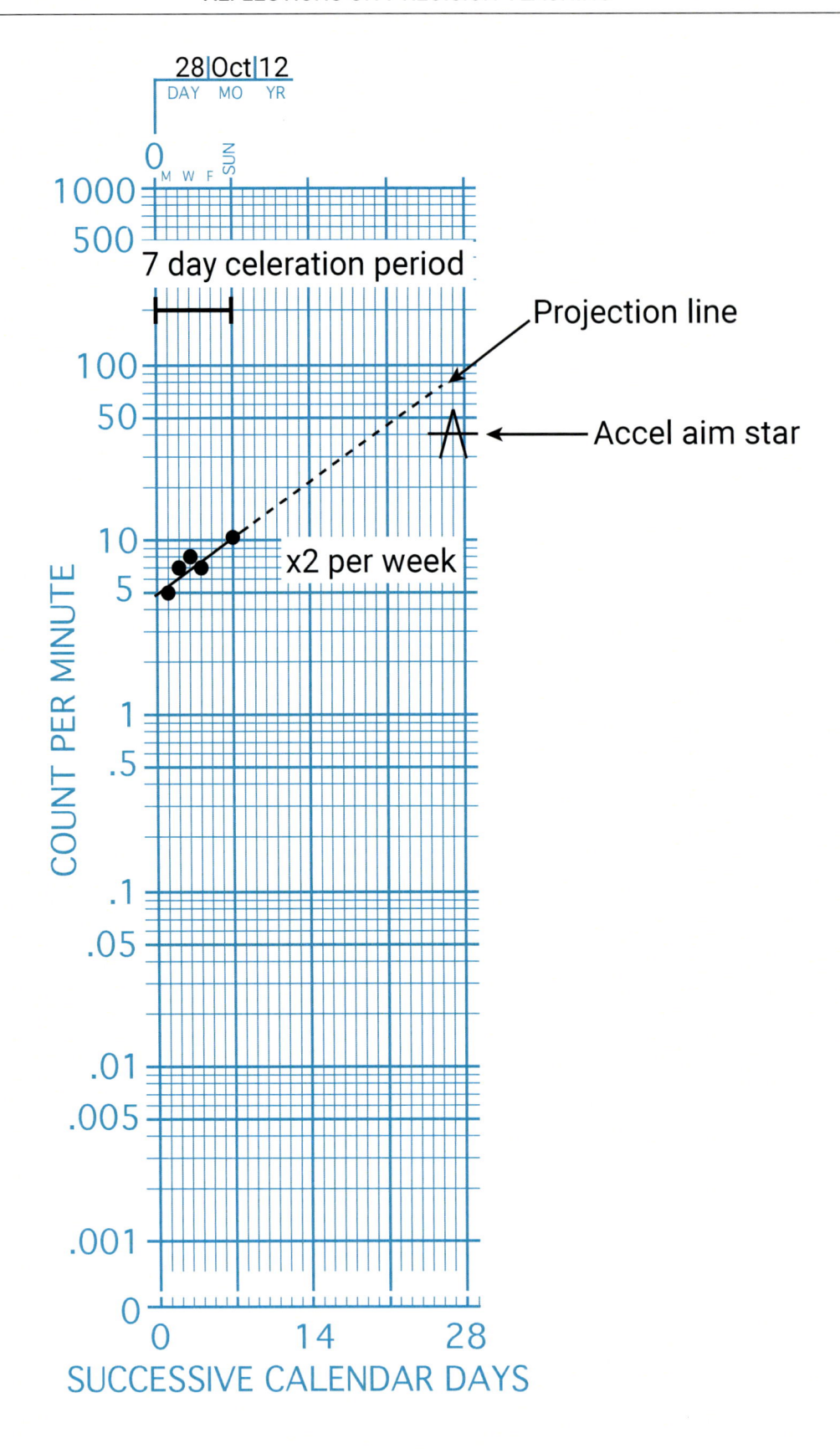

Figure 39. An example of a celeration line on an SCC segment.

The celeration value comes to x2.0 per week. The celeration value communicates a vast array of important information. (1) The x2.0 means the measured behavior, or pinpoint, has doubled in frequency for the celeration period. In Figure 39 the starting frequency 5, doubled to 10 at the end of the celeration period. (2) The x2.0 also communicates the percentage change, a 100% change for the celeration period (a 100% gain of 5 = 10). (3) The celeration period, 7 days on a daily chart, always appears after the celeration value. Knowing the celeration time unit allows the chart reader to evaluate the pace of change over time. (4) The celeration line visually depicts the direction of the measured behavior and where it lies in relation to the frequency aim. By drawing or estimating a projection line (dashed line in Figure 39), the chart reader can quickly evaluate if the behavior will reach the frequency aim in the time frame.

Therefore, anyone using a daily Standard Celeration Chart has a meaningful picture of change clearly visible for all to see. Additionally, all the math behind the celeration value helps the chart reader appreciate the dynamics of the behavior change. Does the celeration rise to a level the chart reader determines as significant? Does the celeration follow a trajectory that will lead to successfully meeting the frequency aim or goal? Also, and I cannot understate this, the Standard Celeration Chart is *standard*. In other words, every celeration value will have the same meaning for every chart reader.

Celeration, use it for all the learners!

People have asked me if I have a favorite blog that I have written. The following entry, I rank in my top 3 favorites. People would leave comments and tell me what they thought about the content when I used to blog. The forthcoming blog received many positive comments. It felt good to discuss decomposition and remind people that we need to act as better stewards of the planet. But the analogy to celeration, especially deceleration, really works. Most people think of deceleration as decreasing, but that doesn't work technically. *Decrease* lives in the add/subtract world whereas *deceleration* or decay lives in the multiply/divide world. Deceleration shows us how fast a quantity (behavior, money, etc.) has disappeared. Deceleration on the SCC provides incredible information and a fitting perspective on what has happened and what lies ahead.

Entry: Decay rates and celeration

How often do we discard trash each day? I ate breakfast this morning and had a yogurt (in a plastic container) and then a Del Monte grapefruit cup (cup made of plastic). Later I mailed some items and used my label maker which produced a label and a plastic piece that when in the trash. After going to the post office, I opened my PO box only to find three pieces of junk mail which joined the garbage can. I could go on describing the trash I produced and I know you can relate to my story when you think of your own life and your relation to refuse. What I would like to draw your attention to follows; how long it takes for objects to decompose when we discard them.

As an environmentally conscious person I frequently worry about our relationship with our planet. But I do not directly intend to lecture anyone on their trash producing habits. Instead, I want to focus on decay rates involved with decomposition. Let's start with the term decomposition. Decomposition refers to how substances break down into simpler forms of matter. For every single substance, decay rates occur as an exponential function. An exponential function simply means a quantity changes (grows or decays) by a fixed percent per unit of time. For example, an exponential increase (growth) in a population of people might come to 3% growth every year. As an example, if the city of Denver (Colorado) had 619,000 people living in it in 2012, a 3% growth would do the following:

Current population in 2012 = 619,000

619,000 x .03 = 18,570 (new people)

So...

619,000 + 18,570 = 637,570 (new population in 2013 with a 3% growth rate).

What about decay rates we see in decomposition? Same process but we use division.

How long does it take for a banana peel to decay? We would need to figure out the decay rate. To do so, we need a unit of time for our calculation. We could choose minutes, hours, or days. Then we need to factor in the process that gives us the percentage for the decay rate. In the case of a banana, bacterial growth act on the organic material causing it to decompose. When the bacterial organisms multiply and work on the organic material, the more organisms created (exponential increase), the more quickly the item (like the banana) will decay. Of course, much factors into decay rates like temperature and humidity (which impact the rate of growth for the bacteria).

Different types of substances decompose at different rates due to the processes that act upon them. Look at the following infographic and observe how long different forms decompose. The items have different decay rates because each substance has a different chemical structure; the active agents involved in the decay directly influence the decay rate. For organic material, bacteria and other lifeforms hasten decay. But for inorganic material like glass and plastic, chemical decomposition occurs. Or perhaps, chemical change would more accurately describe what happens. Nevertheless, glass and plastic change forms but do not decompose like the banana peel. A plastic bag will break down into simpler components, and again, depending on the circumstances and environment factors take an exceptionally long time to change.

CHAPTER 5 : INSIDE THE SCC

HOW LONG DOES IT TAKE TO DECOMPOSE?

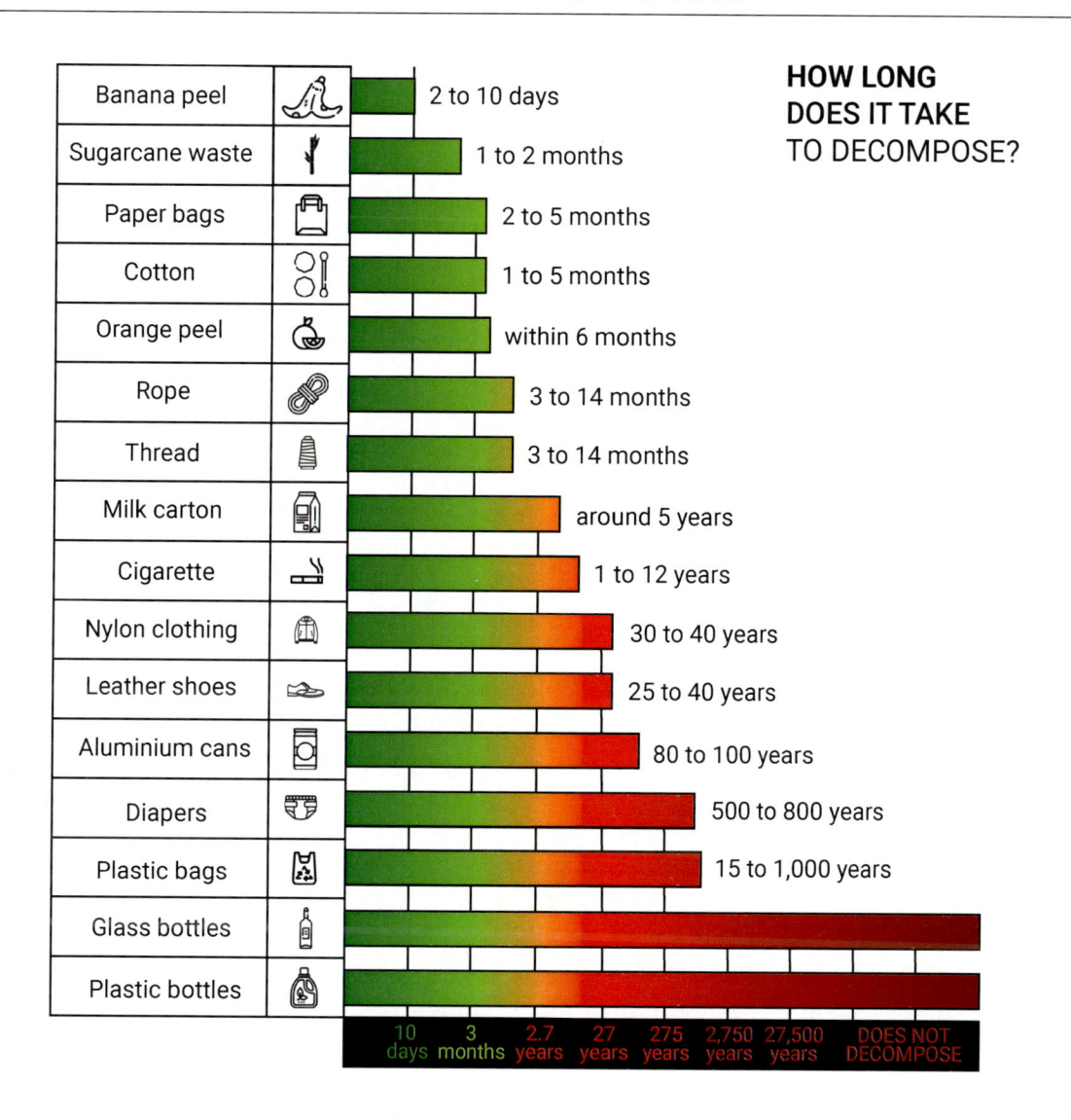

Banana peel	2 to 10 days
Sugarcane waste	1 to 2 months
Paper bags	2 to 5 months
Cotton	1 to 5 months
Orange peel	within 6 months
Rope	3 to 14 months
Thread	3 to 14 months
Milk carton	around 5 years
Cigarette	1 to 12 years
Nylon clothing	30 to 40 years
Leather shoes	25 to 40 years
Aluminium cans	80 to 100 years
Diapers	500 to 800 years
Plastic bags	15 to 1,000 years
Glass bottles	
Plastic bottles	

Scale: 10 days | 3 months | 2.7 years | 27 years | 275 years | 2,750 years | 27,500 years | DOES NOT DECOMPOSE

Figure 40. An infographic showing different items and the length of time involved with decomposition.

I write this post on decay rates because I do have deep concerns about trash and what we do as a society to recycle and reuse finite materials, but also, I want to draw your attention to a direct corollary with Precision Teaching. We have a change measure called "celeration." Celeration refers to how much a quantity changes (grows, decays) over a time period. For the daily Standard Celeration Chart, if a quantity grows, which we call acceleration, the value represents how much it has multiplied for a week. Let's say I started off the week with 20 behaviors in a minute. If I have a celeration of x2.0 per week, then at the end of the week my quantity of 20 behaviors/minute will have grown or accelerated to 40 behaviors/minute (20 x 2 = 40).

The same holds true for decay rates or deceleration. If I started off the week with 100 behaviors/10 minutes, and I have a celeration of ÷2.0 per week, then at the end of the week I will see a 50% reduction and have 50 behaviors/10 minutes (100 ÷ 2 = 50). Just like I described above with the decay rates for organic materials, many factors would affect celeration when

RICK KUBINA | 99

it comes to behavior change. Such reasons vary and require an in-depth analysis. For now, let's take a moment and marvel at the wonderfully informative celeration change measure!

Whatever personal interest you have in behavior change, actions that lead to losing weight, learning how to play the guitar, biting your nails less, or some other personal project you desire a change in, celeration gives you the measure to say exactly how that behavior changes across time. Perhaps you hold a personal or professional stake in the behavior change of someone else. Maybe you have a child who needs to learn to read better, or a neighbor kid coach to play better soccer. Or you might have a professional stake in helping a child hit peers less or eat more food. Celeration not only plays the role of your best friend when examining and evaluating behavior change, but functions as a critical, indispensable measure for everyone serious about determining the effects of an intervention.

Why is celeration so important? Let's go back and look at the decay rates for trash. If we control the conditions affecting decay rate such as temperature, humidity, and available oxygen, we end up with predictable, consistent decay rates. The previous example portrays science at it best; controlling variables and then receiving consistent information regarding nature. How long until a banana peel decomposes? Under specified conditions: 5 days. What about an orange peel? Again, under specified conditions: 3 months and 15 days.

Decay rates tell us how long we can expect to have the trash we put in landfills, fields, lakes, and oceans will remain with us. Likewise, celeration tells how long behavior takes to grow or decay. Concerned with how long it will take your child to learn to tie shoes? Celeration gives us a standard line (slope) along with a number telling us exactly how much shoe tying has changed. Anything we find important, any human behavior, we can put on a chart and look at its celeration. The growth and decay rates (we call both celeration) provide the chart reader immediate, critical information showing and quantifying change across time. Like the decomposition rate infographic above, one day we can produce similar posters for learning showing what procedures produce for outcomes we find important.

※

If I said it once, I said it a thousand times; the world needs celeration! In fact, I led with that as my blog title. I first learned about celeration as the greenest of green undergrads at Youngstown State University back in 1986 (my first class with Steve Graf). I still have the notebook from that class and occasionally refer to some of the examples Steve shared. I had other classes in behavior analysis in which the professors shared data in nonstandard linear graph presentation. I sensed something amiss. But young Rick had no way to articulate the problem. I started using PT and the SCC to learn my SAFMEDS in Steve's class, track my weightlifting, and improve my golf game. I would show my charts to Steve, and he always had me measure the celeration and say what it meant. Steve's lessons resonate with me to this day. In the following entry, I again tried to use reason and logic to show why people should adopt celeration to understand their data better and enhance decision making.

Entry: Why the world needs celeration

One of the major contributions Precision Teaching (PT) has made lies in a standard measurement unit called celeration. It makes sense a measurement unit would rise to the top of the achievement list because PT fashions itself a measurement system (Lindsley, 1997, 1999). And the measurements have centered on human behavior. If you read this blog and find yourself measuring the behavior of other people (e.g., clients, students, yourself), celeration takes center stage as part of the scientific analysis of time series data.

We can compare trend lines on a nonstandard linear chart and celeration lines on a Standard Celeration Chart. Trend lines, also referred to lines of progress or celeration lines, have three functions: 1. describing the performance patterns in a series of data; 2. predicting the future performance of a series of data; and 3. describing the effects of an intervention on a series of data (White, 2005). The trend or celeration line directly informs the chart reader when it comes to making judgements about progress and the degree of change. Two options exist for representing how much change has occurred: using words or using numbers.

Measurement

Taking a step back, let's first examine a measurement unit or unit of measurement (same term but some people order their coffee black while others order black coffee). A measurement unit refers to a specific amount of a physical quantity that becomes the standard for all other similar physical quantities. As an example, length refers to a measure of something from one end to the other. Your friendly blogger has a body length measured from the bottom of my feet to the top of my head. How do we describe my bodily length? We call it height if I stand up and measure from the bottom of my body to the top (72 inches or 6 feet, if you wanted to know).

To answer how we have come to measure parts of our physical universe we could examine the history and development of measurement. The short answer; a group of people (e.g., natural philosophers, merchants, and later, scientists) developed standard units to precisely define the measures we use in everyday life. You can access the standard measures from different sources (discussed later).

We rely on standardized measures so we do not get cheated when we buy products. If you go to your local grocery store and buy milk for $2.99 (€2.16 for all those readers in Europe), how much should you get? The enterprising clerk might give you "a lot of milk" for your money. The next time you purchase milk from the farmers market a kindly Amish salesperson might also give you "a lot of milk" for your $2.99. The Amish salesperson has a different idea what "a lot of milk" means and you receive more this time than the last. Imagine the worldwide chaos that would ensue? Everywhere you go you never know how much milk your $2.99 would procure.

In the United State we know what $2.99 gets us, a gallon of milk. (Author's note: That number worked in 2014 when I wrote that blog, now in 2020, a gallon of milk costs $3.27, on average). The rest of the world uses liters, but the upside remains the same. Because we have standard units of measurement, commerce doesn't look like the wild west where everyone makes up stuff and measures differ from one person to the next. Ask yourself, do you want to live in a world where no standard units of measurement reign supreme? Stated differently, do you want to live in the 10th century where the King of England had to declare that people do not use "false weights and wrongful measures" under threat of intense corporal punishment or death?

Standards

The International System of Units, http://physics.nist.gov/cuu/Units/ or SI (abbreviated from French Le Systeme international d'unites), encompasses a set of measures used almost universally in trade and science. Table 8 shows dimensions people may like to measure (under the Measurement column). For example, we all keep track of time. Eating meals, showing up for work, watching our favorite TV shows, and figuring out how much we owe for our monthly cell phone bill all represent facets of time. We can do all of the previous activities because we measure time as a physical quantity or unit (second column in the table below). A second represents a universal unit for capturing time. We have 60 seconds in a minute, 60 minutes in an hour, 24 hours in a day, 7 days in week, 4 weeks in a month, 12 months in a year, 10 years in a decade, 10 decades in a century, and 10 centuries in a millennium. The sequence of time strikes us as wonderful order!

Measurement	Physical Quantity or Unit	Descriptive Adjectives
Length	Meter	Short - Long
Mass	Kilogram	Light - Heavy
Time	Second	Momentary - Long time
Electric current	Ampere	Mild shock - Strong jolt
Temperature	Kelvin	Cold - Hot
Amount of substance	Mole	A little - A lot
Luminous intensity	Candela	Dark - Bright

Table 8. Physical quantities and standard units contrasted with descriptive adjectives.

First, we recognize everything starts with the second. People who have adopted the second as a standard unit of measurement have a sense of scale. We understand the difference between a 30-minute television show and a three-hour lecture. We perceive the lifetime of a person measured in years (maximum lifespan = 120 years) versus the staggering immensity of time involved with the lifetime of our Sun (maximum lifespan = 10,000,000,000 years). Standards give us a sense of scale by imposing order within our measurements.

Take a moment and closely examine the first two columns. You will quickly come to appreciate standard units of measurement because the spectacular growth of our technological culture rests with the common language of units. If we didn't have standard units try to imagine the present state of our society by using only the third column for doing science, trade, and commerce. Just open a book and look at life in the 10th century and before.

Standard units of measurement make your life run smoothly. Standard units of measures (and their derivatives) touch you when you go to the doctor, fill up your car with gasoline or diesel, buy coffee, drive to work, and stand on your scale (and smile because your healthy life style shows up in numbers). Does anyone want to live in a society where everything previously mentioned goes away and instead adjectives provide a subjective impression of nature? Asking someone how to dress and they respond with "It's really warm" provides very little specific information. Of course, asking your friend from Norway instead of your friend from Florida will influence how you dress and what warm means to your friends. Likewise, imagine going to your doctor prescribes a medicine and says take a little of it each day. Does a little mean a teaspoon (5 milliliters), a tablespoon (15 milliliters), a fluid ounce (34 milliliters), or a cup (240 milliliters)?

You get the picture. Society, and your life, would function very differently without standard units of measurement. We don't want to move from an age of technological splendor back to the dark ages. Standards make life better for everyone.

Standard Units of Measurement on the Standard Celeration Chart

Back to trend and celeration lines. Look at the figure below. The same data appear on a section of a nonstandard linear graph and a portion of the Standard Celeration Chart. The dimensions of both figures have the same physical and numerical scaling. Each data display clearly portrays the dataset and allows line fitting. For each figure I used the split middle technique to fit the trend and celeration line respectively. When looking at the lines, both have two distinct features, which directly factor into analysis of the meaning of the line.

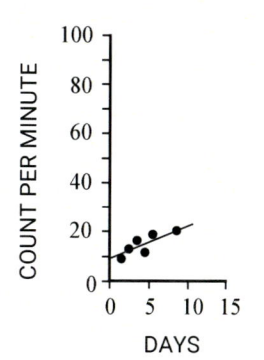

Trend line on a nonstandard linear graph

Celeration line on a Standard Celeration Chart segment

Figure 41. A linear graph and SCC segment with trend lines.

When contrasting the two lines in Figure 41, the first determination made concerns the slope. Clearly both lines have an upward slant. A difference will never exist between trend lines on a nonstandard linear graph and celeration lines on a Standard Celeration Chart. If one line has an upward slope so will the other.

Feature	Trend Line on a nonstandard linear graph	Celeration Line on a Standard Celeration Chart
Slope	Described as upward, flat, or downward.	Described as upward, flat, or downward.
Magnitude	"qualitatively estimated as high, medium, or low" (Kennedy, 2005, p. 197-198).	**Numerically determined with a celeration value (Pennypacker, Gutierrez and Lindsley, 2002).**

Table 9. A comparison of trend and celeration on linear graphs and SCCs.

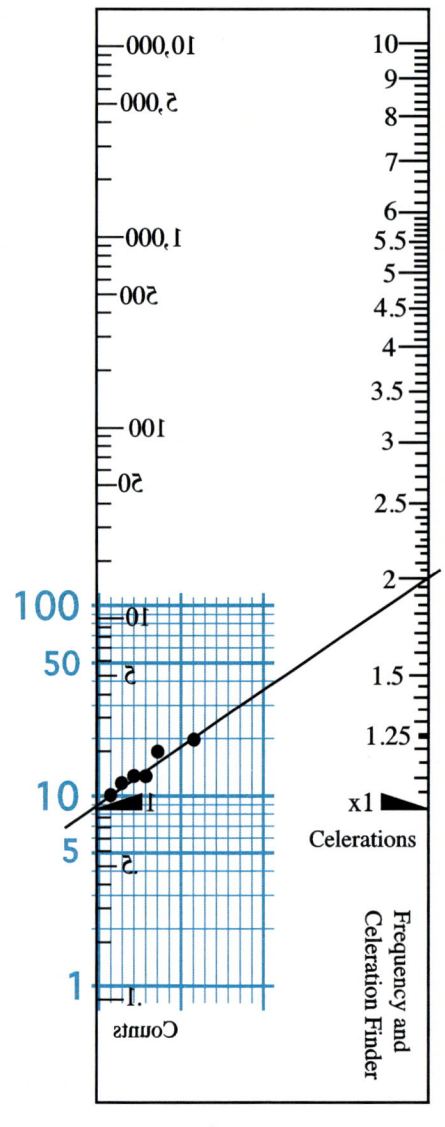

Figure 42. A finder used to reveal celeration

The magnitude of the trend requires a judgement. The individual assessment yields a qualitative value. In Figure 41, I estimate the trend as medium. With the SCC we do not need to rely on a subjective impression. We can measure the line and express the magnitude of growth with a number. Figure 42 shows how a finder reveals the celeration value. Note, when we extend the line it goes through the hatch mark labeled with a 2. Therefore, the celeration value of the line = x2.0 per week (when on a daily per minute chart). The x2.0 per week means the behavior has doubled or increased by 100% per week. Looking at the figure you see the first data point starts at 10 and the last data point ends at 20. Doubling 10, or 10 x 2, equals 20.

Celeration, then, refers to a unit of behavior change everyone can use. The unit of change expresses the quantified magnitude of growth or decay. For different situations celeration precisely tells the chart reader the speed at which behavior has changed. Table 10 lists a few examples of behaviors and celeration values.

Behavior	Celeration Value	Judgement
Writes answers to addition facts	x1.1 per week	10% growth per week. Falls below acceptable growth rates for Precision Teaching.
Says swear word when asked to do work	÷1.1 per week	9% decay per week. A change rate that means the decel pinpoint will stick around for a long time.
Types word on wireless keyboard	x1.55 per week	55% growth per week. Shows a fast change of learning how to correctly type words.

Table 10. Behaviors or pinpoints, the celeration values and precise interpretation.

With celeration the standard unit of change maximizes judgment of the effect through quantification. The celeration value states exactly how fast the change occurred. The symbol (x or ÷) shows the direction of the change. The multiply symbol will denote growth or an upward slant of the line while a division symbol signifies decay or a downward inclination of the line.

As mentioned previously, trend lines describe performance patterns in a series of data and communicate the effects of an intervention on a series of data. Examine the previous table above but without celeration.

Behavior	Trend	Judgement
Writes answers to addition facts	Slowly increasing	A low increase signals a positive change, but one that may not rise to level of acceptability.
Says swear word when asked to do work	Slowly decreasing	A low decrease in trend communicates a weak effect.
Types word on wireless keyboard	Moderately increasing	Moderate increases suggest acceptable change.

Table 11. Behaviors or pinpoints, the trend, and a general interpretation. *Or rapidly increasing?

What rule determines the difference between moderate and rapid? The judgement made for the trend line on a nonstandard linear graph provides information. The information, however, does not compare with the precision imparted by the celeration line and celeration value on an SCC. If someone ever tells you data on a linear graph doesn't differ from data on an SCC, you will know otherwise. A stark and critical difference exists with the trend line and the subsequent effects of judgement.

The social sciences have used nonstandard linear graphs and trend lines for a long time. Researchers made discoveries and helped many people change their behavior. The present blog does not disparage trend lines and suggest they have no positive purpose; clearly the data say otherwise. The main point lies in what we might aspire to as a science and to recognize our present limitations. The scope and depth of analysis and judgement of change dramatically improves with celeration. If one argues against celeration as a standard unit of behavior change then that person argues for nonstandardization and less precision. As an applied scientist or a concerned citizen of behavior change, ask yourself what do you prefer, standard units of measurement or imprecise, subjective estimations?

I wrote the following entry as a way to correct an inexactitude I previously made in another blog. The paper SCC has 20 celeration periods. Those 20 celeration periods appear in all Standard Celeration Charts. Understanding their nature provides one with a well-rounded understanding of the order inherent in all charts. Plus, readers can check off "celeration period" from the list of PT nomenclature.

Entry: The celeration period

In a previous blog post I used the term "celeration period" in a rather cavalier manner. In Precision Teaching, however, celeration period has a distinct meaning. Namely, the celeration period refers to a fixed length of time on a Standard Celeration Chart (SCC). With four different types of charts in the SCC family (i.e., Daily, Weekly, Monthly, Yearly), each chart has its own celeration period. For the Daily chart, the celeration period = 7 days, or one week (see Figure 43). The Weekly chart has a celeration period of one month. The Monthly and Yearly chart, respectively have celeration periods of six months (or half year) and five years (or half decade).

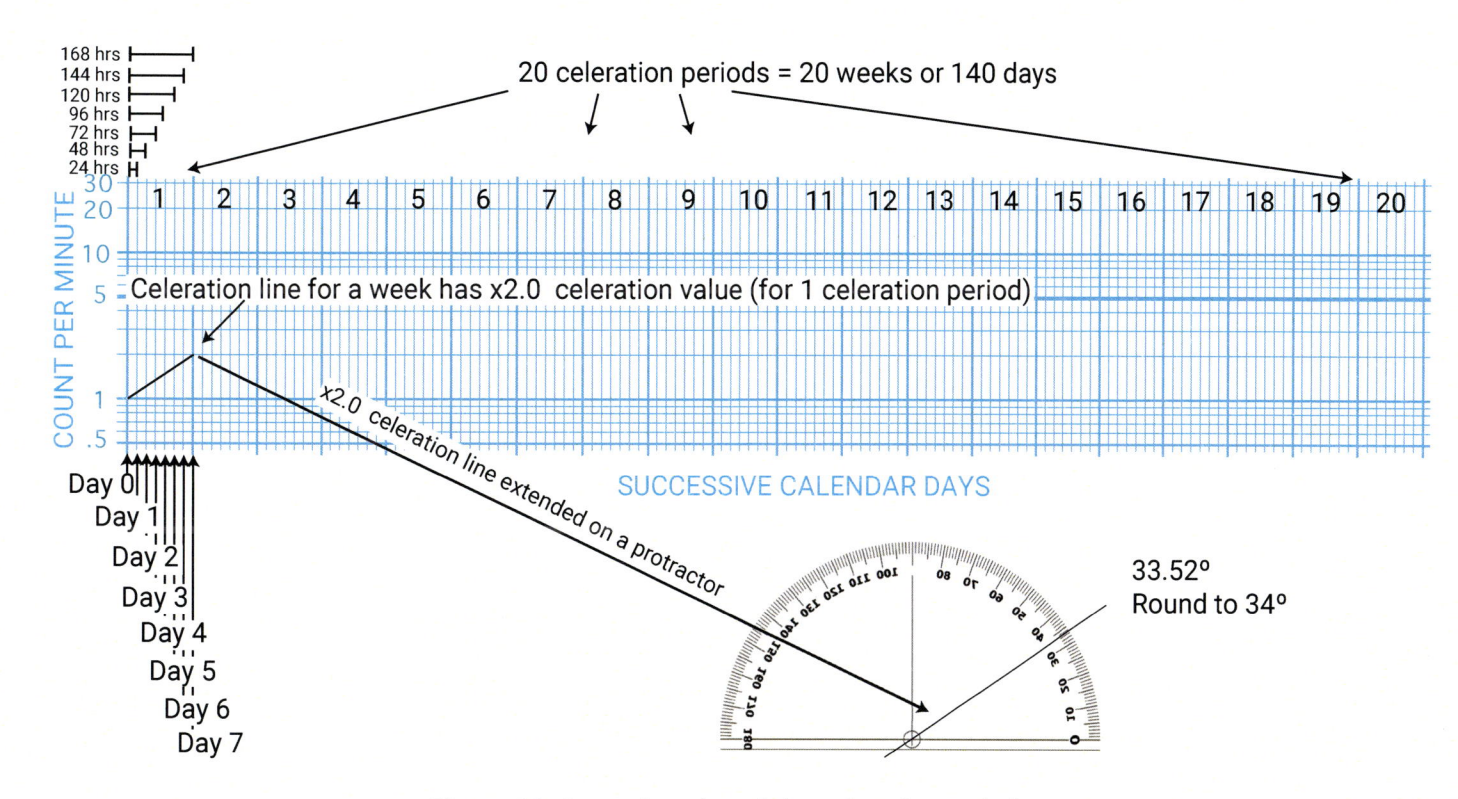

Figure 43. An explanation of the celeration period.

A celeration period for one week appears in the cross section above. Notice the celeration line technically starts on day 0 (recall all thick lines represent Sunday whereas the other thin lines cover Monday through Saturday). On the Daily SCC if we measured 24 hours of time, we see the time frame starts at day 0 and goes to day 1. Then another 24 hours from day 1 to day 2 gives us 48 hours (see top of Figure 43 and hours). At the end of the week, we have a total of 168 hours and the celeration line stops on a Sunday line. Therefore, everyone using the Daily SCC to analyze the daily behavior will first see learning changes in one celeration period (1 week or 168 hours).

Learning = Celeration = minimum of 5 data points (though some prefer a 7-9 data point minimum)

Performance = Frequency = 1 data point

Therefore, on any chart you can see performance and performance change, which means looking from one data point to another. The change in one dot to the next tells you precisely how much a performance has improved, worsened, or maintained. To see learning changes, we have celeration, which tells us precisely how much a series of performances have improved, worsened, or maintained. With the Daily SCC a celeration period forms the nest where performance frequencies grow. I do not know who is the bird in my previous analogy but let's just go with it.

Each chart has 20 celeration periods. If you look at the cross section of the Daily SCC you will see the 20 celeration periods. If a celeration period equals 1 week then 20 celeration periods cover 140 days. On a Daily SCC that covers quite a bit of ground! As a person interested in behavior change you have a lot of real estate to monitor learning changes.

One final note, the geometry of the chart contains standard angles which have mathematical significance. Notice how on the figure above the x2.0 celeration appears on the protractor. You will see the line almost perfectly matches a 34-degree angle; the line falls slightly below 34 to 33.52 but we round up and refer to it as a 34-degree angle.

All of the charts in the Standard Celeration Chart family have the 34-degree angle across each celeration period which means the change has doubled. So, if we start at 1, as in Figure 43, and we double the performance, we end up with 2 (1 x 2 = 2). On the Daily SCC the doubling coupled with the standard 34-degree angle helps chart readers instantly spot significance growth (i.e., acceleration) and decay (i.e., deceleration).

If you want to employ a visually driven, informationally intensive, data monitoring system, consider the power of Standard Celeration Chart. The SCC offers celeration lines with a slope containing valuable quantification. Additionally, the data move within celeration periods giving the chart reader clear vision and a perspective forged in time.

I wrote about different data features of the SCC and had to understand them well to explain them. The following blog celebrates my first attempt to explain bounce. Concepts like bounce have layers. And as I read different books and articles, I worked hard to share and extend a growing understanding of bounce. I also had many conversations with my dear mentors (i.e., Steve Graf and John Cooper). Plus, I took every chance to hit up other PT greats such as Clay Starlin, Malcolm Neely, and Owen White. I hope what I learned then does justice to the source material I read and the advice many people provided.

Entry: Bounce on the SCC

Today we discuss an incredibly important characteristic of learning, bounce. Bounce, a Precision Teaching term for variability, refers to the degree to which a behavior varies over time. We can only see bounce for multiple data points across time, bounce does not lie in a single data point. The larger the bounce the more erratic the behavior. Seemingly "out of control behavior" will translate to high bounce. One day the behavior occurs one or two times and the next day it occurs 40 or 50 times. As an example, I had the chance to inspect the Standard Celeration Chart (SCC) of young man with autism spectrum disorder who had a behavioral target of "aggression." Aggression referred to behaviors that included hitting, kicking, pushing, and biting. By the way, aggression makes for a very poor pinpoint.

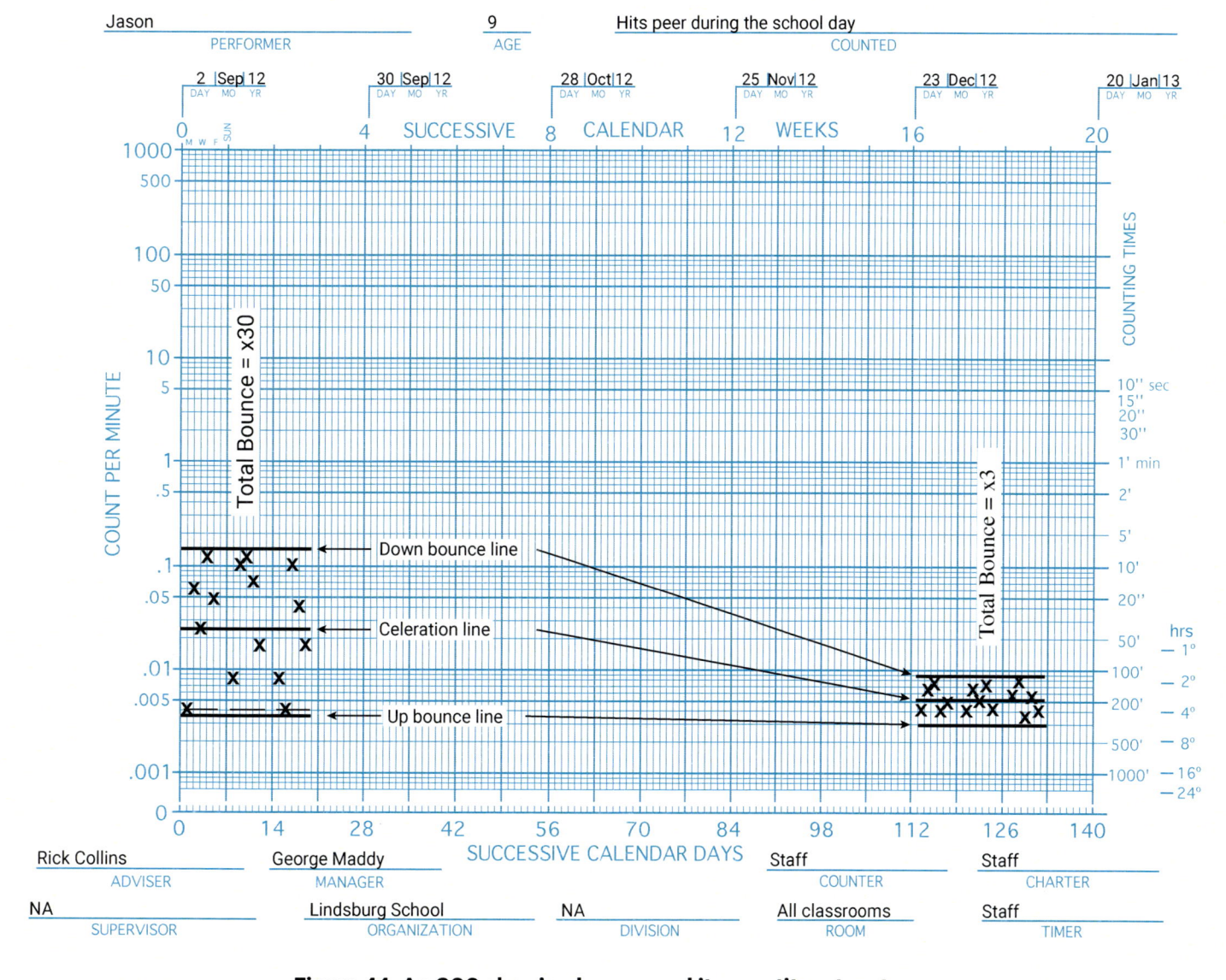

Figure 44. An SCC showing bounce and its constituent parts.

On the chart the total bounce value came to x30.0 (see Figure 44 – counting time = 4 hours). A x30.0 total bounce value describes the relative multiply units of frequency distance found on a SCC. In other words, we have a bounce envelope comprised of a down bounce line, celeration line, and up bounce line (though the actual bounce envelope covers the distance from the up bounce line to the down bounce line). The frequency distance for the "hits peer during the school day" pinpoint (i.e., behavior) falls within the x30.0 bounce envelop measured from the up bounce line to the down bounce line. Note the up bounce and down bounce lines appear opposite for accel data. (*Author's note*: Down bounce means what happens on a bad day. For decel behavior that would occur up top. But for accel behavior a bad day happen opposite and the line rests on the bottom. Likewise, up bounce shows what happens on a good day so for decel behavior the up bounce appears on the bottom and for accel data the up bounce line has its position above the celeration line).

Figure 44 shows total bounce at x30.0. The individual data points bounce all around the celeration line. From the up bounce line to the down bounce line the individual behavioral frequencies (recorded data points) fall within the x30.0 spread. With the up bounce line resting on the .004 frequency line (the frequency line for a behavior with a counting time of 4 hours or 240 minutes) and the down bounce line on the .15 line, the range within the envelope is between 1 and 30 instances of "hits other" and everywhere in between. Having such a large bounce value means one day "hits other" could occur 1 time for the observation period or up to 30 times during the next day (for the 4-hour observation period).

If you had Jason in your class and he performed the pinpoint "hits peer during the school day" once in 4 hours on Monday but the next day he had 23 instances of hits other, what would you think? Such a crazy swing in frequency makes it seem like you can't predict Jason's behavior. Wild swings in the frequency of behavior become known by inspecting large bounce envelopes. With the SCC, you can also put on a number on it. The power of the picture and number, the total bounce value, puts a hard core scientific measure in the hands of the teacher. The teacher knows the behavior has very high bounce (namely, a x30.0 total bounce, no need for adjective like very high).

And as a teacher who must help Jason, the task moves to accounting for the variable(s) at play leading to a x30.0 total bounce value across the three weeks. Behavior occurs as the product of an orderly function of a large number of variables. When we see a large bounce value, the controlling variables might appear episodically. But that doesn't mean we can't identify the controlling variables. And when we implement interventions, the total bounce value will tell us if we found those variables controlling behavior.

Look to the right of the x30.0 total bounce and see the x3.0 total bounce. The stability and regularity with the spread of data instantly communicates a behavior under control. In other words, the controlling variables for the behavior shows up through the spread of the behavioral frequencies (measured pinpoints). The science of behavior considers behavior a lawful phenomenon. The charted frequencies and how much they bounce speak to the orderliness at play in the person's current environment. And we can see it all on the chart.

Most behavioral journals do not present information on variability. And if they do, readers will have a hard time understanding the information due to the subjective terms used (e.g., highly variable). What exactly does highly variable mean? And with nonstandard linear graphs (NSLG) the visual presentation will vary itself from article to article due to the extreme idiosyncrasies of the graph design. For those who use the SCC, however, bounce yields a standard visualization and a number expressing the degree of variability. Why doesn't everyone use it?! In the following entry I attempted to describe bounce with examples and also further define the value of using a better variability measure.

Entry: Do you know bounce?

In a previous blog post we spoke about three features you need. No, three features the world needs when understanding behavior change: celeration, bounce (variability), and outliers. We now turn our attention to bounce.

Variability refers to measured behavior, which occurs at different frequencies across time. Precision Teachers used the term "bounce" because the performance frequencies bounce around on the chart.

What varies and bounces around? Aside from me on the dance floor, think about any behavior we might measure. Say a student raising their hand in class. One day we might observe a frequency of 3 hand raises. The next day 2, the following day 4, and then 4 and 2 on the last two weekdays. So, we have the following observed frequencies:

Monday	3
Tuesday	2
Wednesday	4
Thursday	4
Friday	2

The next week we measure the behavior for 5 more days and measure the following:

Monday	3
Tuesday	2
Wednesday	3

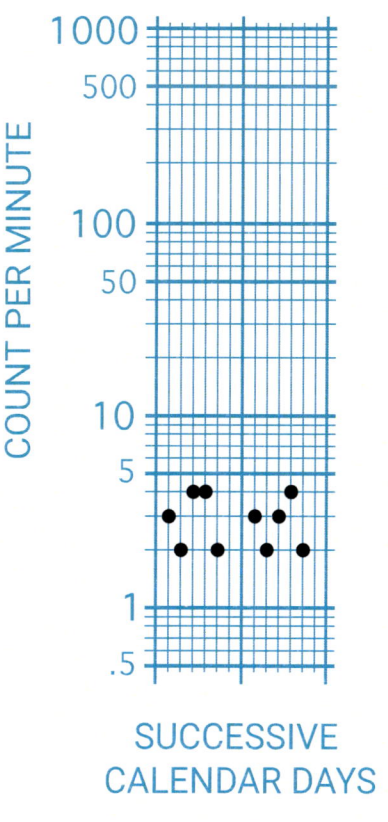

Figure 45. Performance frequencies bouncing around the chart.

Thursday	4
Friday	2

Look at the frequencies in Figure 45 and note how those frequencies bounce around like no one's business!

Why doesn't the student raise their hand 3 times every day we measure the behavior? Because human behavior varies. And it varies for all sorts of reasons. The causes can reside within the instructional environment. Perhaps the teacher ignores our student more one day than the next?

Other reasons for variability occur within the student. The student may feel sick, which affects the likelihood of them raising their hand. Or the questions asked by the teacher may have uneven difficulty so some days our student knows the answer while other days they do not. We could go on. But whenever we measure behavior across time, we see certain properties: celeration or the speed of change, and bounce, the variability or consistency with which the behavior occurs.

How does bounce help us understand the pinpointed behavior? Bounce shows how much control exists in the measured data. From a classic book on behavioral research, Parsonson and Baer (1978) wrote: "A highly variable baseline...suggests that potentially controlling variables occasionally were in effect" (p. 120). In other words, the larger the spread of data, or the more bounce we see, the less control we have.

Look at the two different data sets. The first data set shows the frequency of a student leaving their seat during class over one week. The second set of data shows another student's frequency of leaving their seat. With the greater bounce we can see that we have much less control in the instructional environment for student 1 than student 2.

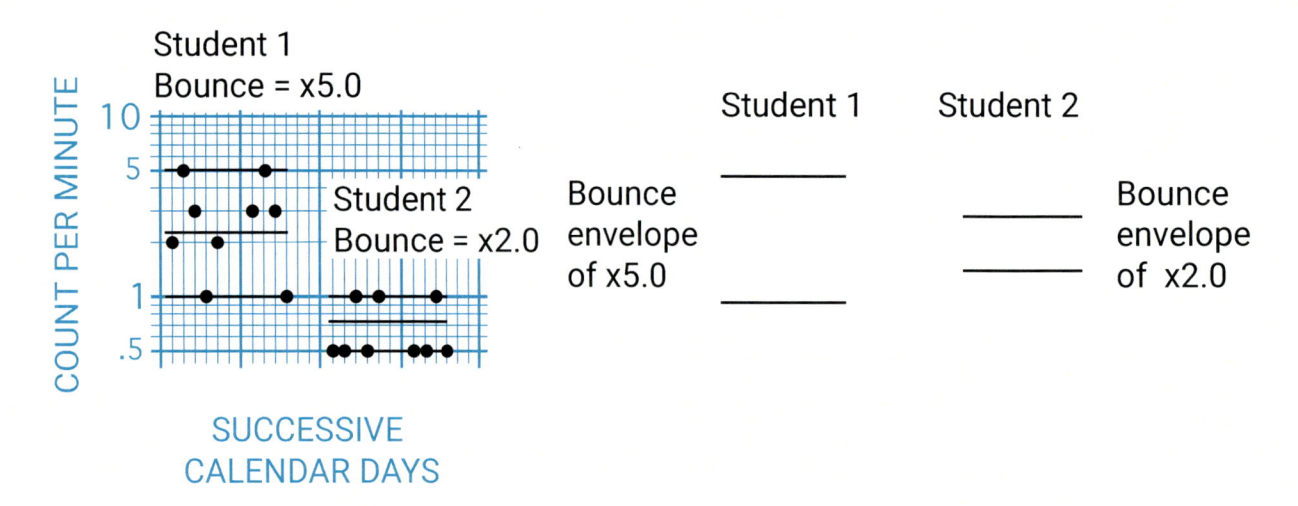

Figure 46. A cross section of the SCC comparing the frequencies of two students leaving their seats during class.

And by control I don't necessarily mean teacher power. In science, when we use the word control, we mean influence. A teacher can arrange a classroom so the influence of what students do occurs due to different environmental variables. For example, a sign posting the classroom rules can influence student behavior as much as a teacher speaking directly to the student.

Why use the SCC for bounce?

Figure 46 shows us bounce. Not only can we see bounce, but we can quantify it. For example, the first student has a bounce value of x5.0. The bounce value states that within the envelope the data will vary from smallest to highest by a ratio of x5. A x5 bounce indicates a moderate degree of variability.

The second student has a smaller bounce envelope of x2.0. A x2.0 bounce value suggests strong control. Looking at the SCC we can see that each day student 2 leaves the seat between 0 and 1 times. The consistency or regularity in the tight bounce envelope communicates performance frequencies varying very little. We know exactly how much they vary by the bounce value of x2.0.

We can compare values and see the degree of difference between performers. A x5.0 bounce value is x2.5 greater than x2.0. Those values tell the teacher student 1 has more than double (almost 3 times) the variability of student 2.

If someone asked you why we should use an SCC for bounce or variability instead of a nonstandard linear graph (NSLG) tell them, we have three very substantial reasons.

1. Behavior lives in the multiply world. Behavior will maintain the same multiple whether it accelerates or decelerates (Lindsley, 2010). With a NSLG all bets are off. The variability or bounce envelope will change depending on which way the behavior changes.
2. Bounce has a numerical value. With numbers, we can qualify change and therefore better understand what is happening. We want numbers, we don't want to rely on less precise means like using words (e.g., small variability, moderate variability, large variability).
3. A standard chart means once we come to recognize bounce, we can quickly ascertain the degree of control we have just by looking at the SCC.

Bounce, a visual and quantitative indicator of control. Let's always forge our analyses in the rich metrics of the Standard Celeration Chart

∞

A within condition analysis contains different components with which chart readers can understand their data at a deep level. Celeration, bounce, level, and the improvement index round out the top four major parts of data set level analysis. I wrote previously that very few people use variability and bounce to analyze their data. Almost no one uses the improvement index, even within the PT community few people report values or discuss in research or practitioner articles (according to a comprehensive survey of all Journal of Precision Teaching & Celeration issues). Awareness may promote more adoption with specific and, hopefully, the suite of amazing SCC metrics.

Entry: A behavioral metric for quantifying improvement

At the time of writing this blog, a headline on CNN reads "Dow sinks below 23,000; Nasdaq flirts with a bear market; and oil is in free fall." The Dow Jones Industrial Average (DJIA) and Nasdaq both represent important stock exchanges. In fact, many people consider the DJIA as a financial barometer of the world. Therefore, the Dow taking a dramatic downturn makes the mainstream news and causes headaches and worry for investors.

The DJIA has 30 stocks from United States companies. For many years the Dow had a simple calculation: summarize the stock prices of all companies and divide by the number companies in the index. For example, the Dow started with 12 companies, and if all their companies' stock price combined to $10,000, then the average would come to 833.33 ($10,000 ÷ 12). Now the Dow uses a more complicated weighted average. But what does the Dow and index calculations have to do with behavior?

The improvement index

An index serves as an indicator of something. As discussed previously, the Dow and the Nasdaq indicate how well the stocks in their portfolio perform. Investors have a quantifiable figure to gauge the "health" of the market. Unknown to many behavior analysts, there exists a quantifiable figure to determine how much improvement occurred over time.

"Improvement" cuts across all ages, occupations, and positions. Elementary school students, college athletes, professional musicians, and surgeons all engage in behaviors that may improve or deteriorate.

Take the example of a basketball player shooting free throws. The player who shoots from the free throw line has a number of corrects (balls through the hoop) and incorrects (balls not through the hoop). A traditional measure of skill would appear as a percentage. For instance, 15 shots correct and 5 shots incorrect = 75%. Improvement, then, would occur if the accuracy went beyond 75%.

But increases in accuracy from one data point to the next provide only a simple conception of improvement. Namely, that of the person becoming more accurate. The improvement index evokes a much greater appreciation for skill development.

The following data show a high school player, Mack, who practiced shooting free throws. Mack shoots as many balls as he can in a one-minute counting time. The data show a rich display of information across time. The dots represent corrects and the X's incorrects.

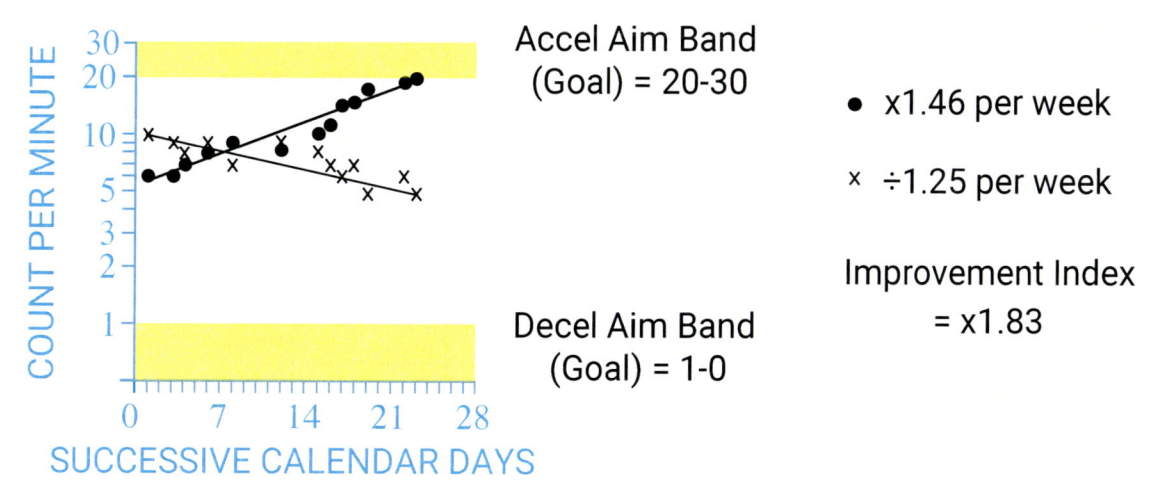

Figure 47. A standard Celeration Chart segment showing corrects and incorrects for shooting free throws.

A behavior analyst could also view improvement by looking at the Standard Celeration Chart data for other data features:

1. The direction of corrects and incorrects. Do they trend towards the aim or goal?
2. The speed at which each data path changes. Does the speed with which accel (corrects) and decel (incorrects) data change meet acceptable thresholds?

The data in Figure 47 reveal that both data paths move in the direction of the aim band. Furthermore, across time, the corrects accelerated 1.46 times per week (a 46% weekly growth rate) while incorrects decelerated by ÷1.25 (or decayed by 20% each week).

A very sophisticated way to discern how much progress happened falls in the domain of the improvement index. The improvement index uses both the celeration value for the corrects and incorrects and then forms a ratio. The resulting value directly quantifies the degree to which a behavior became better or worse.

Mack's x1.83 improvement index communicates the extent to which his free throw shooting improved. Stated differently, Mack's ability to shoot free throws in practice improved by 83%. Just like the Dow Jones Industrial Average, the improvement index combines data (growth and decay rates across time) to provide a sensitive metric for behavioral improvement.

With the improvement index behavior analysts can (1) quantitatively assess improvement or deterioration, (2) objectively compare improvement across people, and (3) have a scientific standard for which all behavior analysts grade interventions in terms of the amount of improvement produced.

Conclusion

Analyzing behavior makes for an exceptionally challenging task. The task becomes even more taxing without ready, quantifiable markers of behavior change. The improvement index presents a means to monitor and judge how much a behavior advanced or progressed. With the improvement index behavior analysis may one day have benchmarks indicating socially significant improvement. Until then, every behavior analyst can put their data to work by displaying it on a Standard Celeration Chart and examining the improvement index.

I find the topic of outliers fascinating. The topic has significance from several areas. Outliers in math means a value that lies outside of the other values. We can look at outliers mathematically and when we place them on the chart all sorts of interesting things happen. First, we can easily spot outliers whether high or low. Second, we can apply some cool math to outliers and indicate their probably of occurring. And third, figuring out why the outlier happened in the first can uncover real gold. The following blog entry describes my first attempt to explain outliers from a PT perspective.

Entry: How bizarre

Malcolm Gladwell wrote a book on the subject. Statisticians tell us they are a mistake. And a brewing company claims it as their namesake. You guessed it; this blog we will discuss those strange things we call outliers.

The term outlier has different meanings depending on who does the defining. In statistics, an outlier refers to an observed data point very distant from the other observed data. Statisticians believe outliers can come from variability but also may result from a measurement error (many statisticians want to remove outliers from the data set).

In geology, an outlier means a younger rock formation occurs with older rocks. And with people, an outlier describes a person excluded from a group. In statistics, geology, and people, an outlier represents something standing apart from the other usual, typical things.

In Precision Teaching, outliers also share aspects of distinct separateness. Specifically, outliers communicate

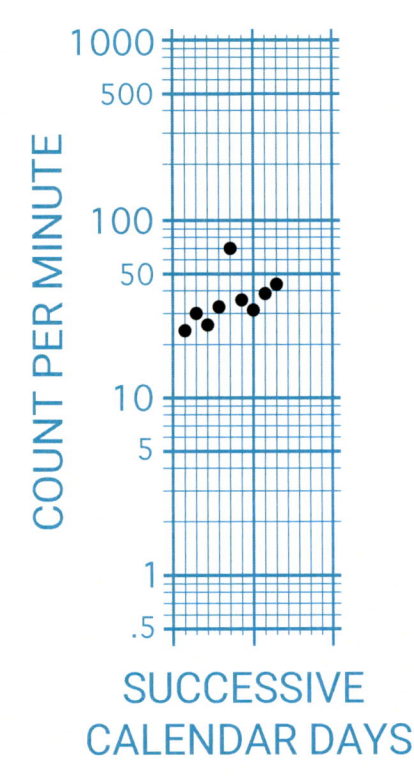

Figure 48: A cross section of a Standard Celeration Chart showing an outlier (highlier)

an exceptional performance. Outliers have two flavors, exceptionally high and exceptionally low. Thus, some use the terms highliers and lowliers to directly communicate what type of outlier has taken place.

Ogden Lindsley, the founder of Precision Teaching, early on recognized the importance of outliers and used the whimsical names "peach" and "lemon" to describe very high and very low performance frequencies. Looking at the figure below can you spot the outlier?

What do outliers do?

If you see an outlier, welcome it to the fold. Outliers provide a superb opportunity to gather information. In the case of a highlier, we learn about the conditions that help usher in exceptionally positive change. Then, we gain insight into how we can help dramatically accelerate growth and learning.

When we see a lowlier, we again acquire important knowledge. Namely, what to avoid in the future. Lowliers show us conditions that negatively affect behavior. One day we have a person learning like no one's business. The next day, boom! The person has an out of nowhere terrible performance; one you have never seen before, and one you hope to never see again.

Outliers do not happen often so when they do, we must immediately investigate. True, some outliers can occur because a person committed a measurement error. Also, sometimes people enter in the data and miss a digit making a performance look like an outlier. But true outliers do come to pass. And like a rare sighting of a comet, we must take notice and make swift inquiries into what happened.

The likelihood of outliers

If you have a checklist of all the awesome things you can do on a Standard Celeration Chart (SCC) you now have another entry. We can calculate the probability of an outlier occurring based on its distance from the bounce envelope.

What does probability tell us? Let's say you found a $5.00 bill as you went for a walk around New York City. The probably of finding a $5.00 bill comes to 1 in 5,000. That means you have a 1 in 5,000 chance of finding a 5 spot. Your chance of a finding a gold bar in New York City comes to 1 in a 1,000,000,000,000 (1 trillion). You have a chance to find a $5.00 bill, you have almost no chance to find a gold bar lying around.

Probabilities tell us the same thing on the chart. If you have an outlier with a 1 in 1,000 chance of occurring you might not find that so unusual, it can occur though we would classify it as rare. But the more improbable the chance of that outlier occurring, the more we need to see why it happened. Figure 49 shows the distance a data points lies away from bounce envelope and the probabilities of it occurring.

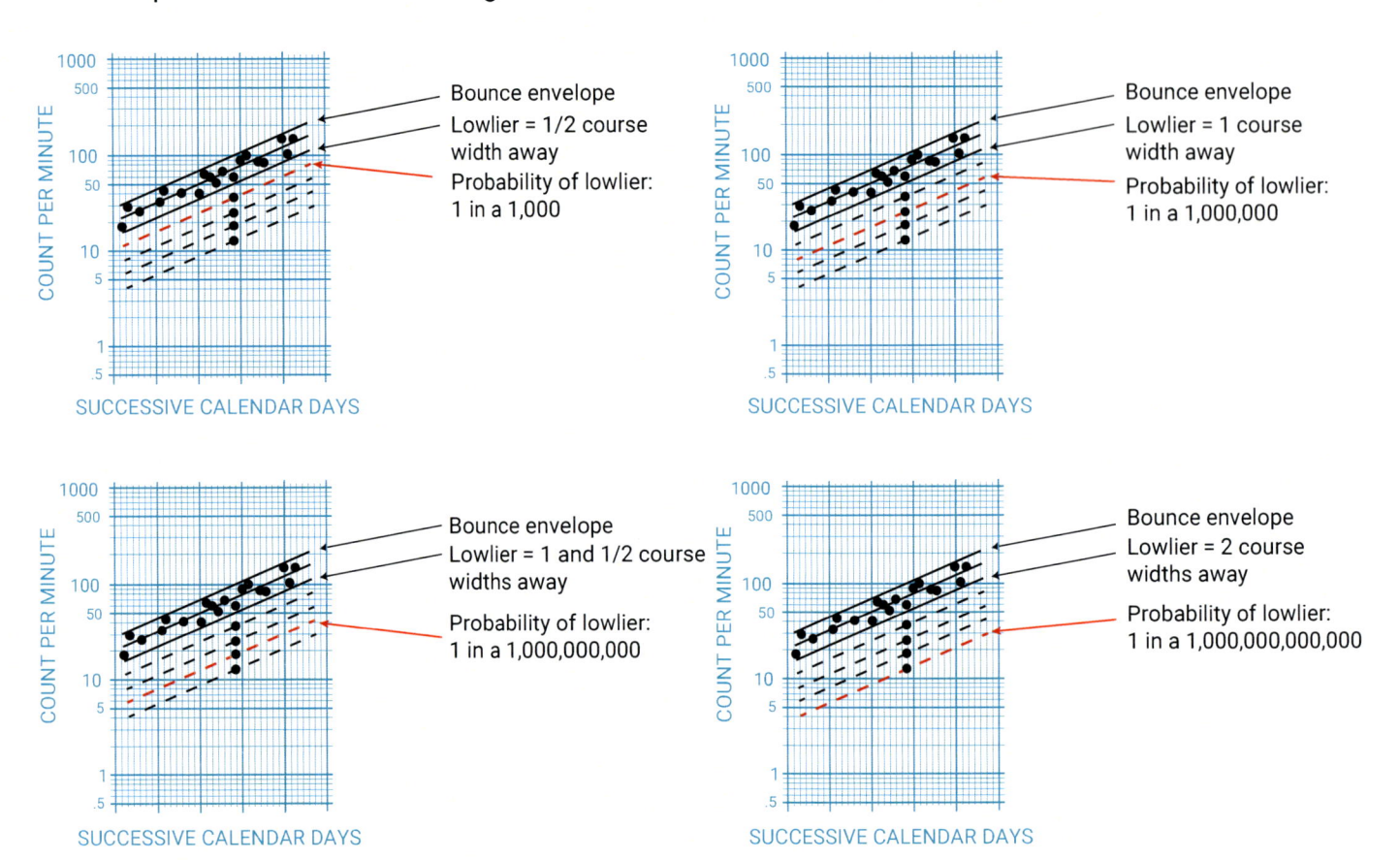

Figure 49. Distance away from the bounce envelope corresponds to the probability of occurrence for the outlier (lowlier). A course width = the size of the bounce envelope.

We have much to learn from outliers. When placed on the team with celeration, bounce, level, and improvement index, outliers give us that much more analytical power to understand behavior, solve problems, and create a potent, exciting learning environment.

∽

Somehow, I picked up a habit of going to Box Office Mojo each Sunday and reviewing the weekend box office. The revenue, reported in the millions, for each film led to many interesting analyses. For example, looking at the budget for a film and how much it made reveal the popularity of a movie (range - bomb to blockbuster). I have admired many of Hollywood's products while scratching my head at others; I guess everyone is a critic! I read an article once about pirated movies and thought it would make a great topic for discussing projections. The following entry presents a common and less common method for making projections on the SCC.

Entry: Illegal Oscar Screeners: The Standard Celeration Chart projects an end to piracy

Movies and Screeners

If you like movies, you find yourself in good company. The national box office for 2016 came in at 11.2 billion dollars. The number of tickets sold driving such big numbers: 1,296,674,369. As of today's writing, the top 10 Hollywood movies have generated 3.4 billion dollars by themselves.

Around the water cooler, people talk about the latest Star Wars or Avengers movie. But in Hollywood, talk turns to money such as ticket sales, revenue, and how to extract more money from movie goers and the licensing of their content. Yet Hollywood has long battled piracy and the illegal sharing of content in today's digital age.

According to the file sharing news site Torrentfreak, the top 10 pirated movies of 2016 included titles such as Deadpool, Star Wars: The Force Awakens, and Finding Dory. The money lost through file sharing websites reaches into the billions.

During December of each year, Internet pirates look forward to "Screener Season." Industry insiders who vote for Oscar nominated films receive DVD or digital "screeners" showcasing films that studios hope will receive attention, and nods, for an Academy Award nomination.

The pre-release screeners get leaked to file sharing sites, and then anyone with an internet enabled device and the proper software can download or view movies either still showing or not yet released. Needless to say, Hollywood has agonized for years over trying to stop illegal sharing of their content.

A recent article illustrated the trend of screeners with a simple bar graph. The figure shows the calendar year and the number of leaked Oscar nominated films. All the leaked films show up on file sharing websites and studios lose money. According to Figure 50 what trend do the data show?

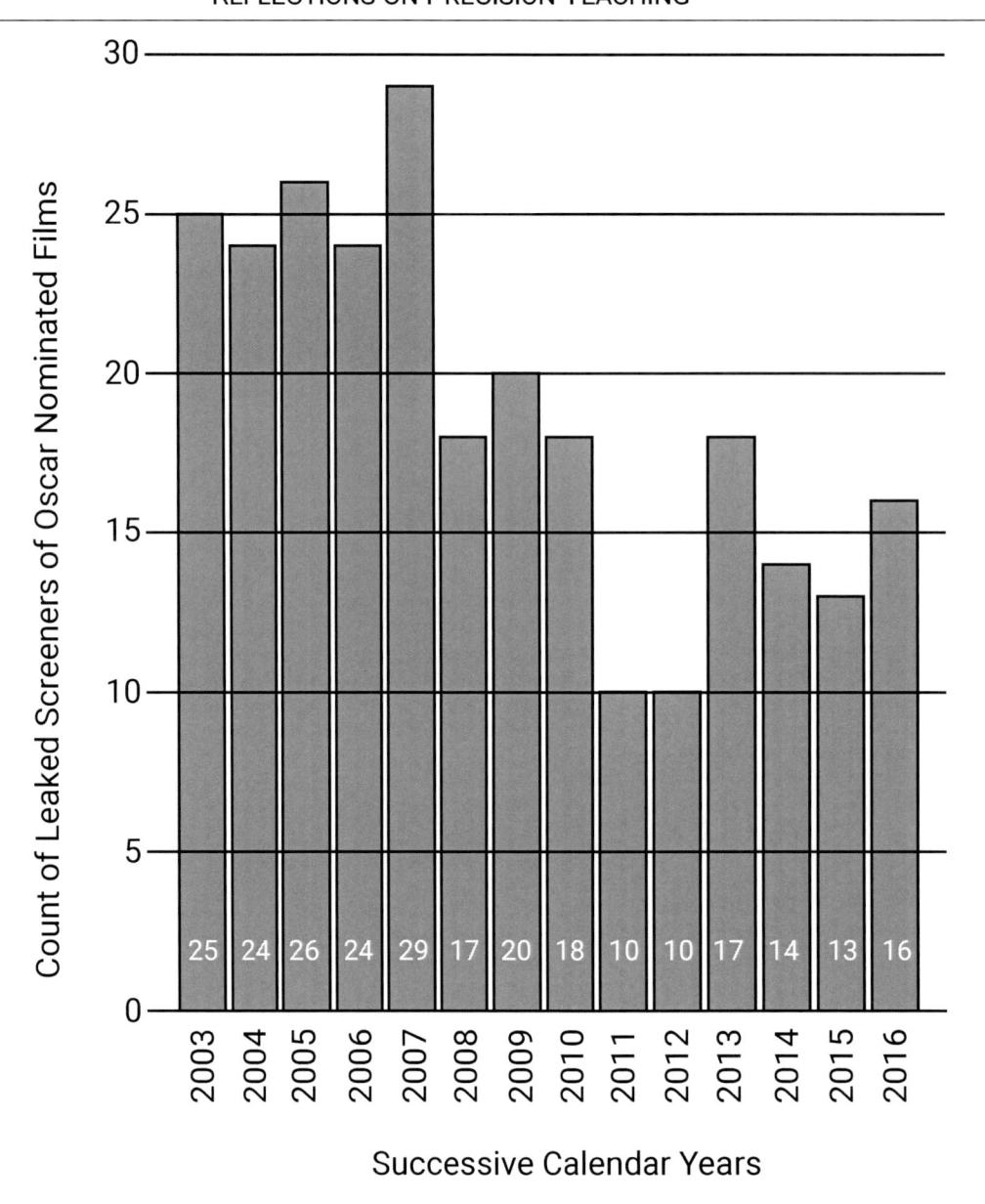

Figure 50. A column graph showing the number of leaked screeners of Oscar nominated films (Source: torrentfreak.com).

The SCC

The data from the figure above come from Andy Baio, an Oscar piracy watcher. And with the data we can transform the bar graph to a Standard Celeration Chart or SCC. The Yearly SCC below better handles the data due to its rate-of-change purpose.

Each vertical line designates a calendar year. The scale along the vertical axis provides a ratio view of "count per year." Therefore, the X's or deceleration data on the SCC illustrate the yearly leaked Oscar screeners starting at 2003 and ending at 2016.

Chapter 5 : Inside the SCC

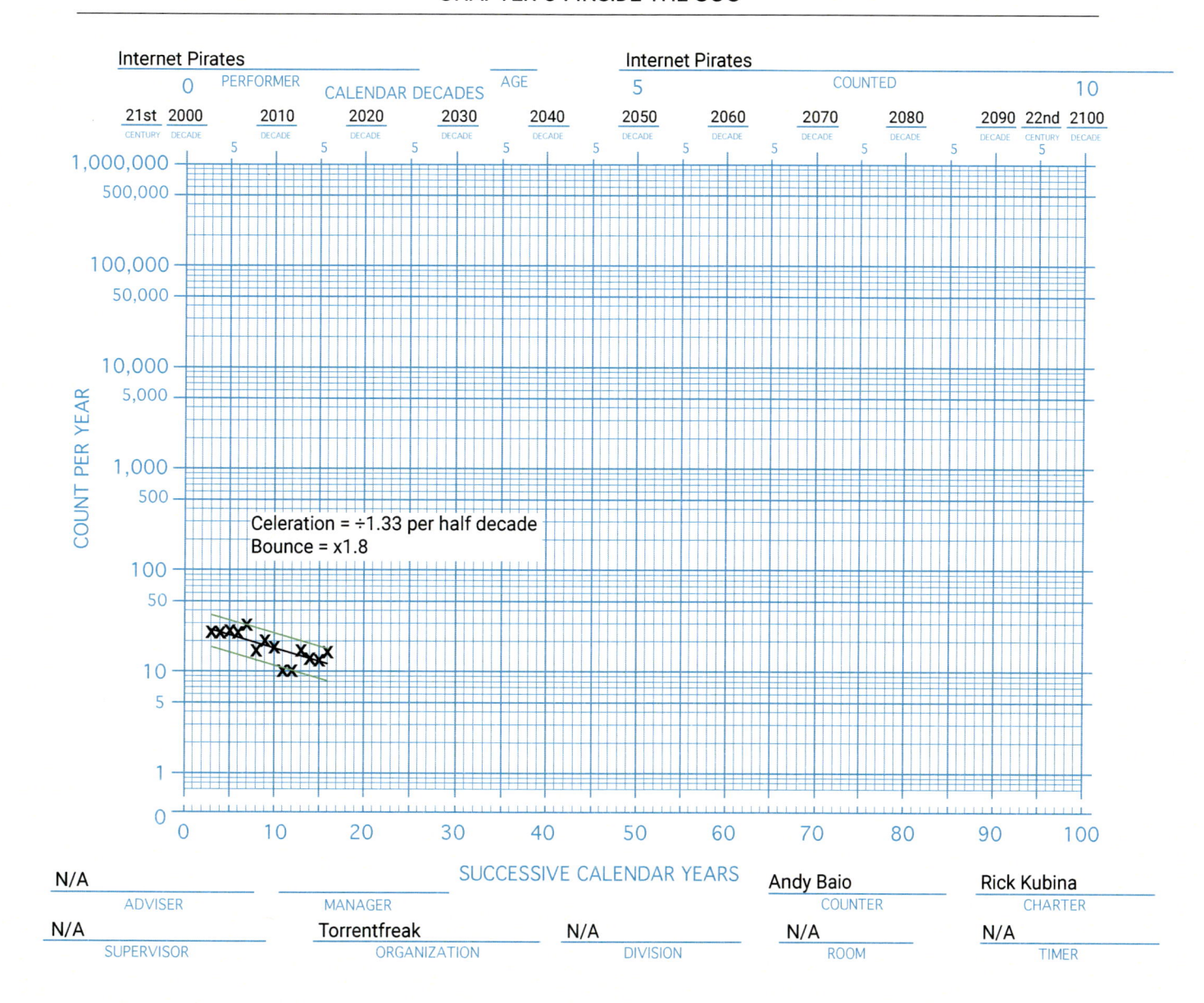

Figure 51. A Yearly SCC displaying "Leaked screeners of Oscar nominated films per Oscar year."

The X's show a downward trend (i.e., black line in Figure 51). The trend line represents a measure called "celeration." Celeration, the root word of acceleration and deceleration, communicates the speed of change. Specifically, the data decelerate by ÷1.33 per half decade. In other words, every 5 years the data decay by 25%. The decay rate offers a value expressing the speed at which the leaked screeners decline. The faster the decay rate the faster the measured quantity disappears and moves toward 0.

Another interesting feature of the data appears in the "bounce." Bounce displays how much the data vary. The green lines, or bounce lines, visually depict the envelope capturing the degree of data dispersal. The bounce value then quantifies the data distribution.

Across time the number of leaked Oscar nominated screeners vary by a factor of x1.8. The bounce value of x1.8 suggests stability. The closer the bounce value moves towards x1.0, the lowest bounce value, the more unchanging and regular the data become.

The visualizations of bounce and celeration along with their values tell a data story. The tale recounts what happened and where the data lie in the present. Namely, Internet pirates who leaked screeners of Oscar nominated films did so quite regularly for many years, but the activity steadily declined. The rate at which leaked screeners disappear has occurred at 25% per half decade for the last 13 years.

The future

The SCC has an amazing gift for all those who would partake of it, projecting data into the future. A projection differs from a prediction. A projection simply takes existing data and estimates where it will occur in the times ahead. A prediction refers to a process whereby a scientist makes a quantitative statement asserting what will happen under fixed conditions. "Prediction" also has meaning in regard to statistics and everyday judgements.

The SCC bestows two special type of projections, a celeration projection and a bounce projection.

Celeration and bounce projections

The celeration line describes how fast a data set changes. The projection of the celeration line forecasts where a behavior, pinpoint, or measured quantity will appear in the future.

Figure 52 has a celeration projection line (i.e., black dashed line) that extends forward showing how the future data set will continue to decelerate. Based off the ÷1.33 celeration value, the projection reveals that screeners will reach 0 in the year 2072. Hollywood insiders seeing such projection will not like the outcome. Another 55 years of leaked screeners makes for an unwelcome predicament.

The celeration projection line projects when the measured quantity will reach a specific quantity in the future. Stated differently, the forecast presents a specific date and value for the entire data set. The screeners reaching 0 in 2072 serves as an example of how a chart reader would see the ensuing quantity and finishing date.

The SCC not only forecasts a specific quantity and time, but with the bounce line projection delivers an area projection. The area covers the range from soonest to the latest when the future event will take place.

Chapter 5 : Inside the SCC

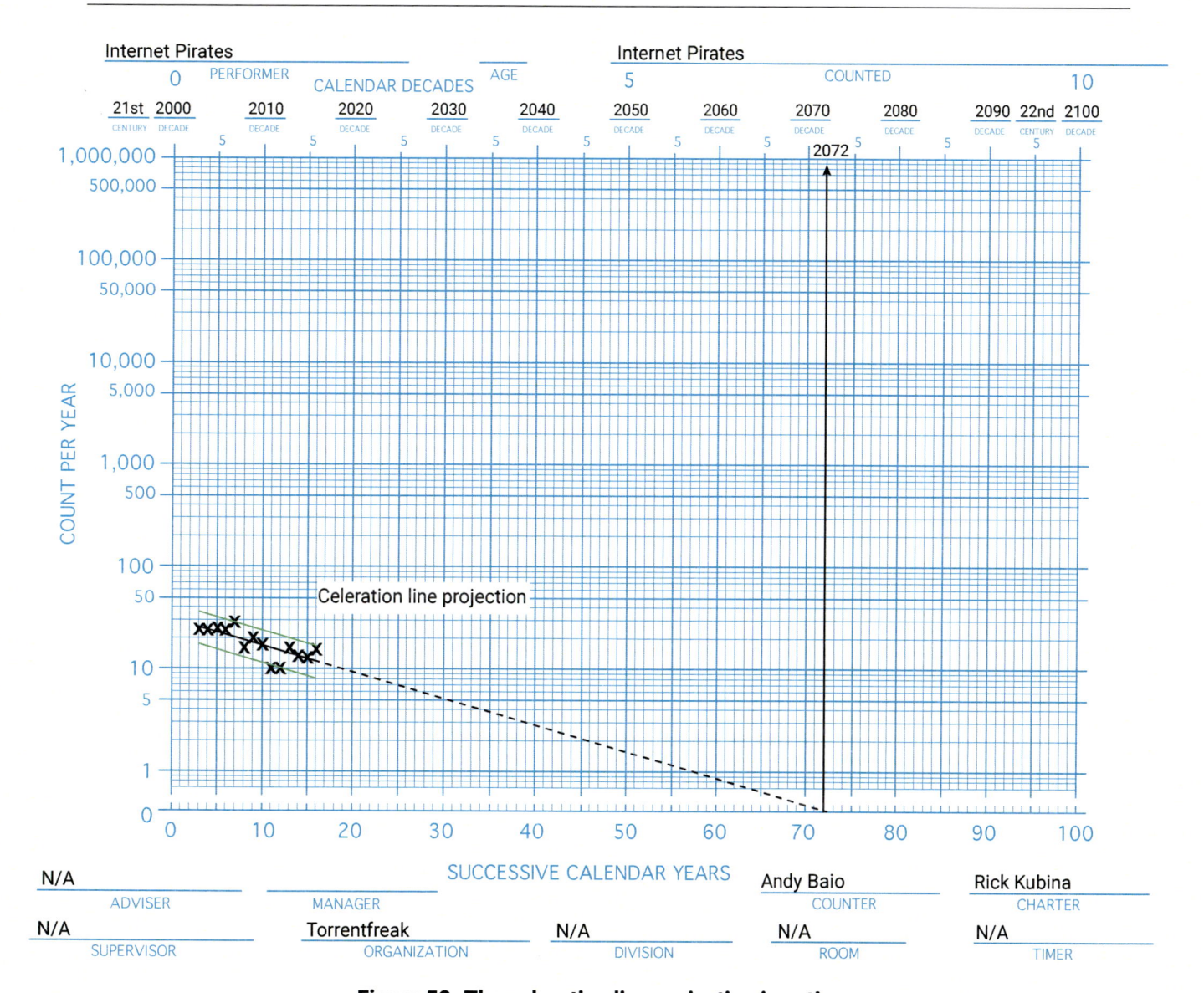

Figure 52. The celeration line projection in action.

Figure 53 shows the area forecast. Two dashed projection lines issue forth from the lower and upper bounce line. The lower bounce line projects the screeners reaching 0 in 2066. But the higher bounce line continues until 2077. Therefore, the bounce projections yield a range where leaked screeners will reach 0: 2066 to 2077.

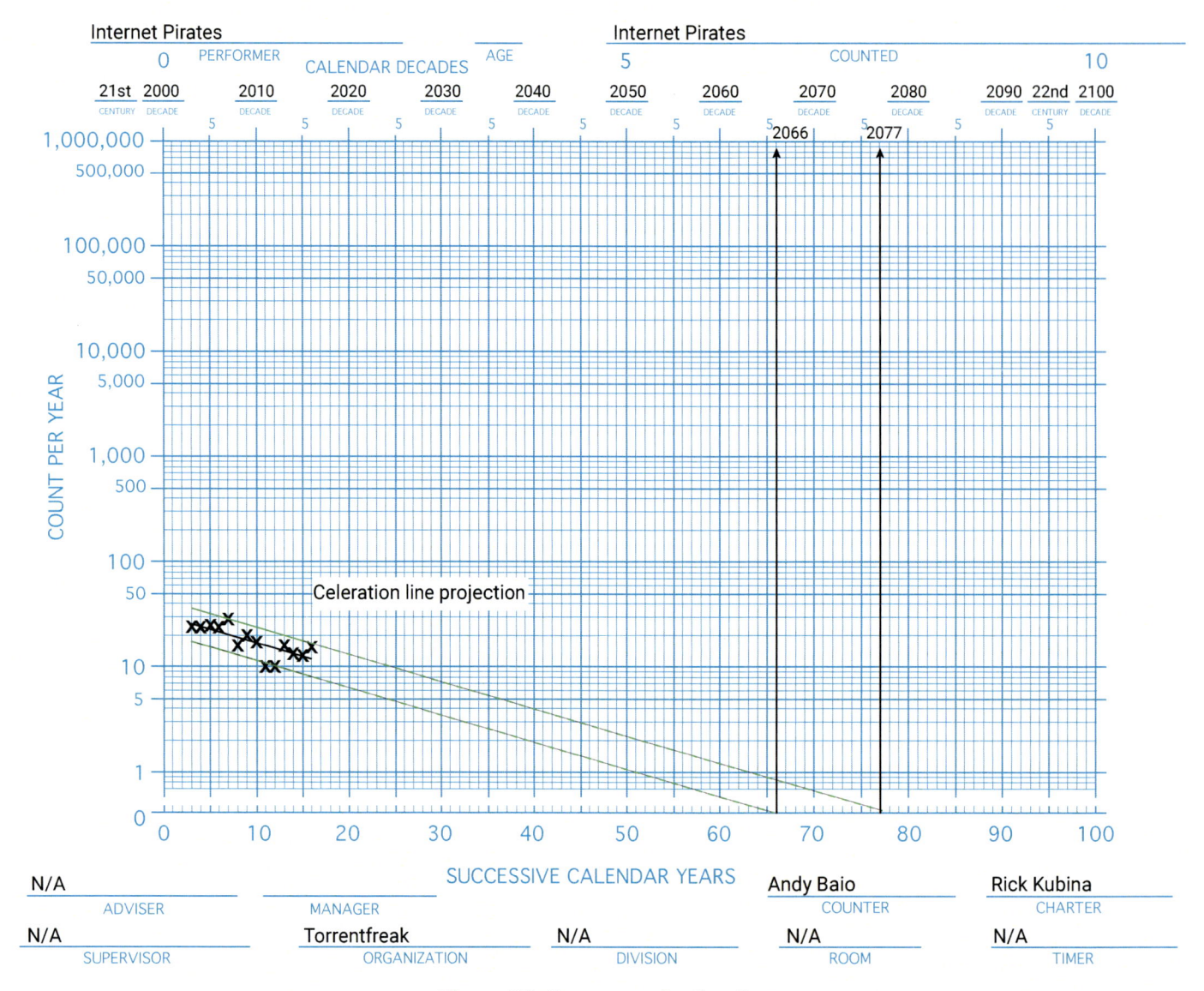

Figure 53. Bounce projection lines.

Conclusion

The SCC equips all chart users with a disarmingly simple yet powerful tool, the ability to project specific and ranged future targets. The utility of forecasting when and how much something will occur in the coming times confers significant benefit. As with the case of sharing illegal screeners, the data show an unacceptable outcome for pirated content: years of continued sharing and lost profits. People in the movie industry could try interventions, place them on the SCC, and then observe their effects. A prescription for success involves examining the data in terms of the past, present, and future.

Based off of the last entry you can tell I have a thing for movies. The next blog fell right into the category with one of the names of a learning picture, jaws. I still remember that movie as a child of the 70s and the effect it had on my swimming behavior. But learning pictures have long held esteem in the PT community because of their handiness and practicality. I always liked the fact the students came up with the name for learning pictures. Some have aged like jaws but they all still work. And a new generation of students has come up with their names - long live learning pictures!

Entry: Jaws, Snowplows, and Dives: Using Learning Pictures for decision making

In the summer of 1975 the movie Jaws hit the theaters. Jaws told the story of an idyllic seaside community with a shark problem. The shark had an insatiable appetite that involved humans as the main course.

The iconic movie poster depicting the single-minded eating machine evoked a sense of dread. The open jaws of the massive shark swimming towards an unsuspecting swimmer foretold of a frightening outcome.

The well-known Jaws image entered the collective consciousness of the nation. Parodies, commercials, and even political cartoons made use of the open-mouthed shark. And in 1977, teacher Pat All and her 7th grade class went on to use the imagery for a very different and productive purpose, one of the names of a "learning picture" (All, 1977).

Learning Pictures – A Precision Teaching technique

Precision Teaching (PT) traces its roots back to B. F. Skinner. The founder of Precision Teaching, Ogden Lindsey, explained how PT inherited a standard visual display (the cumulative recorder, which sparked the Standard Celeration Chart) and a universal dimensional quantity for behavior (rate or frequency).

Contemporary behavior analysis has become very popular as an applied method for helping people with autism spectrum disorders. However, PT began in earnest in public schools. Lindsley described how PT supercharged classroom learning:

"High performance aims and custom-tailored prescriptions maximize learning. Least costly and most effective learning occurs with classroom performance timed, counted, and charted daily by the learners themselves. Least costly and most effective learning improvement changes occur with chart-based decisions made weekly by the learners and their teachers" (Lindsley, 1992, p. 51).

Students self-charted their data and decided if they needed help. A student could ask the teacher for a change or could come up with their own intervention and run it by the teacher.

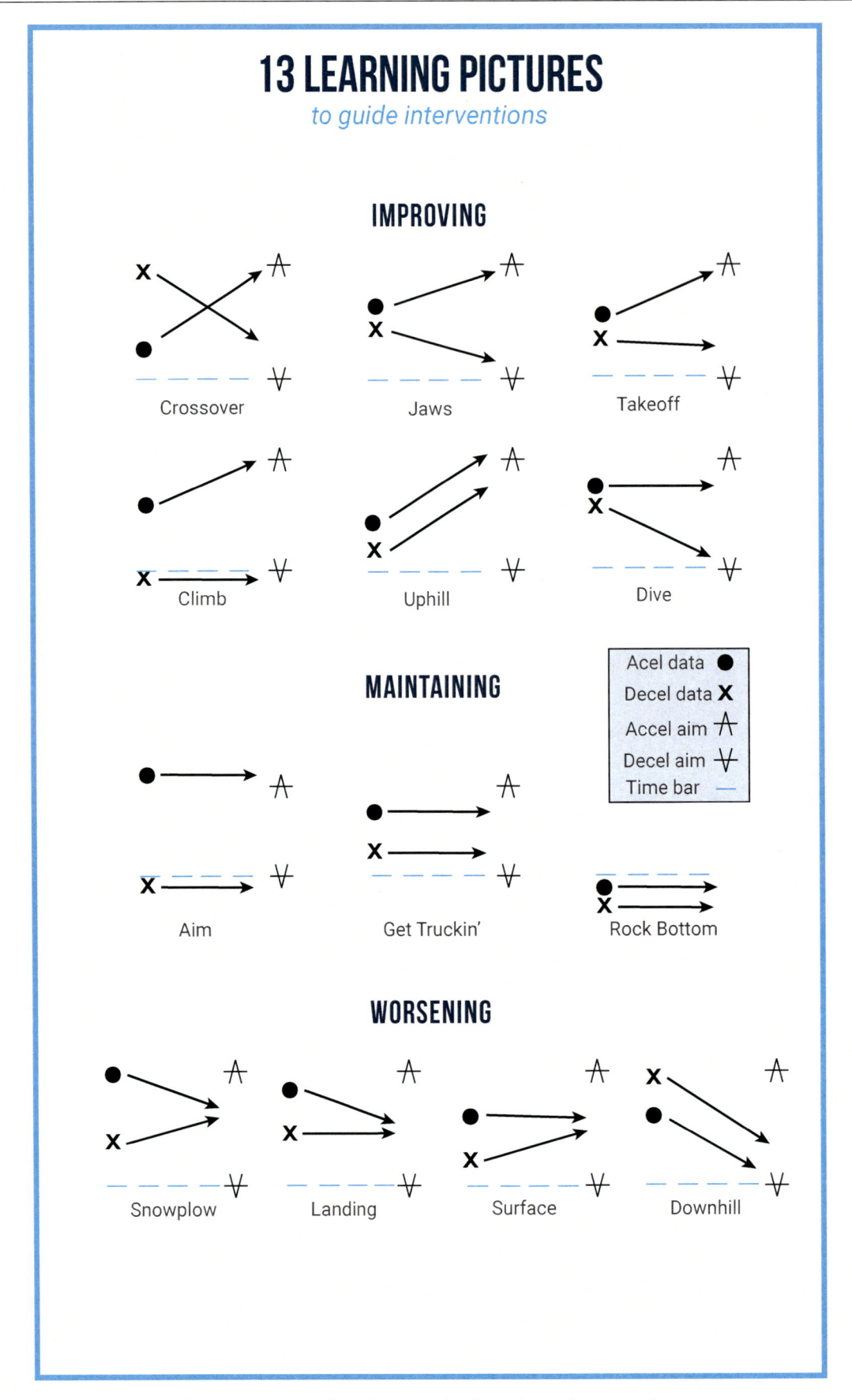

Figure 54. Learning pictures in three broad categories.

The students became aware of their progress and when they needed help through "learning pictures" (also called behavior change pictures; Kubina & Yurich, 2012). The learning pictures emerged after the students charted corrects (acceleration data) and incorrects (deceleration data) on their Standard Celeration Charts.

Precision Teaching emphasized the measurement and monitoring of acceleration and deceleration behaviors at the same time. On one hand a behavior can have corrects and incorrects (called an accuracy pair). On the other, a behavior targeted for deceleration can have a corollary behavior set for deceleration (called a fair pair).

Figure 54 provides a recreation of Lindsley's original 13 learning pictures. In the Figure, the arrow line symbolizes acceleration data (with dots) or deceleration data (with x's) moving through time. The celeration line visually communicates the speed and direction of behavior change. The A (accel aim star) and inverted A (decel aim star) represent the aim or goal. And the blue horizontal dash depicts the time bar capturing the counting time or interval for observing and tallying the behavior (e.g., 1 minute).

Three broad categories describe progress change. Behavior change can improve, worsen, or stay the same and maintain. Students with improving pictures continue their current program or intervention. Students with worsening pictures ask for help. And students with maintain learning pictures evoke different actions depending on where the behavior paths lie (discussed in detail later).

Lindsley described how the 7th grade students came up with the names in 1977. The students named Jaws after the wide-open jaws of the shark famous in a thriller movie the prior summer. Snowplow, Uphill, and Downhill came from the positions of snow skis while skiing. In Climb, Takeoff and Landing the correct celeration line is the flight of an airplane and its related error line is the surface of the ground. In Surface and Dive the correct line is the surface of the sea, and the error line is the path of a submarine (Lindsley, 1990, p.13).

The first four improving pictures (Cross-over, Jaws, Take-off, Climb) have accel data growing and moving towards the accel aim. The decel data advance towards the decel aim or maintain. However, the fifth learning picture, Uphill, has decel data growing also. A teacher would monitor such a pattern because the growing decel data indicate the student learning the incorrect form for performing a skill or behavior.

The last improving learning picture, Dive, has decel data trending in the right direction and accel data flat. While the behavior technically improved, the teacher must keep a watchful eye on the data to make sure the accel data moves upward towards the aim.

The maintaining learning pictures suggest two different responses/decisions. The aptly named "Aim" indicates the student's performance reached the aims for the accel and decel data. The goal shifts to maintaining the mastery condition across time.

On the other hand, Get Truckin' and Rock Bottom propose the student do something different. The lack of learning in the middle of the chart for Get Truckin' and the languishing performance for Rock Bottom reveal a problem. In both cases the direction of the accel and decel data point to a lack of progress.

The worsening pictures expose a problem necessitating immediate remediation. Namely, the deterioration of progress. In the case of the Snowplow, the student knew something but across time unlearned what he or she knew. A real snowplow signals relief for those who live with snow, but the Snowplow learning picture suggests the opposite!

Landing and Surface tell a similar story but in different ways. Landing shows a worsening condition as accel data decelerate but decel data maintain. Surface shows the accel data maintain but the decel data accelerate. In both cases the behavior change has degenerated across time.

The fourth worsening learning picture, Downhill, looks like what would happen if someone rolled a ball down a hill. The ball would descend and pick up speed. The Downhill learning picture demonstrates such an outcome. The decel data move downwards which speaks to a positive result. Yet the accel data follow the same path, a very unwelcome event.

All learning pictures help students, teachers, parents, behavior analysts, and anyone else on the behavior change team recognize key patterns. The visual evidence points to different states of progress: improving, worsening, or maintaining. And depending on what learning picture emerges, the teacher or responsible behavior change agent can decide more quickly and soundly.

Learning pictures – The past to the present

At the time of this blog, learning pictures have turned 41 years old. The 7th graders who named the pictures would find themselves in their early 50s! The validity and utility of learning pictures, however, has not changed. Yet many new students and even practitioners might not appreciate the dated references like Get Truckin'.

The student names of the universal learning patterns may change, even though the patterns do not. For example, a new crop of students at the Haugland Learning Center, a charter school for students with an Autism Spectrum Disorder came up with their own names for learning pictures (Guild, 2015). Some of the new names include Climbing the Mountain, Stuck in the Mud, Belly Up, and The Race.

The specific names of the learning pictures do not particularly matter. The effect of naming the specific patterns, however, does have real power. Naming learning pictures inspires confidence in the decision making process and leads to ownership of the charted data.

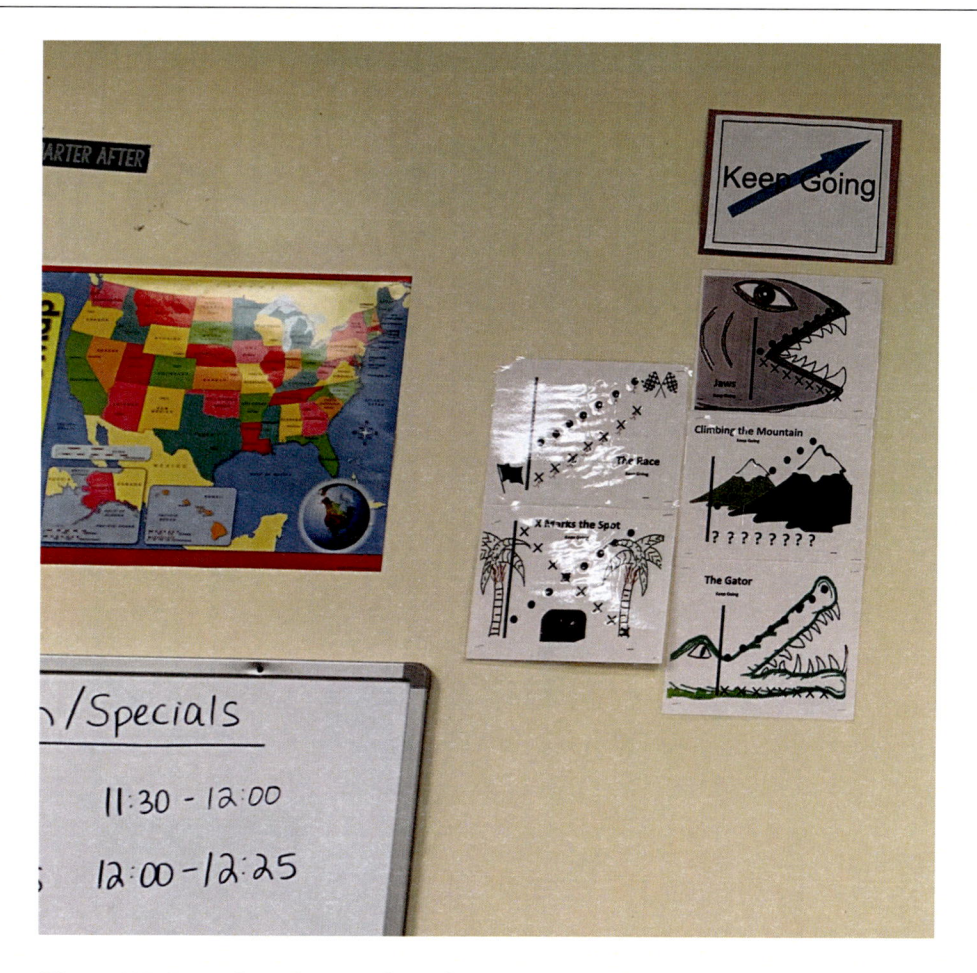

Figure 55. Learning pictures in a classroom at Haugland Learning Academy.

Conclusion

Learning pictures appear on a Standard Celeration Chart as a result of charting acceleration and deceleration data concurrently. In the 1970s, students discovered the patterns that emerged helped them understand if they needed help or could continue to make progress. Naming the learning pictures had a practical application by facilitating decision making. More importantly, the students formed a community around learning showcased on a standard visual display.

While the previous section highlighted how learning pictures helped students, the same benefits hold true for behavior analysts and other behavior change agents working in a clinic or a home. The knowledge of learning pictures advances informed data monitoring, promotes data intimacy, and most importantly, improves decision making.

Dimensional quantities such as duration reflect behavioral counts with alacrity. Yet many people new to the SCC have a hard time with duration. The reason? Most people have their vast experience working with a graph that has only one vertical axis. As a result, when duration lessens, the data move from top to bottom. But on the SCC duration lessening moves in the opposite direction, from bottom to top. Such movement causes confusion sometimes. The SCC has two vertical axes. The right vertical axis has time moving from 24 hours up to 1 second. In the following entry, I enjoyed recounting a successful data story that also demonstrated how duration works on the chart.

Entry: How to Stop Thumb Sucking & Unwanted Toddler Behavior: Using Duration on the Standard Celeration Chart

Sarah joined the world like most other babies do, an uncomplicated pregnancy and a natural birth. Her parents, Mike and Diana, delighted in her arrival. Diana lobbied Mike to name the baby Sarah after her a beloved grandmother. Mike readily agreed.

Sarah grew and hit many developmental milestones. She engaged in behaviors typical of a toddler: playing with blocks, imitating the actions of her peers, and laughing at silly faces. Sarah enjoyed her parents and family as they did her. At the age of three, however, Diana and Mike noticed Sarah sucking her thumb habitually. Sarah had a thumb sucking problem.

Thumb sucking itself does not pose a problem. Indeed, thumb sucking normally occurs in children and tends to disappear as they age. Yet children who suck their fingers beyond 2 to 4 years of age can experience several severe problems according to the American Dental Association:

- Misshapen mouth
- Improper development of the roof of the mouth
- Misaligned teeth

Thumb sucking can also attract social stigma for children who continue to engage in the behavior as they age.

Intervention plan

Sarah spent time at a daycare facility as both her parents worked. The daycare had many excellent staff who supervised the children. Ms. Ashley had Sarah in her class and noticed the thumb sucking problem almost immediately. After consulting with Sarah's parents, Ms. Ashley came up with a plan. First, she needed to collect baseline and document the degree of the problem.

Ms. Ashley observed Sarah during playtime. Playtime lasted 1 hour from 8:00 AM to 9:00 AM. During that time, Ms. Ashley had a timer and recorded the duration of thumb sucking.

Duration = "The elapsed time between the beginning and ending of a behavior" (Johnston & Pennypacker, 2009)

Duration = "The total extent of time in which a behavior occurs" (Cooper, Heron, & Heward, 2020)

Sarah sucked her thumb on and off during playtime. Ms. Ashley started the timer when Sarah placed her thumb in her mouth and stopped the timer after the thumb came out. The total duration for the one-hour daily observation came from all instances of starting and stopping across the hour.

Standard Celeration Chart (Data Display)

Ms. Ashley took the total duration of thumb sucking and placed it on the Standard Celeration Chart (SCC). All of her analysis occurred on the SCC and provided an abundance of visual and individual statistical information. The chart excels at analysis, interpretation, and communication of basic and applied experimental results.

First, a quick tutorial on the SCC. Notice the chart has dual vertical axes. The left vertical axis displays Count Per Minute. The left axis comes into play when someone wants to know the know the count, expressed as per minute, for the target behavior. Every observed behavior will have a count.

The right vertical axis contains a series of Counting Times, or the time interval spent counting a behavior. The right vertical axis also shows time for duration, latency, and a unique symbol called a counting time bar.

The Standard Celeration Chart accurately represents time. If time lessens or becomes shorter, the data (e.g., duration, latency) go up. Conversely, if the time interval lengthened, the data move downward illustrative of more time.

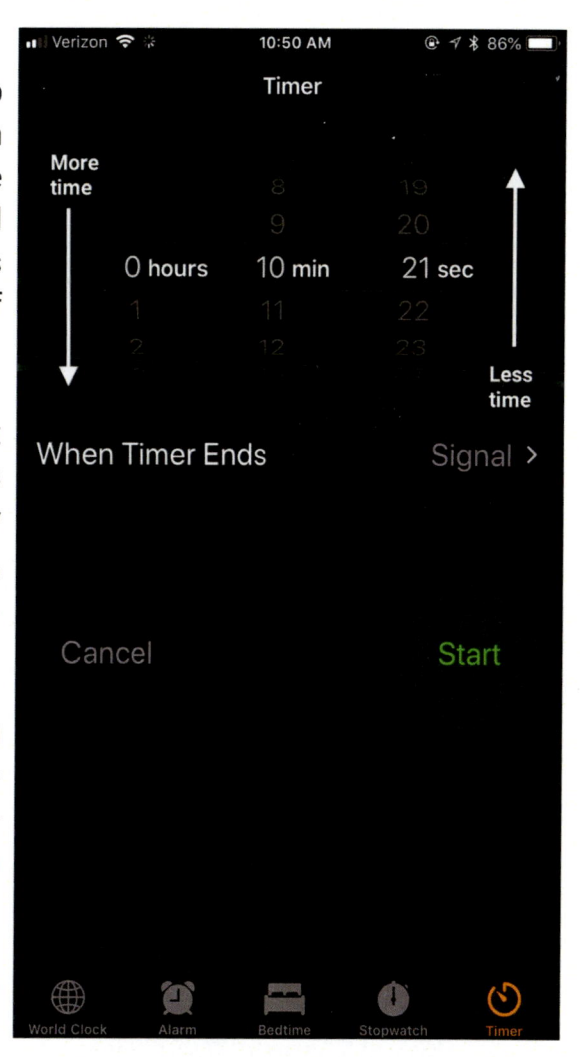

Figure 56. A screenshot showing a timer with spinner to shorten or lengthen the time interval.

Take the example of a 60-second duration taken on Monday. The next day the duration reduced to 30. The SCC visually conveys the smaller amount of time by having the data move upward.

People familiar with viewing duration on a single axis linear graph tend to have an opposite perspective. Linear graphs start at 0 and the data rise as more time appears. Therefore, duration data trending upward communicates an expansion of time, the opposite view of the SCC.

An analogy may help remind people of how duration works on the chart. The screenshot from a timer app demonstrates that more time means moving the spinner down while less time moves up.

The SCC in Figure 57 has Sarah's thumb sucking duration data. Note the labeled blanks surrounding the SCC. The labeled blanks impart vital information regarding behavior (Performer, Age, Counted), data recording (Counter, Timer, Charter), management (Manager, Adviser, Supervisor), and the place (Organization, Division, Room) where measurement occurred.

The daily SCC also presents all behavioral data in real calendar time. A client who missed a day due to sickness or the weekend would have white space on the SCC. The analysts would see the person did not attend the session (or someone did not measure the behavior for a given day). Notice that Sarah went away for vacation with her parents and the annotation lines communicate Sarah's absence. On the SCC the backward slash (\) symbolizes duration. Each duration data has an associated time shown on the right vertical axis.

Data analysis

Analysis of the SCC data offers behavior change agents a rich assortment of outstanding visual and statistical information. The information appears in a standard format, so all chart readers quickly orient to essential chart elements. First, Sarah's SCC immediately relays the who, what, and where of the intervention.

Sarah, a 3-year-old (Age), has a target behavior where she sucks her thumb during free time (Counted labeled blank = Free-do sucks thumb during free time). The "Free-do" in Counted labeled blank represents a "learning channel."

The responsibility for counting, timing, and charting the behavior falls to Ms. Ashley as indicated in Counter, Timer, and Charter labeled blanks. Ms. Ashley also serves as the Manager or the person who works with the Performer, Sarah, on a daily basis.

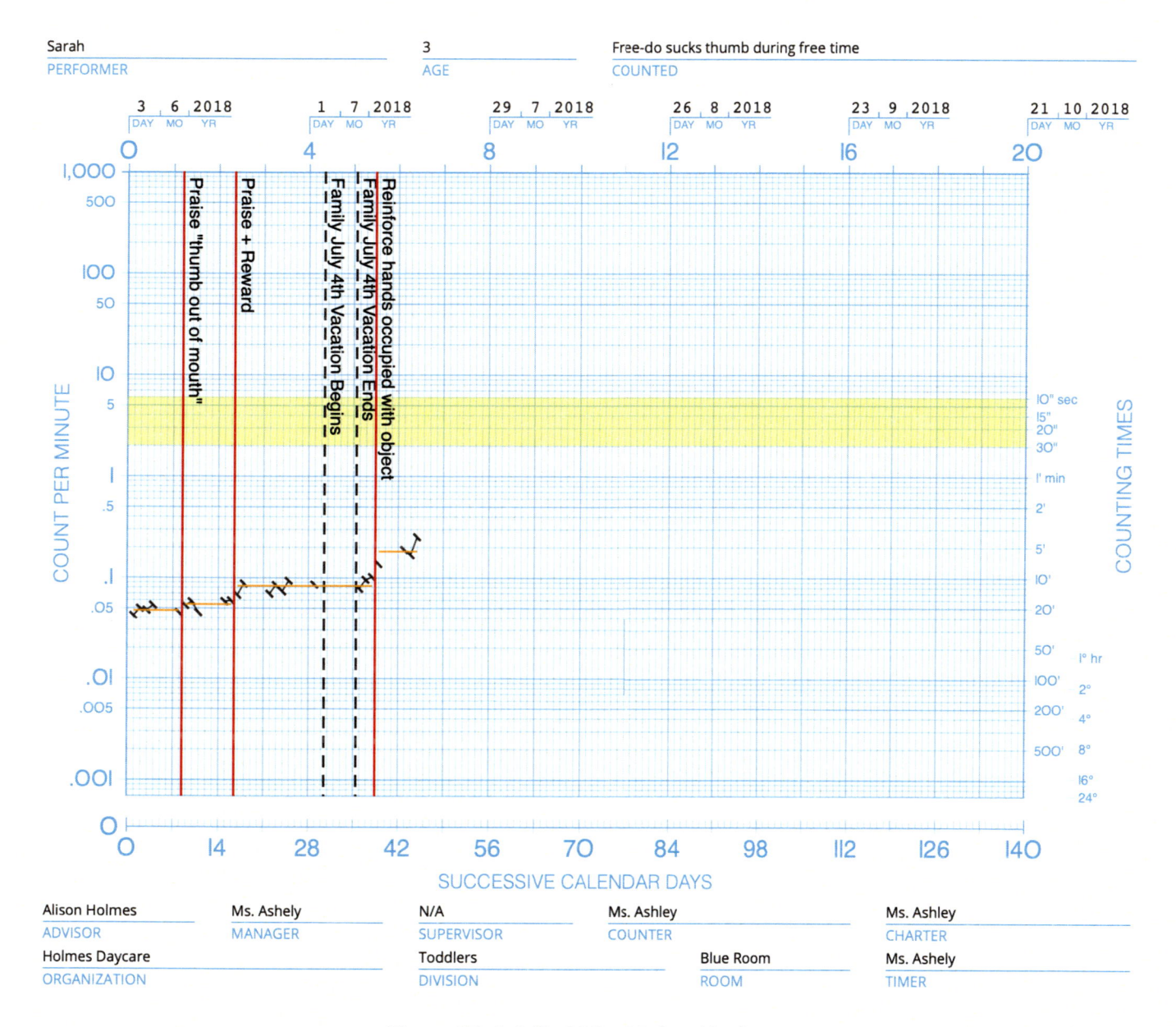

Figure 57. A daily SCC with Sarah's data.

The Adviser examines the data on a weekly basis and provides advice. Alison Holmes, who owns the daycare center, fills the role of the Adviser. A Supervisor would see charted data on a monthly time frame. No one has assumed that role for the current project.

The last pieces of information concern where the charted project takes place. Observation and intervention occur at Holmes Daycare (Organization), in the Toddlers Division in the Blue Room (Room).

The second significant part of the chart, the inside, contains data, conditions, goals, and all other relevant qualitative and quantitative information.

To begin, the yellow aim band across the chart spans 30 to 10 seconds. The aim band represents the goal or where Ms. Ashley sets intervention success.

The duration data start off in real time and each data point depicts a day's worth of observation. By looking at a duration symbol and moving across to the right vertical axis, chart readers can determine the interval of time.

The duration data move across time in response to the current condition. The first condition begins with baseline. The celeration line drawn across the data shows almost no movement (i.e., looks flat). The lack of progress sparks Ms. Ashley into action and she implements her first intervention, delivering praise for instances when Sarah does not have her thumb in her mouth.

Visually inspecting the second condition exhibits a slight trend upward. On an SCC, duration trending upward means the total time for the behavior shortens.

Still, the gradual slope of progress indicates a need for change. Therefore, Ms. Ashley implemented the second condition, praising Sarah for when her thumb did not enter her mouth and giving her a small reward at the end of the session. The data show the second condition lasted over two weeks which included an absence due to family vacation.

The last condition Ms. Ashley enacted called for the specific reinforcement of instances where Sarah had her hands occupied with a toy, other functional objects, or appropriate activity (e.g., clapping games). The last condition worked. The data show a sharp acceleration. Furthermore, the dotted line projects Sarah will make her goal in less than a month.

Quantification = Next level analysis

The previous description of data contained only a visual analysis. However, the SCC also provides a full range of vital, precise statistics that portray changes across time. The SCC segment, Figure 58, has orange level lines fitted to each dataset per condition.

The quantification allows a behavior change agent to expertly determine the speed of behavior change (celeration) and the average amount of behavior change (level) for each condition.

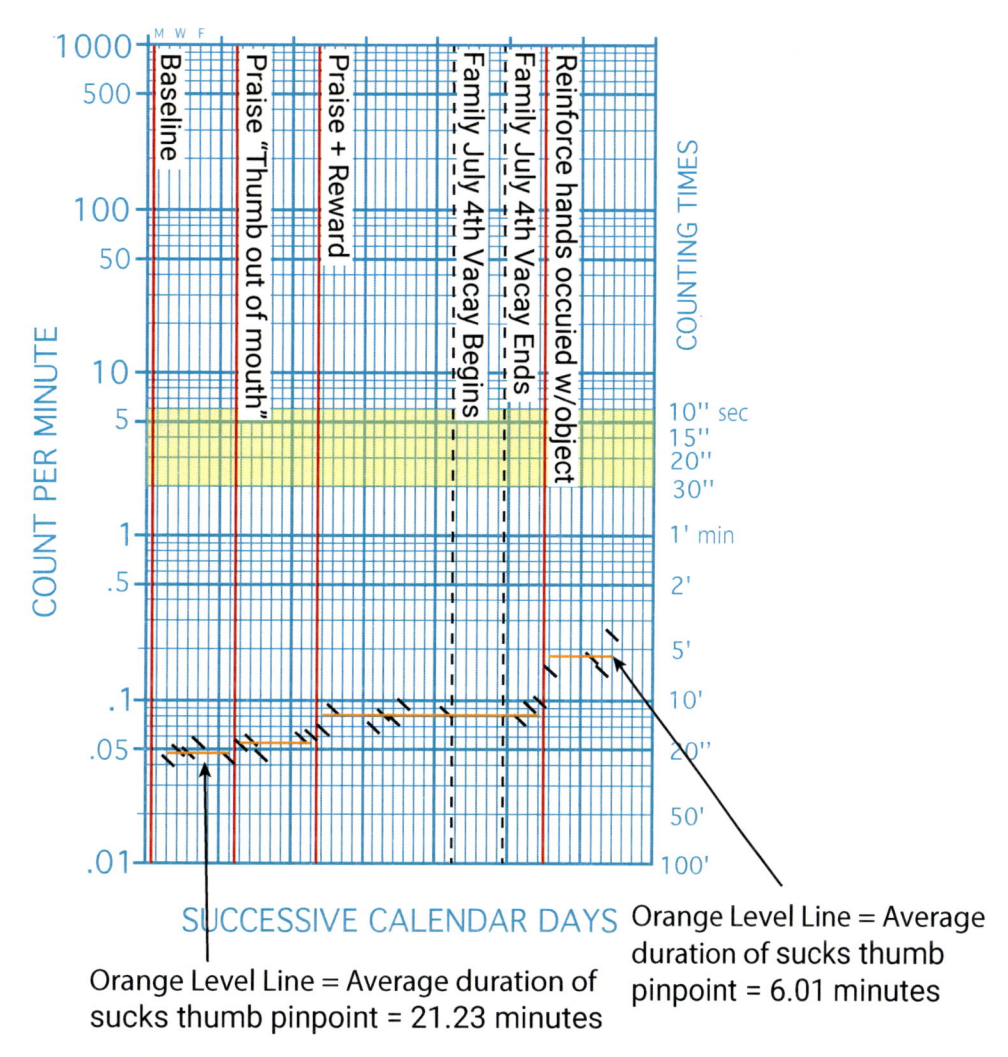

Figure 58. An SCC segment with level lines.

Table 12 lays out the quantitative values for both celeration and level. The level values capture the average duration for each condition. The level numbers quantify the orange lines shown in the figure above.

	Baseline	Praise Intervention (#1)	Praise Intervention (#2)	Reinforcement Intervention (#3)
Level	21.23 min	18.54 min	12.11 min	6.01 min
Celeration	x1.02 per week	x1.13 per week	x1.08 per week	x1.77 per week

Table 12. Level and celeration values for Sarah's SCC.

On average, in baseline, Sarah sucked on her thumb for 21 minutes and 23 seconds during the one-hour observational period. Stated differently, 1/3 of the time Sarah had her thumb in her mouth.

Each successive condition has an intervention. The level contributes to an understanding of how much the amount of thumb sucking changed. Praising the thumb out of her mouth led to an average of 18 minutes and 54 seconds of the behavior. The next intervention, with a reward component, shortened the average time even more to 12 minutes and 11 seconds. The last condition worked very well, reducing thumb sucking to only 6 minutes and 1 second.

While levels help behavior change agents get a handle on the average amount of behavior in a condition, the celeration values show how quickly the behavior changed across time. The higher the celeration value, the faster the duration data changed. When duration data accelerate, that means shorter and shorter durations.

The behavior in baseline barely changed at all. Anything at x1 celeration stays the same, and x1.02 per week differs very little from x1 per week.

The second condition had a celeration of x1.13 per week. In other words, duration length changed by growing 13% each week. Expressed in a different way, the durations got shorter or lessened at a weekly rate of 13%. While the next condition (i.e., Praise + Reward) didn't yield a celeration as fast as the previous condition, the higher level indicates the intervention had a more positive impact. The final condition evoked the fastest change and highest celeration value, x1.77 per week.

Conclusion

The science of behavior contains a treasure trove of applied interventions ready to help children like Sarah. The Standard Celeration Chart equips behavior change agents with a robust measurement system that engenders analysis and subsequent decisions by virtue of a standard chart and a full array of individual behavior change statistics.

Ms. Ashley helped Sarah (true story, different names) stop her thumb sucking by trying several interventions and analyzing her data in a time efficient way. The personalization of data and rapid decoding of information promoted behavior change, aided problem solving, and facilitated the reduction of an unfavorable behavior. The SCC can help all behavior change agents navigate behavioral outcomes and exercise data science for individuals.

Chapter 6

More SCC Goodness

One of the themes that may have become apparent involves my deep respect and awe for Precision Teaching, especially the Standard Celeration Chart (SCC). I have found once professionals (e.g., behavior analysts, teachers, coaches) truly understand the import and utility of the chart, they cannot unlearn the concepts nor can they accept inferior graphs. The emerging commitment surprises some people outside the PT community. Pessimists and haters will refer to SCC users as a cult. Not coincidentally, I have heard the pejorative directed at me during a past conference's Q&A session by a leading voice in the ABA field.

Cults imply people blindly follow a charismatic leader or a set of unorthodox beliefs. But the cult accusation appears disingenuous and not credible when we turn our eye to science. For instance, chemists would find themselves a cult because of their devotion to beakers. Beakers have precision, standard forms, and function (e.g., holding waste fluids, preparing solutions, aiding experiments). Physicists, biologists, astronomers, and many other scientists use standard equipment and procedures due to their experimental effectiveness. Applied practitioners and experimenters in schools, clinics, and home settings who use the SCC have the same drive and goal. But with the added weight of directly working with fellow humans, the SCC facilitates superior outcomes which confers a set of positive feelings to the chart that aided the changes.

The specific capabilities of the chart came through in entries shared in the previous chapter, Inside the SCC. The blogs in Chapter 6 highlight several advantages SCC users receive and talk more about what I call "chart goodness." I wrote the next entry back in 2012 and wanted to draw attention to relative change. The combination of knowing the technical features of chart, how to use it, the basis for its preeminence, and why to use it, create a special attraction for those who strive to help people achieve their learning and behavior change goals.

Entry: More on relative change

In the Precision Teaching Book (Kubina & Yurich, 2012), a great deal of information surrounded the difference between absolute amount and relative change. The Standard Celeration Chart offers relative change; arithmetically scaled line chart uses absolute amount of change. To demonstrate the value we gain with relative change, please answer the following questions. If Bill Gates found a $10.00 bill, and a single mother of five children living in extreme poverty also found $10.00, who has received a more significant impact to their personal wealth?

If a 42-pound, six-year-old girl came down with strep throat and a 220 pound, 35-year-old man also has the infection, who would significantly benefit by adding a daily, 180 mg dosage of Azithromycin (for five total days)?* Which atrocity had a bigger impact, the 40,000,000 deaths from Mao Zedong's rule where he starved his people and led a civil war or the 40,000,000 deaths from the 13th century Mongol Conquests?

Absolute amount of change says Bill Gates and the single mom both have $10.00 more. Absolute amount of change also would note the six-year-old girl and the 35-year-old man both experienced the same milligram dosage, and the Mao Zedong rule and Mongol Conquest held equal catastrophic weight in terms of death toll (i.e., 40,000,000). You can probably see the problem already. And arithmetically scaled line charts use absolute amount of change to portray and communicate the significance of educational change without context of or relation to where the change starts from.

Approaching the previous questions and embracing context provided by relative change we gain whole new perspective. If Bill Gates' net worth comes to $56,000,000,000 and the single mom has a net worth of $100.00, finding a $10 bill would mean almost nothing to Bill Gates whereas the single mom has just come into a windfall. A 42-pound, six-year-old girl receiving a therapeutic dose will have a significant outcome whereas a 220-pound, 35-year-old man may likely remain sick because the same dosage acts differently within his body due to weight. The Mao Zedong rule and the Mogul Conquests each killed 40 million people. When scaled for population size, however, Mao Zedong maintains a mid-20th-century equivalency of 40 million people who lost their lives while the adjusted Mongol Conquests would have led to 278,000,000 deaths making it the second most deadly atrocity in the 20th century (Pinker, 2011). Context matters. And with relative change we see the world differently than with absolute amount of change.

*Azithromycin dosage guidelines: Children should take 12 milligrams (mg) per each kilogram they weight. For a 42-pound girl the recommended dosage works out to roughly 180 mg a day. Dosage recommendations for adults – 500 mg on day one and 250 mg for days two through five.

Learning about the SCC and using it professionally and personally for so many years led to one of the great love affairs of my life. That might seem like a bold admission, but as Carl Sagan once wrote, "When you're in love, you want to tell the world!" The simplicity and complexity both await people interested in the chart. I have continued to learn more about the SCC and how it reveals the dynamics of behavior change and learning. The powers of 10 and subsequent orders of magnitude account for one of those understated, unfamiliar features of the chart. Yet once people see them and understand the potency of classifying and inspecting data in orders of magnitude, a new way of thinking emerges. I enjoyed sharing some of that wonder and perspective-altering knowledge with the following blog.

Entry: Powers of 10 are sexy

Would you like to nerd out with me? Good, let's do it. And we start by officially recognizing we have completed an order of magnitude with today's blogpost! Yep, todays topic deals with powers of 10, also called orders of magnitudes, and we find them a sexy topic.

An order of magnitude helps deal with size or scale. Let's take an example. Think of an ant. Now think of an average adult. We can quickly conclude based on powers of 10 that the adult is three orders of magnitude taller than the ant.

For my fellow nerds who love math, let's see how the numbers work. We place average height of an adult about at 1.7 meters (5 feet 7 inches). When we round 1.7 to the nearest power of 10, we round to 10^0 or 1. Recall 10^0 doesn't mean 10 x 0 = 0. Rather, the exponent tells us how many zeros we need to add to 1. So, for 10^1 (or 10 multiplied 1 time) we add one zero to 1 and have 10. And 10^2 gives us 100 (we add two zeros to 1 or 10 multiplied 2 times, 10 x 10), 10^3 equals 1,000 (add three zeros to 1). But if we have 1 or 10^0, we add zero zeros to 1.

Now back to our little friend the ant. The size of an ant works out to about 3.4 millimeters. If we translate millimeters to meters, like our 1.7-meter human, 3.5 millimeters = .0034 meters. If we round .003 to the nearest power of 10 we get 10^{-3} or 10 to the negative 3. So now we can easily compare our ant to our human.

    Ant height = 10^{-3}

    Human height = 10^0

From -3 to 0 we have move foreword by three exponents. In other words, the human has three powers of 10, or three orders of magnitude of height, on the ant.

The power of powers of 10

Precision Teaching (PT) deals with behavior change, as do you. PT places behavior on the Standard Celeration Chart (and I hope you do too). Because of its special scaling, we can see the orders of magnitude or powers of 10 up along the vertical axis. On Figure 59 see the vertical axis for the count only chart and the daily per minute chart.

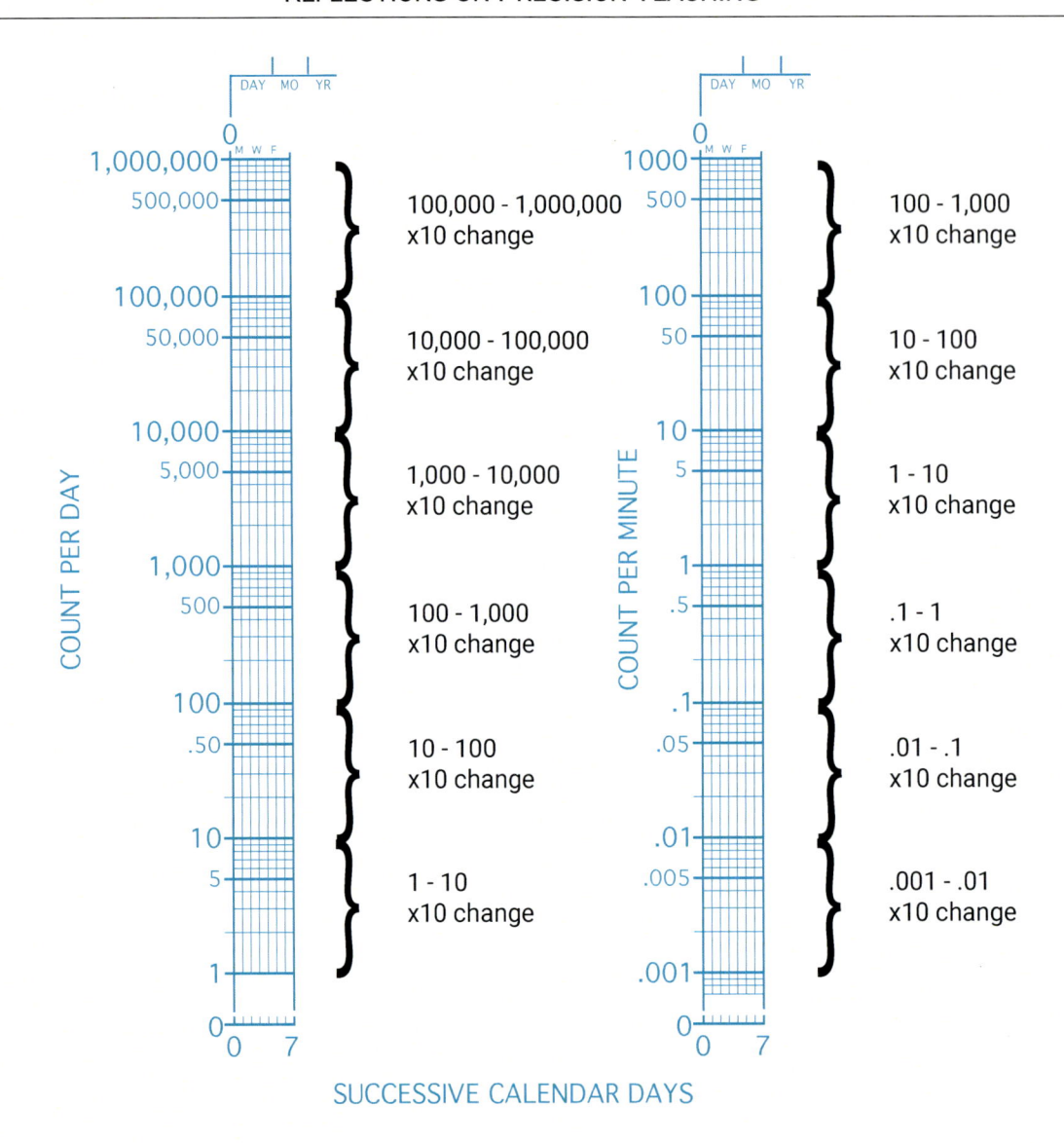

Figure 59. Two vertical axes from two different varieties of daily charts: the count only Standard Celeration Chart and the per minute Standard Celeration Chart.

Notice how each order of magnitude changes by moving up one power of 10. Viewing behavior on such a scale allows us to easily analyze and compare different data quickly. Therefore, we can make decisions about data just as fast.

Let's put the last statement to the test. You can visualize the difference between the height of an ant and human and quickly come to appreciate a three order of magnitude change. In behavior, think about a child who can only speak 1 word a day. Then compare that behavior with a child who can speak 1,000 words a day! Literally the difference of speaking vocabulary between an infant (12 months old) and a toddler (3 years old).

And what about behaviors we would like to get rid of? A smoker takes approximately 10 puffs of smoke from a cigarette (American Cancer Society, 2014). A pack contain 20 cigarettes. So, a pack a day habit = 200 puffs of smoke. Let's say in a week a smoker consumes 5 packs of cigarettes and takes 1,000 puffs per week. Compare that to a person that takes one drag off a friend Friday night (only one puff of a cigarette per week).

Examine the two people and see what a three order of magnitude change reveals. The difference between a heavily addicted smoker and one who we might would call an experimenter. Furthermore, imagine what type of intervention would we need to apply to the 1,000 puff a week smoker and the 1 puff a week smoker to get either one to quit smoking?

As soon as you start charting and comparing behavior on a true scale, you will discern the orders of magnitude difference between behavior. The amount of transformative power necessary to grow or decay a behavior immediately jumps out at the chart reader. The knowledge the SCC imparts continues to impress me. And who thought I couldn't blend the terms sexy, math, and the Standard Celeration Chart in one blog!

Many business books describe metrics and analytics. Businesses learned through big data that metrics and analytics could meaningfully impact the bottom line, help land new customers, and guide companies to an expansive, profitable future. Unfortunately, few metrics and analytics find their way into the classroom, clinic, and home settings. And yet, Precision Teaching has an abundance of metrics that feed analytics to answer profoundly important questions about behavior change. The following entry describes metrics and analytics and then shows Precision Teaching's very own metrics and analytics.

Entry: Metrics and analytics: The key to better understanding behavior

In the business world, metrics and analytics play a critical role in understanding consumers. Most specifically, businesses hope to understand consumers' behavior so they can market products. And the purpose of marketing ends with consumers exchanging their money for a product or service - in other words a sale.

Whether people like it or not, every time they browse the Internet through smartphones, tablets, or computers, each web page visit generates data. Businesses then pore over the information to better understand how to market and sell something.

Metrics and analytics

Businesses use metrics and analytics to accomplish a variety of tasks. When applied to marketing, for example, metrics and analytics provide insight into consumer behavior. But how does a metric and analytic differ?

Metrics refer to some standard of measure. How often do people click on cat picture memes in one month? How many Starbucks coupons did consumers download to their phones in a week? Or how many people submitted an online application for a telemarketer job?

Metrics provide counts. Metrics also serve as a useful means for tracking counts. In summary, metrics provide insight based on the tangible enumeration of what people do.

Analytics concern using information and logical analysis to answer specific questions. How do we get cat lovers to buy certain cat toy? Which new coffee flavor should Starbucks develop? What type of person will likely make a good telemarketer? Analytics answer important questions.

The business world can't live without metrics and analytics. But what about people concerned with helping change behavior and improve learning? Can metrics and analytics provide useful/helpful information to behavior change professionals?

Behavior change and interventions

Behavior change and learning do not happen spontaneously. Events in the environment must occur in a way to promote change. As an example, a child takes a bite of a jalapeño pepper and quickly learns something about the pepper. If the child experienced a strong dislike of the flavor, in similar conditions the child has a reduced probability of taking a bite of the spicy plant.

The arrangement of events and how they systematically affect behavior fall under the principles of reinforcement and punishment. The understanding of how reinforcement and punishment work forms the basis of behavior change procedures.

Behavior analysts attempt to enact positive change and use interventions (i.e., behavior change procedures) to drive learning. The term intervention describes any planned process or program focused on behavior change. Science labels an intervention with a more technical term, the independent variable.

Interventions can range from simple to complex. A simple intervention might entail a contingency where each time a shy child starts a conversation with a peer, the child's behavior contacts reinforcement. Complex interventions could include using a well-designed multi-component curriculum to teach a student to read.

The implementation of an intervention most often plays out on a time series visual display. A line graph can show behavior moving across time to the beat of an intervention. The eloquent design of line graphs function as a "comprehensive yet simple means of recording, storing, representing, communicating, and above all, analyzing behavioral data (Parsonson & Baer, 1986).

An instrument for quantification and metrics

The formal system for examining the effects of interventions on behavior has emerged in single-case design (Cooper, Heron, & Heward, 2020). Behavioral experiments of all types occur in the flow time. Similarly, outside of formal experimental designs, behavior change professionals working in homes, clinics, and schools also endeavor to understand how well an intervention produces change. And the workhorse for understanding experimental effects all mainly appear on a simple line graph, the most common visual display used in behavior analysis (Cooper, Heron, & Heward, 2020; Gast & Lane, 2014).

The simple line graph relies on visual analysis. Visual analysis refers to the inspection of data in regard to characteristic data patterns: level, trend, and stability. Changes that occur in line with the intended direction of the independent variable (i.e., intervention) lead the visual analyst to determine an effect has occurred.

By way of illustration, a child who infrequently raised their hand during class in baseline receives an intervention of attention upon raising their hand. If a flat trend in baseline occurs, and then a sharp rising trend appears in the intervention condition, trend analysis suggests an effect. Level and trend analysis also occur concurrently. When a predictable pattern across time emerges, the behavior analyst feels more confident the intervention had a reliable effect.

Metrics

- The Standard Celeration Chart or SCC offers another visual medium through which to view behavior change. The SCC has a number of features behavior change professionals would find useful:
- Standard visual display of data
- Engineered to give prominence to rate of change data
- Ratio scale shows relative change
- Uniformity of rate change growth across time illustrated by straight lines
- Ability to quantify important individual change statistics (e.g., trend, level, variability)
- Proportional comparisons of data with different statistical magnitudes (i.e., low frequency versus high frequency data)
- Metrics from the chart provide data that quantify different behavior change features

Figure 60 depicts a segment of the Standard Celeration Chart, that shows the same data analyzed for level, trend (called celeration on the SCC), and variability (called bounce on the SCC).

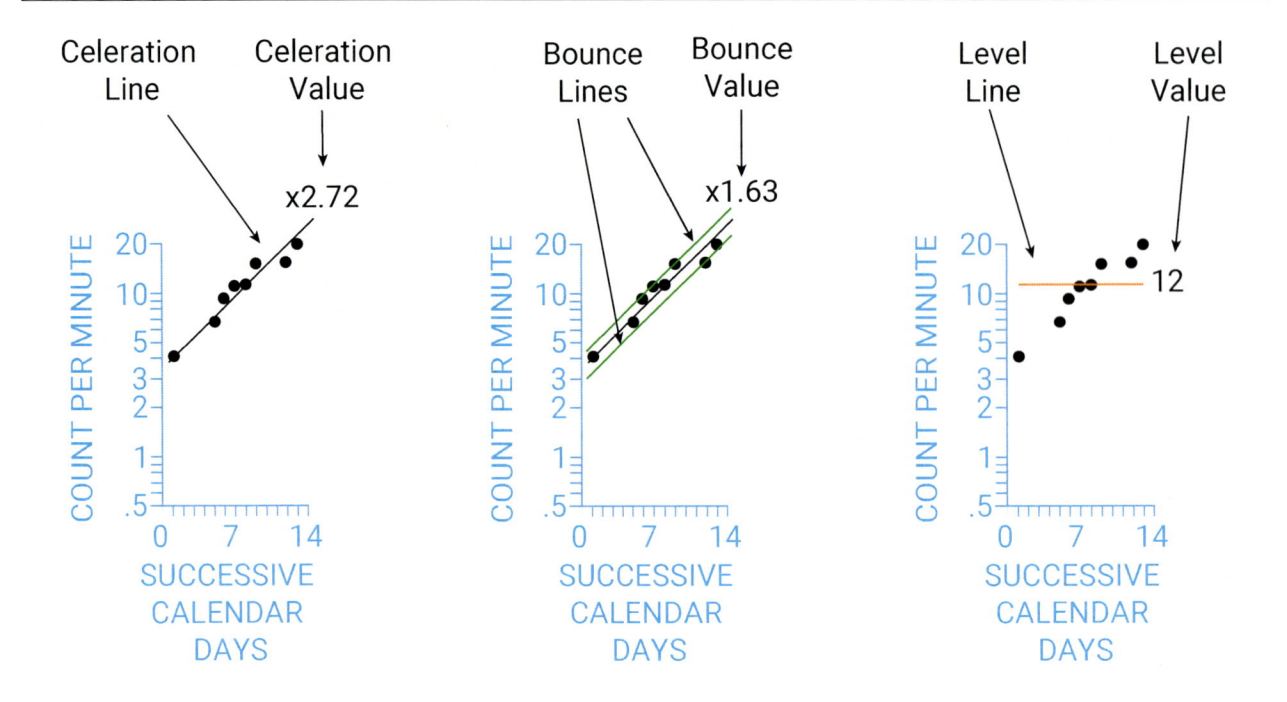

Figure 60. Three different SCC visualizations and subsequent metrics.

The celeration value tells the chart reader how fast the behavior changed. For instance, a student learning signs to communicate may pick up new signs very quickly. A metric such a celeration clearly states how fast the student learns new signs.

Stated differently, all behavior change professionals can have a "learning rate." The speed at which someone learns serves as a speedometer. If a person doesn't meet the threshold for learning fast enough, then the behavior change professional can modify or implement another intervention to speed up learning.

Another useful metric reveals itself in the bounce value. The term "bounce" comes from Precision Teaching (PT) and means variability (each individual performance data point will bounce around from day to day). Bounce offers a metric stating how much control an intervention exerts. Take the example of high school student learning how to balance chemical equations. If performance data do not vary greatly day to day, the student's behavior has consistency or stability.

Stability suggests strong control from the intervention. Just like a stable government or stable economy has forces driving steadiness, so does the bounce metric. The bounce metric offers a number independent of the speed of learning; bounce precisely quantifies the degree of control an intervention has yielded across time.

Level represents the last metric shown in Figure 58. Level conveys the average amount of responding for a given set of behavioral data. Visually, level appears as a straight line drawn across a set of data. The calculation options for level include mean, median, or the geometric mean. The metric, therefore, reflects the typical amount of responding in the data set.

Averages for specific conditions or intervention inform all. When reporting on three different interventions implemented in a quarter, the level shows the average rate of responding for each. The level metrics quickly relay the typical effects for each intervention. Ease of comparison allows the behavior analyst to easily conclude which intervention helped to change behavior the most.

Metrics quantitatively express real properties of behavior. Therefore, metrics acquire power by offering an understandable, comparable unit mirroring a salient property behavior change professionals monitor and analyze.

Businesses use metrics to track consumer behavior and throughputs of advertisements and other tactics aimed at making sales. Behavior change professionals can also use metrics to supplement visual analysis and have a rich understanding of behavior change and intervention effects.

Precision Teaching, metrics, and analytics

As stated earlier, analytics use information and logical analysis to answer important questions. Precision Teaching, along with the Standard Celeration Chart, provides answers to weighty behavioral questions. Has the intervention led to socially significant change? Rather than rely solely on survey questions that ask the client or people who speak on behalf of the client, PT can help behavior change professionals leverage metrics and other facts to provide data-informed answers.

Take the case of a client who steals items incessantly. A behavior change professional who intervenes will have data collected and then graphed. Visual analysis may suggest a decreasing trend, reduced variability, and lower level of stealing as a result of the intervention. By using metrics, valuable information emerges such as the precise speed at which stealing decelerates, exactly how much lower, on average, stealing occurs, and the numerical degree to which variability (i.e., bounce) changed demonstrating just how strongly the intervention functioned.

Metrics form key statistical indicators summarizing the extent and significance of what happened. PT also supplies visual analysis and metrics to uncover overall patterns in the data. Subsequent models emerge that can then provide understanding, prediction, and future optimization of behavioral programming.

How does PT answer the question such as whether an intervention addressing stealing has social validity? The SCC can project exactly how much less the person will steal items in the future. The data speak to the "legs" an intervention will have. PT and the chart can also shed light on time allocation and return on investment.

PT also interfaces with other information sources such scorecards, dashboard data, reports, clinical notes, and a host of other structured and unstructured data. The ability to answer why something happened, predict if it will happen again, and offer the behavior change professional insight they have never thought of before, epitomizes the value of Precision Teaching and the Standard Celeration Chart.

∽

The mathematical relationships made possible by the SCC grant insight and awareness of events that influence behavior change. The concept of multipliers represents one such useful aid. For example, 10x has entered the lexicon of people from business and computing to biology and science. A "10x engineer" means that engineer produces 10 times more than the worst engineer. A popular business book called "The 10x Rule" refers to "massive action" necessary to ensure companies and individuals meet their lofty goals. 10x embodies a multiplier. The following blog describes multipliers and presents a case for their use with behavior change and learning projects.

Entry: Multipliers

Multipliers provide handy information. As an example, for gamblers, multipliers state how much money will grow based on a bet. Figure 59 shows a picture of the poker machine advertising how much money the person could win if they play. The 10x potential multiplier means if the person bet $1.00, they would win $10.00 ($1 x 10 = $10).

Figure 61. Pictures from a video poker and slots machine.

The second picture in Figure 62 comes from a slots game and shows the "Bet Multiplier" the person selected. A Bet Multiplier of x1 means people win whatever they wager. A ¢50 bet x1 returns ¢50 (¢50 x 1 = ¢50). By the way, the payout of $0.00 nicely demonstrates what happens most of the time when people bet slots!

Figure 62. Another video slots machine picture showing a bet multiplier.

Multipliers also help Hollywood studios determine their return on investment. Crazy Rich Asians and Peppermint represent two movies playing at the time of this blog. Crazy Rich Asians cost $30,000,000 (30 million) to make and made approximately $171,000,000. On the other hand, the studio spent $25,000,000 to make Peppermint. Peppermint made $35,000,000.

The multiplier for Crazy Rich Asians came to x4.9. Peppermint had a multiplier of x1.4. The comparison of multipliers quickly and easily allows studios and other interested parties to understand the magnitude of growth immediately.

Hollywood pays so much attention to multipliers due to information regarding initial investment. Compare two movies; Movie 1, an indie film that costs $2,000,000 to and makes $10,000,000. Movie 2, a $200,000,000 spend for a superhero movie that returns $250,000,000. A casual observer might conclude Movie 1 did far worse than Movie 2 because an 8 million return doesn't compare to 50 million.

Multipliers tell a completely different story. The studio immediately sees movie 1 had a x5 growth while movie two a disappointing x1.25. Think of multipliers as amplifiers. The bigger the amplification, especially in terms of behavior and learning targets, the better.

Multipliers for professionals who care about growth

The power of clarity through quantification (e.g., multipliers) eludes many people who work with clients with autism and other disabilities. And the problem stems from the tools available in the profession. Almost everyone who conducts single case experimental design (research) or applies an intervention in a service capacity (applied) employs a nonstandard linear graph.

A linear graph does not lend itself to visually displaying multiply relationships. After all, the linear graph has an explicit construction design geared towards showing absolute amount of change or how much more or less behavior changes. Linear graphs lead to linear thinking. But as Jeff Bezos famously said, "We change our tools and then our tools change us."

Table 13 offers four instances of multipliers in action. The first items to explore appear in Column one titled "Change Metrics."

Change Metric	Multiplier Effect	Explanation
Celeration (Within Condition)	How quickly behavior grows or decays.	A x2.7 celeration value means the behavior has grown 2.7 times (or 170% for the given celeration period. On a daily chart the celeration period equals a week so a x2.7 celeration value describes a 170% weekly growth rate.
Improvement Index (Within Condition)	The extent of improvement measured across the condition.	An improvement index of x3.7 indicates 3.7 times more improvement as measured from the beginning to the end of the condition.
Frequency Multiplier (Between Condition)	The last behavior data point of a condition may jump up, jump down, or stay the same as measured by the first data point in the next condition. The degree of change demonstrates the immediacy of impact.	The x1.6 frequency multiplier value speaks to an abrupt change in the second frequency. The first behavior in the intervention condition rose 1.6 times when compared to the last frequency in the previous condition.
Celeration Multiplier (Between Condition)	Celeration in a second condition may turn up, down, or stay the same when compared to the celeration of the first condition. How much of a departure in rate signifies the overall of speed change.	A x2.0 celeration multiplier expresses 2 times (100%) more acceleration in the second condition when compared to the first condition.

Table 13. Change metrics and their multiplier effects.

Change metrics describe the change of interest and when it applies. Namely, does the metric involve change happening within a condition or between two conditions?

Both types of metrics answer specific questions. What effect would a behavior change professional like to see? Celeration deals with the speed change in a condition. The improvement index reports on the degree of improvement that occurred within a condition.

Between conditions analyses, or moving from one condition and then examining what happens in the second condition, have two effects. One, how much impact did the addition or removal of the second condition have (i.e., frequency multiplier). And two, how much faster does change take place upon removal or the addition of the second condition (i.e., celeration multiplier).

All of the metrics provide a broader, more contextual picture of the change the happened. A behavior change professional eager to evaluate the impact of an intervention instantly see complex data transformed into digestible metrics.

What specific benefits do the four change metrics provide? Table 14 communicates what information behavior change professionals could potentially leave behind.

Issue	Linear Graph	Standard Celeration Chart
A metric showing speed of change	No	Yes
Quantitative evidence demonstrating behavioral improvement	No	Yes
Statistical evidence of the immediacy or impact of a new intervention	No	Yes
An understandable value revealing the speed change from one intervention to a new one	No	Yes

Table 14. Comparison of linear graphs and Standard Celeration Charts.

Conclusion

Multipliers have great value in business, science, and the practice of behavior analysis. Like a Hollywood studio laser-focused on understanding profit, multipliers realized as change metrics convey the extent to which a behavior changed along specific dimensions (e.g., speed, improvement). The transparency and utility of quantifying behavior effects permit behavior change professionals to assess programmatic changes for all clients. And if the change metric (i.e., multiplier) does not meet the threshold of a meaningful effect, the behavior change professional will take action creating and personalizing a new intervention.

We all encounter statistical graphics and data visualization in daily life. The graphics serve as a way to make our life better. High resolution graphics reduce optical noise while providing useful information and narrate a data story. Looking at streams of data on a table with numbers cannot compare to the beauty of well-designed statistical graphics. On a flight to Las Vegas, I used Flight Tracker and found myself immediately admiring the visual display and all the information at my fingertips. The elegance of Flight Tracker and how it transformed complex data into understandable, visually appealing information reminded me of how the Standard Celeration Chart functions much the same way. The following entry came forth as a result of my experience.

Entry: What Southwest's Flight Tracker reminds us about tracking behavior

I recently flew to Las Vegas for a business/personal trip (the personal part had to do with a casino and an unforgiving craps table). Typically, I fly Southwest because of their commitment to efficiency and customer service. Who am I kidding, I love Southwest! They lighten the mood with jokes, allow two free bags, have reasonable rates, and get you in and out the plane in great time.

Other nice features involve free, limited Wifi and services such as "Flight Tracker." Flight Tracker provides important information about the trip so passengers remain in the know. Check out a screen shot showing my flight from Baltimore to Las Vegas.

Figure 63. Flight Tracker from Southwest airlines.

Notice the elegance in the simple yet information-rich interface.

Top section next to Southwest label

- A visual depiction of the plane's progress and remaining time left until the landing.

The upper-left hand section

- Flight number (#) identifying the specific flight.
- Time and distance remaining for the flight.
- An estimate of when the plane will land based on prevailing conditions

The upper-right hand section

- An image of an altitude indicator showing altitude in feet.
- A compass image representing a heading indicator. Informs people as to the exact heading of the aircraft.
- The ground speed image displaying how fast the plane travels relative to the ground (easier to understand for most people than airspeed).

Map section

- Colored map showing where the plane departed, its present location, and the final destination.

I love Flight Tracker. As a behavioral scientist I find visual displays illustrating complex data invaluable. And for people that make their living using statistical graphics to understand nature and act effectively, lessons learned from superior visual displays tell an important story.

Standards matter

Let's start with the Flight Tracker map. Maps work so well because they have standard qualities that do not change from map to map. Effective maps have a scale faithfully representing geographic information. For example, the map of the United States in Flight Tracker conforms to the scale provided by the United States Geological Survey (USGS). The USGS states a line running from "approximately 10 miles south of Brunswick, GA" to "approximately 12 miles south of San Diego, CA" equals a distance of 2,089 miles. Map makers then simply scale by using a ratio of inches to miles and an effectively scaled map emerges.

What do maps tell us about effective graph construction? Maps with a proper scale, well balanced colors, and legible symbols provide accurate information, facilitate comprehension, and lead to sound decision making. Maps simplify the world by providing proportional, consistent information reflective of geographic information. Navigating a trip from your house to your favorite destination can occur seamlessly.

People who wish to access high quality graphed data can take a page from cartographers and insist on a standard visual display with standard colors, symbols, and physical dimensions. As an example, the popular standard visual display, the Standard Celeration Chart or SCC serves as the "go to" graphic for time series data.

Like a map, people who use an SCC quickly detect key information via visual patterns produced by the uniformity and consistency of the standard graphic. When someone uses a map like the one in Figure 63 (in Flight Tracker) no questions surround the visual information showing the states and the aircraft's flight path. Anyone who has read a map discerns the information almost instantly.

Likewise, with the SCC, a number of chart features allow chart readers to immediately understand the data, A straight line on the SCC retains the same value on every chart. The time spent identifying significant trends becomes an easy task. A line with the value of x2.0 per week means the behavior has doubled each week. Anyone who sees a x2.0 angle on the SCC will know they have found something significant.

Better information leads to better analysis and decisions

While I could probably write two or three blogs comparing all the information on Flight Tracker to an effective graph like the SCC, I will focus on one more point. Flight tracker offers passengers three images with standard information: Altitude, Heading, and Ground Speed.

Every person can react similarly to the information presented because each piece of information reveals a standard or fundamental unit of measurement. An altitude of 38,000 ft clearly differs from 14,000 ft. People can understand the magnitude of 38,000 ft off the ground.

Additionally, when a speed of 419 miles per hour falls within a person's senses. We have all traveled in cars and know what 60, 70, 80, and few daring people, 90+ miles per hour. Going 419 miles per hour represents an incredible speed and explains how someone can travel across the country in a mere 5 hours!

The Standard Celeration Chart also significantly aids understanding and subsequent communication of data through qualification. The celeration value says how fast a student learns something. Growing at the rate of x2.0 means every week the student has doubled the amount of learning. People care about how fast things change so they can plan for when the person will arrive at the destination. The SCC provides clear, direct quantitative information linked to the celeration line on the chart.

Conclusion

Flight Tracker works well at what it does, offering elaborate information made simple to passengers eager to reach their destination. The Standard Celeration Chart also conveys data rendered in a coherent, recognizable visual pattern. For those interested in and new to the SCC, consider giving it a try.

CHAPTER 7

Behavioral Production

IN CHAPTER 0 and other chapters, we established a definition of Precision Teaching (PT). PT constitutes a process that involves four steps: Pinpoint, Record, Change, and Try again. The process has served thousands of teachers, students, parents and children, therapists and clients, and various other people. The second step of PT involved using dimensional qualities to capture the recorded data. During the early years, many Precision Teachers recorded behavior in a one-minute interval. Then the Precision Teachers discovered something amazing. The one-minute interval used for assessing student performance spoke volumes about a student's ability to do well later in the curriculum.

A seminal report on 12 presentations given to a Council for Exceptional Children Conference in 1971 contained some intriguing data. Students who did not reach certain frequency thresholds could not progress to more advanced math. Another discovery demonstrated that when students attained a given level of frequency correct and incorrect words read per minute, the students would not progress in oral reading. Other remarkable findings demonstrated that not only did the one-minute interval used to assess students offer incredible diagnostic value, but the one-minute interval, or timing as many people began calling it, also held much promise as a technique to deliver high-quality practice.

The discoveries made in the 1970s fell under a burgeoning concept called fluency, or later behavioral fluency. The outcome of behavioral fluency applies to everyone everywhere. Fluent behavior or skill means the person can perform with high accuracy and proper speed. Fluency confers functionality, ever readiness, and a certain grace. But the way to get there does not come easily. The journey to behavioral fluency lies on the road called practice, or in PT term frequency building.

The present chapter has a number of my musings and lessons learned surrounding practice and advancing behavioral performance. The first three entries all cover a common theme, why and how to practice. One would think education would embrace practice and behavior fluency. One would find themselves wrong with such a logical notion! The fourth entry covers a component of PT that needs more study and promotion, the element-compound relationship. The fifth entry con consists of my blending of performance improvement for one of my personal behaviors, professional writing.

Entry: Don't 'drill' but do 'practice'

In education, wild misconceptions abound with the concept of practice. A quick search of the web yields a host of people stating problems with practice.

"The old "drill the skill" strategy of learning math facts was based solely on memory. Any strategy that is based solely on memory has a weak foundation."

Source: Response: Ways To Teach Math Besides 'Drill The Skill' (http://blogs.edweek.org/teachers/classroom_qa_with_larry_ferlazzo/2014/10/response_ways_to_teach_math_besides_drill_the_skill.html)

"What worries me and should worry you is what happens to children who are subjected to prepackaged curriculums. If I'd left JJ in a school that relied only on skill and drill worksheets to teach reading, I already saw what would happen – she wouldn't be an enthusiastic reader, even a strong reader."

Source: The Case Against Skill and Drill Curriculum (http://imaginationsoup.net/2011/09/the-case-against-skill-and-drill-curriculum/)

"This [preparing for the tests] is all we did for the first half of the year," Marciniak said. "Our teachers focused on nothing else. And it's kind of hard sitting there as you're basically drilled and lectured on nothing but this." This kind of "skill and drill" test preparation is increasingly widespread, especially in urban and rural schools where there are large numbers of students disadvantaged by poverty and where these students too oftenscore poorly on tests.

Source: Sustaining test score gains requires good teaching, not skill and drill (http://thenotebook.org/summer-2004/04778/sustaining-test-score-gains-requires-good-teaching-not-skill-and-drill)

The above quotes express real frustration and concern for the outcome of students. Therefore, the objections to "Skill and drill" come from a context of caring. Yet each of the quotes shows how the authors got the idea of practice wrong.

Drill, skill and drill, drill and kill, practice

In the previous quotes most people used the term "skill and drill." But other derivatives such as plain old "drill" or its pejorative sister term "drill and kill" evoke notions of blind, back-breaking, soul crushing activities that lead to poor academic outcomes and terrible emotional side effects.

It makes sense on the one hand. If we took an enthusiastic, joyful, curious kindergarten student and gave them worksheets for long hours, we have a situation resembling forced labor, not thoughtful teaching. Parents would not want their child squashed by unrealistic work demands. Likewise, teachers do not want to ruin the youthful exuberance and spirit of inquiry.

Therein lies the problem. The terms Skill and Kill, Drill and Kill, Drill etc. have come to represent very inefficient, aversive practice methods. And because those methods make life unpleasant for the student, no one should use them. The logic train, however, has a flaw:

> Drill and Kill harms students.
>
> Drill and Kill is practice.
>
> Eliminate practice so we no longer harm students.

The previous deduction falls under the category of an "improper generalization." An improper generalization contains an inaccurate statement rendering the conclusion false. Let's review.

1. Drill and Kill harm students.

Possibly true. What exactly people mean by the term varies. When someone paints a picture of pushing students to fatigue, harsh conditions, and forced compliance, sure, let's avoid those situations at all costs.

2. Drill and Kill is practice.

Thoughtful, nurturing, and meaningful practice involves four main elements: (a) timed repetition of a behavior or skill; (b) having a quantified, time-based goal; (b) delivering performance feedback after each practice trial; and (d) engaging in a sufficient amount of daily practice (Binder, 1996; Ericsson, 2006).

Drill and Kill fails the test of good practice because it often has no time limit, absence of goals, has a stunning lack feedback and instead may include criticism. Additionally, Drill and Kill will ask students to practice beyond reason.

3. Eliminate practice so we no longer harm students.

Yikes! Talk about throwing the baby out with the bath water! Yes, Drill and Kill has no place in a humane, compassionate, and positive educational environment. On the other hand, an educational environment that withholds and/or completely eliminates practice oppresses true mastery and fluency of content. Can you think of any human, anywhere, at any time that has become fluent with a skill without practicing?

Research shows again and again the critical, absolute essential need for practice in skills ranging from music and surgery, to reading and problem solving. Let's do away with Drill and Kill and champion effective practice in all classrooms!

I have used the term frequency building instead of practice in my professional writing. But blogging requires a different voice and substitution of terms. Blogs reach the technically and non-technically inclined people out there searching for information. The following entry exposes my efforts to write with a less formal tone and inspire people to use better practice methods. I write professionally, but do so in the realm of science. Therefore, I find it an ongoing effort to write better and communicate straightforwardly. I hope you find blogs you have read understandable and impactful.

Entry: Three simple steps for better practice

Do you, someone you work with, or person you care about, engage in practice? If I had to guess I would say yes. People use practice to get better at all sorts of things.

In business, you might find people working at call centers practicing how to respond to specific questions. At the prestigious Weill Cornell Medical College medical students, surgeons, and other healthcare professions practice safety procedures in their Skill Acquisition and Innovation Laboratory. In sports basketball players practice free throws and intricate plays. And in schools, students practice math facts and writing descriptive paragraphs.

If people want to get better at a skill, they can do one thing only, practice. But differential outcomes occur depending on what goes into the practice.

Figure 64. A picture of the Skill Acquisition and Innovation Laboratory.

You can find much written about practice. The legendary coach John Wooden emphasized the absolute necessity of practice in developing masterful skills. Wooden said, "I am not a strategic coach; I am a practice coach." Hard to argue with a person that produced a head shaking 10 NCAA national championships in a 12-year period (he had a stretch of 7 championships in a row - I mean, who does that! Imagine someone winning 7 Super Bowls in a row or 7 World Cups in a row).

Iconic athletes such as Michael Jordan, Tiger Woods, and Tom Brady all have publicly shared their secret to success - practice. The famous hockey player Eric Lindros said, "It's not necessarily the amount of time you spend at practice that counts; it's what you put into the practice."

Yet for all the books written and anecdotal stories shared from people who have mastered their domain, people oftentimes miss the three fundamental features of superior practice.

1. Time practice trials

No one can escape the universal fact that everything people do, they do in time. By using a timer, we place brackets on the practice segments we choose to observe. As a result, we can compare apples-to-apples when we scrutinize the performance data. Examine the following practice scores for a group of students doing letter sound fluency:

13 correct

15 correct

18 correct

20 correct

Would you conclude the practice procedure worked? The data above sure tell us so. Take a second look at the data in time:

13 correct in 30 seconds

15 correct 40 seconds

18 correct 50 seconds

20 correct 60 seconds

What do you think now? When we place data on the Standard Celeration Chart, a chart designed to show human behavior in time, we see a drastically different picture.

The data actually worsens across time because while the total number goes up, it takes longer to achieve the letter sounds. Ignoring time invites misleading data into the decision making process.

2. Commit to a daily number of practice trials

Systematic practice has three terms pertaining to a practice routine:

- (Practice) Schedule: Planning and scheduling of daily practice sessions.

- (Practice) Session: Overall length of the time spent practicing. Includes all elements of practice.

- (Practice) Trial: An instance of one timed application of practice.

Let's examine the well-known athlete (Olympic swimmer) Michael Phelps.

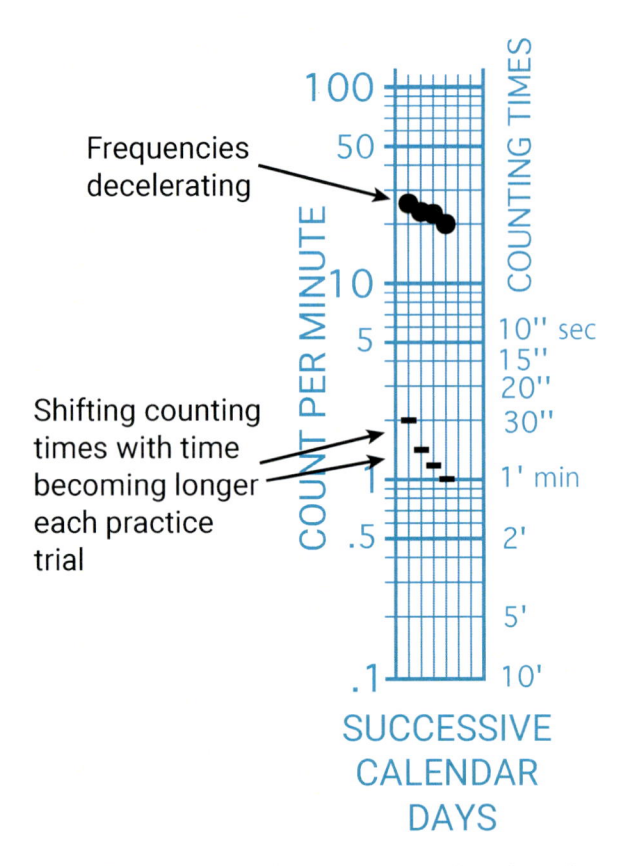

Figure 65. A portion of a Standard Celeration Chart showing practice with letter sound fluency.

Figure 66. Michael Phelps doing his thing. (Source: http://workoutinfoguru.com/wp-content/uploads/2013/06/michael-phelps.jpg)

Each day Phelps schedules his workout routine to include strength training, cardio, and practice on specific skills. During a Tuesday Phelps may workout and have a practice session scheduled for the day. The session involves all the daily targeted practice activities. Two of Phelps practice activities:

- 500 strokes (50 kicks – 50 drill)
- 2000 timed kick stroke

Focusing on one practice activity, we see Phelps does four trials of speed sets (24 X 25 fly on 30 minutes).

Order emerges from Phelps' practice regimen. He has days where he schedules his practice, sessions where he designates his multiple practice activities, and a set number of trials for each practice activity.

By keeping track of how many practice trials a person engages in, data emerge from each timed trial. If performance does not improve, many options now exist. One could increase the number of daily timed practice trials to see if a positive change takes place. Or someone can implement specific feedback within each trial with the resulting data showing whether the new feedback improves performance.

Failing to keep track of the number of daily trials means less information for situations where performance does not improve. Additionally, science demands order! How can we replicate skilled improvements and excellent feats of behavior without knowing how much practice someone must engage in to acquire said skills?

3. Provide feedback after the practice ends

With all the people that golf as a hobby it is a wonder why everyone can't make the pro tour. But just because someone does something a lot doesn't mean they will get better. What would happen if you consistently practiced something in an incorrect manner? You get better at doing it incorrectly!

Reading the scientific literature reveals practitioners and researchers equating practice with going faster or doing more repetitions of a behavior. Effective practice, however, requires the addition of performance feedback. The feedback drives improvement so the next time the person practices the targeted skill improvements may occur.

With golf, hitting more golf balls or hitting golf balls faster compared to game time won't correct a slice or hook (for those not familiar with golf, a slice and hook describe the ball traveling in a hard right or left motion).

When providing practice, coaches or those invested in helping others improve through practice can deliver affirmative feedback (e.g., You hit the golf ball straight), inspirational or motivation feedback (e.g., Fantastic job, you played your scales beautifully), or corrective feedback. Corrective feedback can take three different forms:

- Saying how to do something correctly
- Modeling how to do something correctly
- Guiding a person doing something correctly

Conclusion

Many proverbs, quotes, and phrases stress the vital importance of practice and its outcomes. We have all heard, for example, the adage "Practice makes perfect." Stated differently, to attain excellence at a skill, people must practice. And all practice routines will improve by timing the practice trial, having a set (adequate) number of practice trials completed each day, and providing performance feedback.

I have worked as a Professor in a college of education for 21 years at the time of writing this book. I have directly worked with a little under 1,000 preservice students who would go on to become special education teachers. And I have visited countless classrooms and have seen the degree of practice done in those settings. Both preservice and inservice teachers need to learn about behavioral fluency and how to apply it in the classroom successfully. Parents also have a vested interest in practice because, without it, students will struggle to reach their fluency goals. In the following entry, I tried my hand at creating a checklist for parents and teachers. The checklist contains simple practice elements that lead to prodigious displays of skilled performance.

Entry: Practice - The key to success in school and life

As the new school year approaches, parents and children engage in a familiar set of activities: school clothes shopping, school supply shopping, and checking out classrooms and scheduling assignments.

The time of year holds a mixture of emotions for parents and students alike. Feelings range from excitement and eagerness to nervousness and apprehension. But as parents send their children off to school, one critical factor will play a weighty role into the success of each student - practice.

In fact, next to the curriculum structure and design and curriculum delivery (i.e., instruction), the amount of practice a student engages in holds the most significant impact on success. No one gets better at anything without practice. And if practice does have a presence in the classroom, it may represent drill (read the following for the difference between practice and drill).

How can you tell what type of practice your child receives? The following checklist can help determine the extent to which robust practice procedures occur in the classroom.

CHAPTER 7: BEHAVIORAL PRODUCTION

Behavioral Fluency Practice Checklist

To help you check for properties of high quality practice routines leading to behavioral fluency

#1 Do you witness performers practicing? ☐

Do not send performers off on their own to practice. Good practice starts with a commitment to practice.

#2 Does practice occur in a timed format? ☐

Untimed practice is like trying to keep track of an hour with no watch - it makes no sense! Timing practice adds precision and temporally contextualizes performance data.

#3 Do practice sessions take place daily? ☐

Practicing daily allows for consistent performance, frequent opportunities to correct mistakes, and solidify neural connections.

#4 Do multiple practice trials occur during practice sessions? ☐

One practice trial a day means the next day to shine won't come for another 24 hours. Multiple practice trials facilitate rapid learning.

#5 Do performers receive feedback after each practice trial? ☐

Research shows the importance of feedback for shaping performance. Providing no feedback may result in practicing errors or poor form.

#6 Does the practice program have a fluency aim? ☐

A fluency aim means having a rate or frequency goal. Frequency, or count over time, offers the most sensitive measure possible for gauging performance improvement.

#7 Do practice trials appear on a chart? ☐

Visually displaying performance on a chart allows the public monitoring of growth rates. Additionally, the chart provides motivation and accountability for the performer and practice coach.

Figure 67. The high quality practice checklist.

Practice Checklist

Checklist item #1. To experience the benefits of practice, practice must first occur. Some teachers relegate practice to occasions when they do not monitor or even witness the student working on skills.

The number one culprit of downgrading an active culture of practice? Homework.

Having students practice on their own may work better than no practice, but perhaps not always. Students might practice errors. Students do not receive feedback until much, much later from the time they made the mistake.

Students also can put off homework/practice or not do it at all. If teachers value practice, it must occur in school, in class, and under their watchful eye. Education has many phrases touting teachers as coaching and willing to help. Yet the version of coaching in schools greatly deviates from what good coaching entails.

Checklist item #2. A fundamental truth about humans; all behavior occurs in time. Therefore, the most sensitive measure we have involves counting a skill in time. We call counts over time frequency or rate.

Too often teachers do not time practice and have students work at skills at their leisure. If two students answered 10 math problems correctly, but one took 1 minute and the other 5 minutes, which one has the superior skill?

Because most teachers do not time practice, we will never know or appreciate the difference of skillful performance. And more importantly, decisions concerning competent development proceed unevenly and with obscured information.

Checklist item #3. How often practice sessions take place influences the trajectory of fluency (fluency = the attainment of true mastery defined by highly accurate and well-paced behavior).

Take a look at Tiger Wood's practice schedule:

Tiger Woods Daily Practice Schedule

6:30 AM: One hour of cardio. Choice between endurance runs, sprints or biking.
7:30 AM: One hour of lower weight training. 60-70 percent of normal lifting weight, high reps and multiple sets.
8:30 AM: High protein/low-fat breakfast. Typically includes egg-white omelet with vegetables.
9:00 AM: Two hours on the golf course. Hit on the range and work on swing.
11:00 AM: Practice putting for 30 minutes to an hour.
12:00 PM: Play nine holes.
1:30 PM: High protein/low-fat lunch. Typically includes grilled chicken or fish, salad and vegetables.
2:00 PM: Three-to-four hours on the golf course. Work on swing, short game and occasionally play another nine holes.
6:30 PM: 30 minutes of upper weight training. High reps.
7:00 PM: Dinner and rest.

Picture Source: User:Ytoyoda/botgalleries/Ballsports/2018 July 16-23

Figure 68. Tiger Wood's practice routine.

There is no substitute for the intensity of practice. Athletes, musicians, surgeons, and any person serious about skill develop practice daily. Sadly, in American schools daily practice may not come about due to competing demands or a disdainful attitude towards practice.

Checklist item #4. Some definitions to help explain practice terms:

- Practice Schedule: Planning and scheduling of daily practice sessions.
- Practice Session: Overall length of the time spent practicing. Includes all elements of practice.
- Practice Trial: An instance of one timed application of practice.

A key feature distinguishing good practice from bad involves the number of practice trials that occur in a practice session. Generally, multiple practice trials should take place during a practice session so students have the opportunity to develop skill.

When students do only one practice session a day, it takes another whole day to engage in the skill again. Emerging evidence in world of athletic performance shows sprinting, or doing multiple, shorter timed sessions works as good, and in some cases better, than one long timed duration (true in running, swimming, and in academics).

Checklist item #5. Imagine performing a specific skill each day, multiple times, and with no feedback aside from what you observe? How would you get better at swinging a golf club, singing a song, or writing an essay?

Corrective feedback comes in three forms:

a. Saying how to do something correctly.
b. Modeling how to do something correctly.
c. Guiding a person doing something correctly.

If you observe practice in the classroom, checkmark item number 5 if students receive feedback after each practice trial.

Checklist item #6. Behavioral fluency has a scientific definition: "the fluid combination of accuracy plus speed that characterizes competent performance" (Binder, 1996, p. 164).

To attain behavioral fluency, one must engage in practice. We use the term fluency aim to signify the end point of practice.

A fluency aim has a count placed over time (a metric called frequency or rate). As an example, a fluent typist can keyboard at a range of 60 to 90 correct with 0 to 1 incorrect words per minute. The fluency aim for keyboarding, then, becomes 60 to 90 correct words with 0 to 1 incorrect words per minute.

Oftentimes, teachers use percent correct as a goal for practice. Even 100% for 5 days in a row could make a poor fluency goal. With percent correct, no one knows how many or how fast the student performs thereby shrouding precision.

<u>Checklist item #7</u>. If the classroom you observed contains elements on the checklist, data will exist like ripe apples on a tree. Harvesting the data and placing them on a chart (use the Standard Celeration Chart for the best visual, analytic device) leads to observing patterns suggestive of improvement or lack thereof.

Practice requires careful monitoring so a teacher can make quick, responsive changes if the data so indicate. Likewise, innovations emerge when viewing the magnitude and rate of improvement in conjunction with different practice techniques.

Conclusion

To execute a healthy practice routine geared towards engendering fluency, teachers must directly implement practice. Furthermore, the way in which teachers set up practice routines will strongly influence skill development. We all want students to practice skills, achieve fluency, and become masters in their respective domains. To evaluate the degree and technical adequacy of the practice that occurs in a classroom, use the Behavioral Fluency Practice Checklist and see what turns out.

I have blogged with different groups of people as targets of the content. I wrote the following for behavior analysts and special education teachers. Though other people interested in ramping up behavior production would benefit from the content. And the content goes hand in glove with growing and promoting new behaviors, namely, the element-compound analysis. The skills taught to another person range from simple to very complex. The more complex, the greater the need for a thorough element-compound analysis. I tried to systematically present the element-compound analysis in the following entry as a method behavior change agents could start using right away. By the way, you may have noticed I changed in my later writing from behavior change professional to behavior change agent, but both mean the same thing.

Entry: A behavioral complexity checklist

The branch of science known as chemistry focuses on identifying the properties of substances and how they interact, change, and combine. For example, sodium (Na) and chloride (Cl) come together to form a compound called sodium chloride (NaCl) or its more common name, salt. Chemistry has grown and sheds light on processes that people once thought of as magic.

Behavior analysis, the branch of science that examines behavior, has also made remarkable discoveries that explain how the complexities of behavior emerge. Some of the processes that produce novel behavior appear straightforward, such as imitation. Person one sees person two doing something and imitates their behavior. Now, person one has a new behavior in their repertoire.

More complex processes explaining intricate, generative behavior include stimulus equivalence. With stimulus equivalence, people learn a series of discriminations and some discriminations become related without direct teaching. For example, a child hears the spoken word plane (stimulus A) and has paired it with the written word plane (stimulus B). Also, the written word plane (stimulus B) becomes paired with a toy plane (stimulus C). Then upon hearing the word plane (stimulus A) the child successfully touches the toy plane (stimulus C). The remarkable derived relation of stimulus A to C demonstrates equivalence.

A less well-known method for analyzing and fostering the emergence of complex behavior comes from Precision Teaching and goes by the name "element-compound analysis" (aka component-composite analysis).

Behavioral elements and compounds

Chemistry's core discovery of elements forming a compound also applies to behavior. A behavioral element refers to a behavior that forms a constituent part of a compound behavior. For example, balling one's fist serves as an element of throwing a punch.

A complex multiplication problem serves as another example of a compound behavior with several behavioral elements. Figure 69 shows a complex multiplication problem that requires a long multiplication algorithm (also called grade school multiplication or the standard algorithm). A person who applies the long multiplication algorithm must have the ability to (1) calculate basic multiplication facts (single digit x single digit); (2) regroup or carry numbers in the tens place; (3) adhere to place value for the alignment of numbers in the problem; and (4) complete basic addition facts.

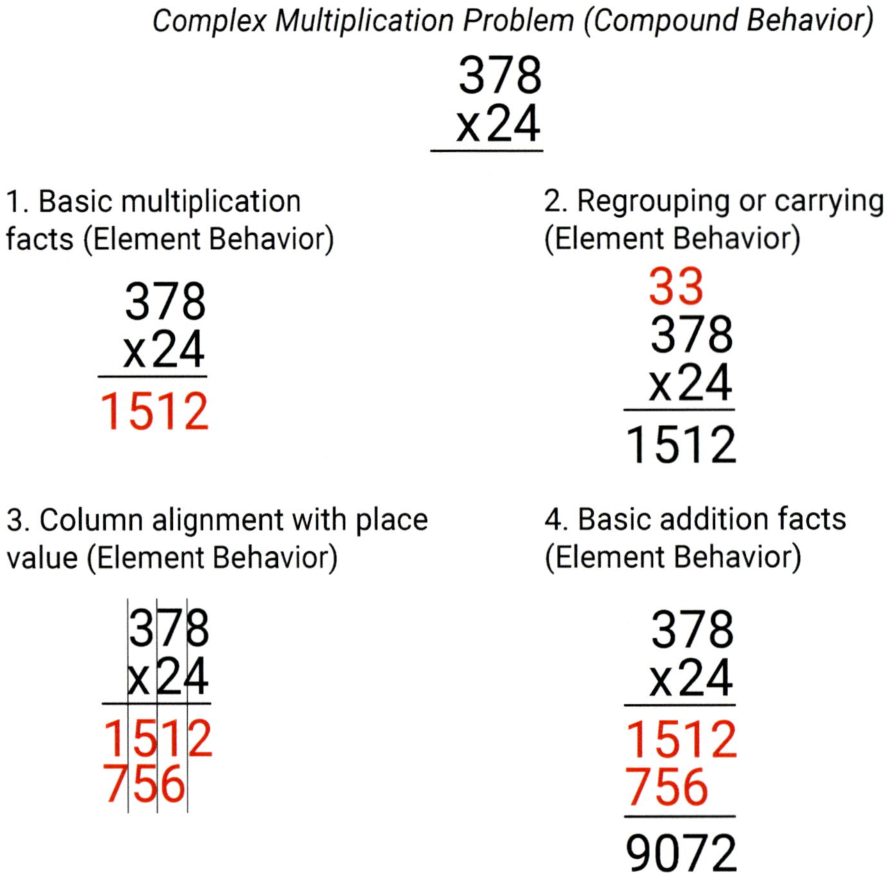

Complex Multiplication Problem (Compound Behavior)

$$\begin{array}{r}378\\ \times 24\\ \hline\end{array}$$

1. Basic multiplication facts (Element Behavior)

$$\begin{array}{r}378\\ \times 24\\ \hline 1512\end{array}$$

2. Regrouping or carrying (Element Behavior)

$$\begin{array}{r}33\\ 378\\ \times 24\\ \hline 1512\end{array}$$

3. Column alignment with place value (Element Behavior)

$$\begin{array}{r}378\\ \times 24\\ \hline 1512\\ 756\end{array}$$

4. Basic addition facts (Element Behavior)

$$\begin{array}{r}378\\ \times 24\\ \hline 1512\\ 756\\ \hline 9072\end{array}$$

Figure 69. A compound behavior and the subsequent element behaviors.

Many complex, compound behaviors will not form without the elements occurring at a level of competency. Trying to apply a reinforcement contingency to the complex multiplication algorithm as above can result in a spectacular failure. For example, a reinforcement strategy that targets student attempts for the long multiplication algorithm will produce little results if the student does not possess a minimum behavioral dexterity with basic multiplication facts. Many educational and behavioral developments benefit from the analysis of the elements within a compound behavior.

Element-compound analysis

Figure 70 presents a checklist from The Precision Teaching Implementation Manual for determining which elements comprise a behavioral compound.

Step 1. The behavior change agent will first look for the targeted compound behavior in a curriculum, assessment (e.g., PEAK: Relational Training System, VB-MAPP), or a single behavior. Choosing the target will occur due to different reasons (e.g., person needs to learn the behavior quickly, person has struggled learning the behavior).

ELEMENT-COMPOUND ANALYSIS CHECKLIST

Compound to Elements: _____

		Yes	No
1	Look for a compound within a curriculum.	○	○
1a	Focus on a single compound behavior.	○	○
2	Identify the target compound as a pinpoint+.	○	○
3	Determine which elements form the compound by generating pinpoint+s.	○	○
3a	Determine frequency aim ranges for pinpoint+s.	○	○
3b	Decide whether pinpoint+s have an optimal order. If yes list the order.	○	○
4	Collect data and determine if elements lead to the compound behavior.	○	○
4a	Modify element frequency ranges or add and/or delete elements if necessary.	○	○

Figure 70. A checklist for the element-compound analysis from *The Precision Teaching Implementation Manual*.

Take the example of an important skill found in the PEAK: Relational Training System book, Direct Training Module – Turn Taking. The goal of turn taking specifies the person's offer to give a turn to another person during a game or toy play.

Step 2. Transforming the compound to a pinpoint+ helps bring precision to the target. Turn taking transformed into a pinpoint becomes: Places Lego toy in peer's hand after 10 seconds of playing with Lego toy in peer's presence.

The previous pinpoint shows the child will give a turn to a peer with a toy after 10 seconds of play. The specificity with the pinpoint clearly communicates that the target behavior includes giving a toy to a peer.

Step 3. The turn-taking pinpoint may have several elements. Figure 71 displays a few important behavioral elements that must occur for the compound behavior. Giving a turn to a peer means the child must value and operate or play with the toy in the first place. Another element pinpoint has the child playing with the toy in the presence of another child or peer. Before a child can give a turn with a toy, having another child next to them forms an important element.

Compound behavior for Turn Taking transformed into a pinpoint:
Places Lego toy in peer's hand after 10 seconds of playing with Lego in a peer's presence

| Operates Lego toy in an appropriate manner | Operates Lego toy in an appropriate manner in the presence of a peer | Places Lego toy in peer's hand upon request from a peer | Places Lego toy in bin in presence of a peer |

Figure 71. A compound behavior and the subsequent element behaviors.

The other two behavioral elements encompass placing the Lego toy in different locations. One behavior, "Places Lego toy in bin in presence of peer" demonstrates the target child can place the Lego in a place. Also, placing the toy in the hand of peer who requests it shows the target child can relinquish the item.

An analysis may reveal the need for additional elements. Also, some specific element(s) may require further sub-elements themselves. A list of what elements constitute behaviors does not exist at present; therefore the analysis falls on the shoulders of the behavior change agent.

Step 3a. All behaviors have a frequency at which the skill becomes functional. For example, "keyboards words while composing an email" becomes functional in the environment at 60 to 90 words keyboarded correctly with 0 to 1 incorrectly keyboarded words in one minute.

In the previous example, the compound behavior and the element behaviors would likely happen during toy play and have a low frequency. Still, when teaching a specific pinpoint, a contrived situation could have a higher frequency with which to judge if the target child's behavior has reached a functional criterion.

"Place Lego toy in peer's hand upon request from peer" could look like a game itself whereby the target child must place a toy in the hand of the peer each time they hear the request. The event could take 3 minutes resulting in a frequency indicative of the aim or goal.

Step 3b. Behavioral elements may take on order for teaching. In Figure 3, for instance, teaching "operates a Lego toy in an appropriate manner" would take place before "operates a Lego toy in an appropriate manner in the presence of a peer."

Step 4. The child learning the element pinpoints requires assessment for the compound behavior (i.e., pinpoint). Sometimes the compound behavior appears spontaneously, which exemplifies generativity. Other times the compound will not emerge until achieving minimum frequencies with all selected element behaviors.

Step 4a. Because so many behaviors of interest do not have readily broken-down elements, behavior change agents will find themselves making modifications. First, changes may occur with the frequency ranges of element behaviors. The element behavior may need to be adjusted up or down depending on how well the element works when applied to the compound behavior. Second, the addition or deletion of element behaviors may also require implementation. If the presence of elements does not appear conducive to the emergence of the compound behavior, the behavior change agent may have missed a critical element.

Conclusion

The science of behavior offers a number of concepts that explain the emergence of novel behavior and generativity. The element-compound analysis serves as a method that may foster generativity but can also shine a light on instances in which a person plateaus or cannot learn a certain complex behavior. The discovery of behavioral elements and their respective compounds illustrates the value and efficacy of behavior analysis to complex skills.

Behavioral production can take many forms. Writing accounts for one behavior I have worked on since grade school and continually try to improve. And I have worked as a professor for 21 years, necessitating my need to produce and guide others to become better writers. I have used PT to help me help others and myself. The following entry describes my personal use of PT and how it has helped me become a better writer.

Entry: To write better chart better

As a university professor, part of my job includes helping students improve their writing. I have worked with bachelors, masters, and doctoral level students. The writing assignments vary between students. For example, at the bachelor's level, students turn in papers that require grammar edits, APA citation formatting, and content feedback.

Masters and doctoral level students also receive similar feedback and receive high-level constructive criticism due to the scope of their work. Masters students learn to write literature reviews and doctoral students write manuscripts that they will submit to journals and other scholarly outlets.

Whether the students find themselves in a course where they must turn in a 1-page reading reaction, an 8-page research thesis, or a 20-page draft, all students must master technical writing. And the challenge to refining writing follows four broad areas: 1. mechanics, 2. writing style, 3. content knowledge, and 4. production.

Writing elements

Mechanics. For technical writing, mechanics range from using quotation marks and oxford commas to APA or MLA citation systems. Everything must follow the system 100% of the time. For example:

Kubina, R. M., Kostewicz, D. E., & Datchuk, S. M. (2010). Graph and table use in special education: A review and analysis of the communication of data. *Evaluation & Research in Education, 23*, 105-119.

Spacing, where periods go, and the use of italics just need learned. Students figure out the system and with practice become proficient. Most of the time errors occur because students don't know the system well, become confused, or do not double check their work (e.g., using a period instead of a comma). The good news? Students can easily look up the rules and master mechanics.

Writing style. Writing style refers to how writers express themselves in text. Developing a sound writing style takes good instruction, lots of practice, and continual revisions and further refinement. At the university I often hear fellow professors lament that their students appear to have never learned to write well or suffer from serious writing flaws.

While high school teachers, middle school teachers, and even grade school teachers receive blame for not teaching writing, the college student needs immediate help. Many books and blogs on writing offer advice. An excellent blog post on writing offered 10 tips:

1. Practice concision and avoid repetitive sentences and drawn out explanations.
2. Write shorter sentences to improve comprehension and readability.
3. Avoid or revise passive voice constructed sentences.
4. Remove all instances of weasel words like "generally" and "most."
5. Steer clear of jargon and instead write clearly and directly.
6. Always use citations when mentioning statistics.
7. Consider using pronouns to create a relationship with the reader.
8. Lead with key insights, do not hide them.
9. Use examples to enhance clarity.
10. Let the reader know where you plan to go with your writing.

Content knowledge. I teach in a special education program. Both my MA and Ph.D. came from a special education program. Additionally, I worked as a professional for a number of years with students with disabilities. Though my 30 years in the field I have acquired specialized knowledge regarding special education (e.g., teaching reading, practicing to fluency, making data-based decisions on visual displays).

Students enter a field and learn about the discipline they have chosen to pursue. When writing a paper the student must do research and acquire specialized knowledge. Sitting down to write about something when the student doesn't have much knowledge will result in frustration and a lack of substance. Writers cannot fake their way through technical content.

Production. Simply put, to write effectively a writer must put in the time. Period. The fantasy about sitting down at the beach, Starbucks, or some other pleasant place to occasionally write just doesn't cut it. Writing requires devoted time, focus, revision, more writing, and more revision.

While this blog post has focused on technical writing, to get an idea of what professional writers in the narrative genre do, check out the daily word counts of some famous authors (for context approximately 250 double spaced words make up a typed page):

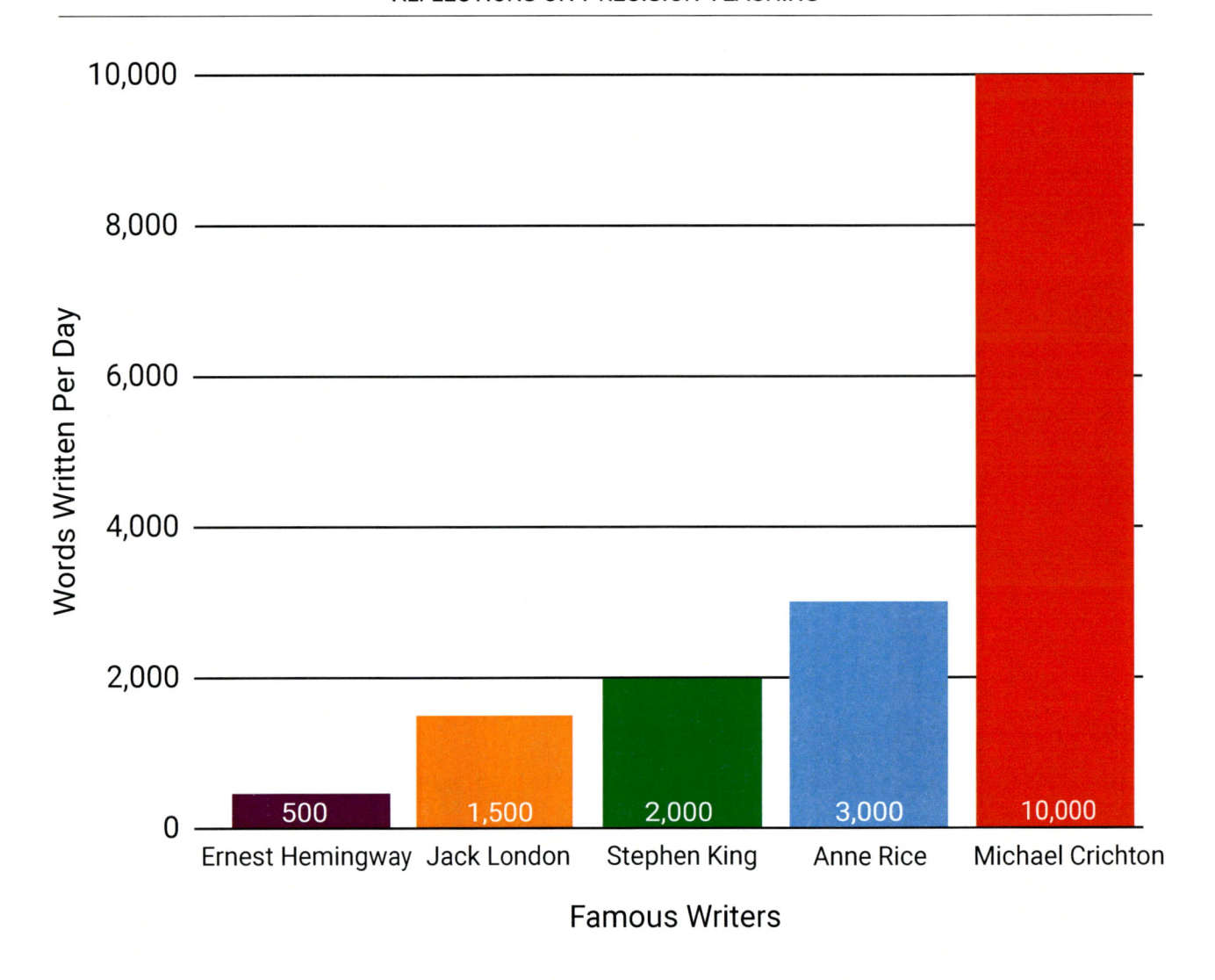

Figure 72. Daily word counts of famous writers.

Stephen King wrote many famous books (would love to hear your favorite). One book that greatly influenced the blogpost author: *On Writing: A Memoir of the Craft*.

King describes his legendary work habits and the importance of goal setting. King set a goal at 2,000 words per day and suggested a book should take around three months to write (~180,000 words). Approaching writing like a job takes discipline but returns tremendous rewards. Having text to edit, to shape, and to share with others means the focus rests on the printed words. Without production, no words, no editing, no shaping, and no sharing.

> *In my experience I have found many students struggle with production. The job of a professor entails nurturing emerging writers. Yet without words on the page no amount of nurturing will help. The most successful strategy I have discovered to help students write more involves having them count words written per day and monitoring their production on a chart. Self-Charting*

Many books and blogs claim to have techniques guaranteed to fix "writers block." But many of the supposed strategies tend to fall on the side of gimmicks. The truth of the matter for production means sitting at a desk, table, favorite workspace, and writing. The most tangible output of writing appears in the number of words written.

Word count/chart method. Counting words written requires a few simple steps.

1. Start a timer.

2. Begin writing.

3. Stop writing when the timer ends.

4. Count the number of new words written.

5. Use track changes for edits and new words written.

6. Record the number of minutes for the writing session and the number of words written.

7. At the end of the day total the time spent writing and the number of words written.

8. Takes the total words for the day and chart them on a Standard Celeration Chart.

9. Enter in a daily writing goal and check progress against the goal.

10. If the data show daily words counts do not meet the goal, try different interventions.

11. Continuing monitoring daily word counts and examine in terms of weekly and monthly word counts.

12. Celebrate success!

In the chart below I share my daily word counts in a monthly view. I enter my data into Chartlytics (Author's note: Now PrecisionX) and have the option of toggling between daily, weekly, monthly, and yearly.

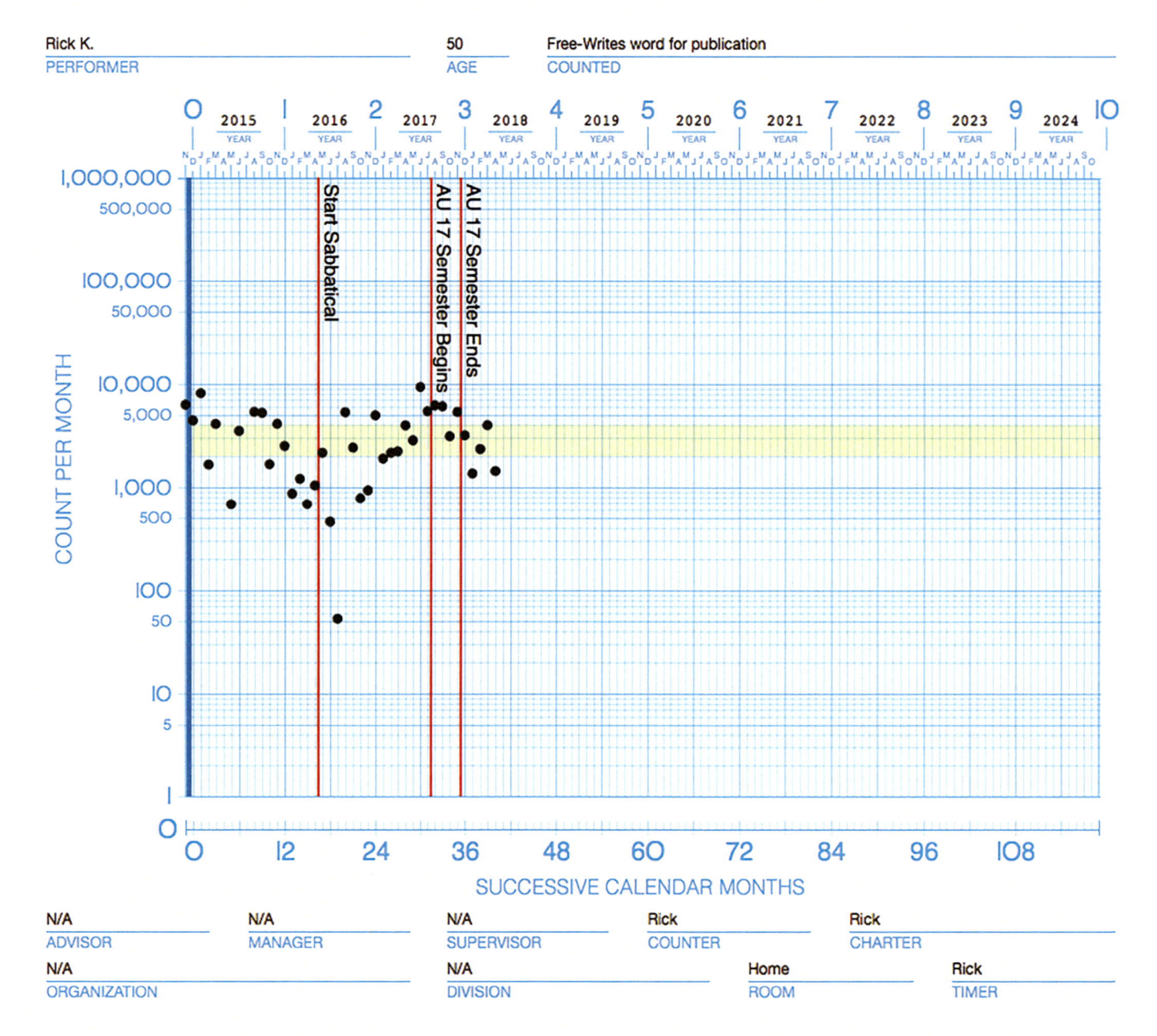

Figure 73. A monthly Standard Celeration Chart showing monthly word counts.

The chart has the summative count of the words I have written each month. The yellow band represents my monthly word count (2,000 to 4,000 words). The chart shows for the last few years I have more months of hitting my aim than less. I have also learned that different types of writing produce different daily word counts. For example, when sitting down to first generate text, my count ranged from 200 to 300 words per 25 minutes (my typical writing block before I stand up to walk around). But when I edit, those counts drop to 50 to 100 words per 25 minute. Also, my average daily total count falls between 150 and 450 words per day. (Authors note: Since the COVID-19 pandemic my daily count has risen to 800 words per day, kind of proud of that number!)

Chapter 7: Behavioral Production

Counting words per day and monitoring word count daily in a monthly view provides insight into my writing habits as well as a sense of accomplishment. Writing steadily each day has aided me in my yearly count of peer-reviewed publications. Figure 74 shows the number of articles published each year before I became a faculty member and my progress as I moved from assistant, to associate, to professor. I have a goal of publishing 3 to 4 articles per year.

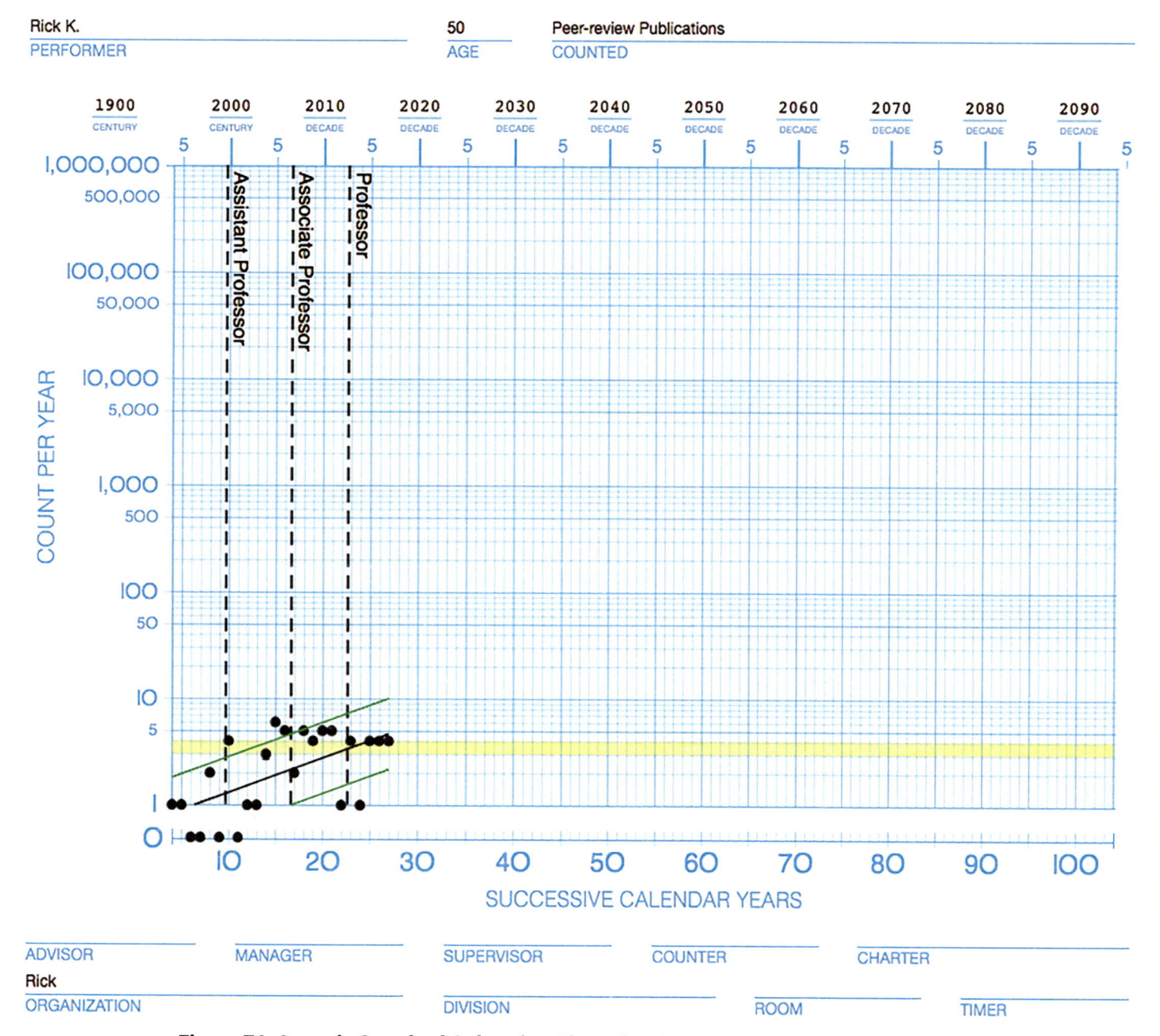

Figure 74. A yearly Standard Celeration Chart showing peer-reviewed publications.

Conclusion

As a doctoral student in my first writing class, I recall a time when our professor asked what we thought of writing. A fellow student famously answered, "Writing ain't easy!" That stuck with me. And through time I have improved my writing. I learned and mastered mechanics through practice and feedback. My writing style improved when I adopted E-prime. My content knowledge came with time and study. And my production has steady increased and stabilized at a range that allows me to remain productive and a contributing member of my field. And an exceptionally helpful strategy for keeping up with production incorporates counting daily words written, charting the total, and inspecting the data on a Standard Celeration Chart.

One of the fantastic innovations in Precision Teaching, SAFMEDS, came from the common intervention practice flashcards. SAFMEDS has rules for how to construct cards, how to order content, and how to practice and assess content. SAFMEDS has taken off in the behavioral literature and has many studies that substantiate it as a powerful method leading to behavioral fluency. And like anything else in science, SAFMEDS continues to receive research and practical attention. I used SAFMEDS in 1986 with my first class taught by Steve Graf at Youngstown State University. I now use them in the classes I teach. The following entry describes SAFMEDS and discusses a study I conducted.

Entry: SAFMEDS

How do people achieve fluency, or true mastery, with content area knowledge? For example, subjects like biology, statistics, physics, and history all possess their own vocabulary and concepts. Mastering abstract information such as the Linnaean Taxonomy (biology), probability (statistics), velocity (physics), or the branches of the government (American history) pose challenges to all students.

Many self-study methods exist which help students, or anyone, learn content. A study surveyed college students and discovered 11 different study strategies. After (1) rereading notes or the textbook and (2) engaging with practice problems, students most often used (3) flashcards (Karpicke, Buttler, & Roediger, 2009).

Many studies examine flashcards and their benefits. For instance, flashcards have helped young children learn to read better, aided medical students' acquisition of terms, increased university students' psychology exam scores, and even heightened patients' understanding of diabetes and medication adherence.

Flashcards continue to attract the interest of researchers and practitioners due to their effectiveness, adaptability, and portability. Yet even with the previously stated benefits and popularity of flashcards, several factors limit their potential.

1. Almost all flashcard practice trials have no set timed practice interval. In other words, students practice in an untimed manner.
2. No uniform performance goals exist. Student may practice to some accuracy criteria (e.g., 80%, 90%, 100%).
3. Flashcards lack instructional design. Creating flashcards comes with no set of rules and each deck contains widely discrepant methods for presenting target content.

Flashcards morph into SAFMEDS

In 1978, Ogden Lindsley and Steve Graf pioneered a practice and assessment procedure call SAFMEDS (Potts, Eshleman, & Cooper, 1993). SAFMEDS stands for Say All Fast, a Minute Every Day, Shuffled. In other words, learners:

- See the front of the card and *Say* the answer.
- Practice with the entire set or *All* of content in the deck.
- Attempting to learn the content *Fast* instead of slow results in steeper celerations or faster learning.
- Assess or practice in timed units such as a *Minute* or other consistent interval (e.g., 20 seconds).
- Practice the content and assess progress *Every Day* instead of weekly or some other protracted time period (e.g., monthly).
- *Shuffle* the deck instead of practicing the cards in order.

SAFMEDS forms an instructional and assessment method that has generated a host of studies demonstrated the superiority and utility over flashcards and other self-study practices.

Like flashcards, SAFMEDS have considerable adaptability to different content areas. Some SAFMEDS research include:

- Branch, A., Hastings, R. P., Beverley, M. & Hughes, J. C. (2018): Increasing support staff fluency with the content of behaviour support plans: An application of precision teaching. *Journal of Intellectual & Developmental Disability, 43*, 213-222.
- Chapman, S. S., Ewing, C. B., & Mozzoni, M. P. (2005). Precision teaching and fluency training across cognitive, physical, and academic tasks in children with traumatic brain injury: A multiple baseline study. *Behavioral Intervention, 20*, 37–49.
- Mason, L. L., Rivera, C. J., & Arriaga, A. (2018): The effects of an avoidance contingency on postsecondary student SAFMEDS performance. *European Journal of Behavior Analysis, 19*, 62-71.

- Peladeau, N., Forget, J., & Gagne, F. (2003). Effect of paced and unpaced practice on skill application and retention: How much is enough? *American Educational Research Journal, 40,* 769 – 801.

A study conducted by your friendly blog author demonstrates how SAFMEDS can help behavior change agents improve understanding of important Precision Teaching concepts such as movement cycles.

SAFMEDS and movement cycles study

Staff who work with people with disabilities such as autism spectrum disorder, intellectual disabilities, and learning disabilities can employ Precision Teaching to enhance measurement, decision making, and communication of data among team members and stake holders. Precision Teaching has four steps: Pinpoint, Record, Change, Try Again.

The first step consists of creating a pinpoint. And at the core of the pinpoint exists a movement cycle. Movement cycles contain two parts, an observable action described by an active verb, and the object that receives the action.

The essence of every behavior originates in a movement cycle. Composing an essay would translate to "writes essay" (action verb + object that received the action). "Aggression" could include several movement cycles: hits staff, slaps face, or scratches arm. And complex behavior such as "joint attention" may encompass aims gaze, points finger, or follows gaze.

To help staff learn movement cycles, Kubina, Yurich, Durica, and Healy (2016) worked with several special education teachers and board certified behavior analysts at a school serving students with autism spectrum disorders. All participants had a maste's degree in applied behavior analysis or a related field (i.e., psychology, special education), coursework with behavioral measurement, and experience with behavioral observation.

The experimenters crafted two SAFMEDS decks with pictures depicting students behaving. The picture on the front of the card had a corresponding movement cycle (i.e., two words = active verb in the simple present tense + object receiving action) on the back of the card.

Figure 75 came from one of the decks. The student had a specific behavior participants needed to translate into a movement cycle. In the picture circles and arrows directed attention. The larger circle showed a hand while the smaller circle centered on two fingers. The arrow portrayed downward motion. Therefore, if the participant said "presses toy" the experimenters would score the response as correct.

Figure 75. A picture of a card taken from a movement cycle deck.

The participants made many competing, incorrect responses to the SAFMEDS cards at the beginning of the study. Participants might say the incorrect active verb (push instead of press), use the incorrect verb tense (pressing, present progressive tense, instead of presses, simple present tense), choose an incorrect object receiving the action (saying piano instead of key), or not use the proper action + object involved with the action (saying "He is hitting the doll").

Additionally, the participants performed the assessment task slowly, with hesitations, or skipped answers outright. Across time, however, the participants increased their frequency. The participants practiced saying their answers and self-correcting their responses. The participants also practiced on the whole deck each day and shuffled it before a practice trial.

Figure 76 illustrates skill progress. In baseline, all the participants made more incorrect than correct answers. Furthermore, incorrect responses accelerated in baseline, a worsening condition for saying movement cycles.

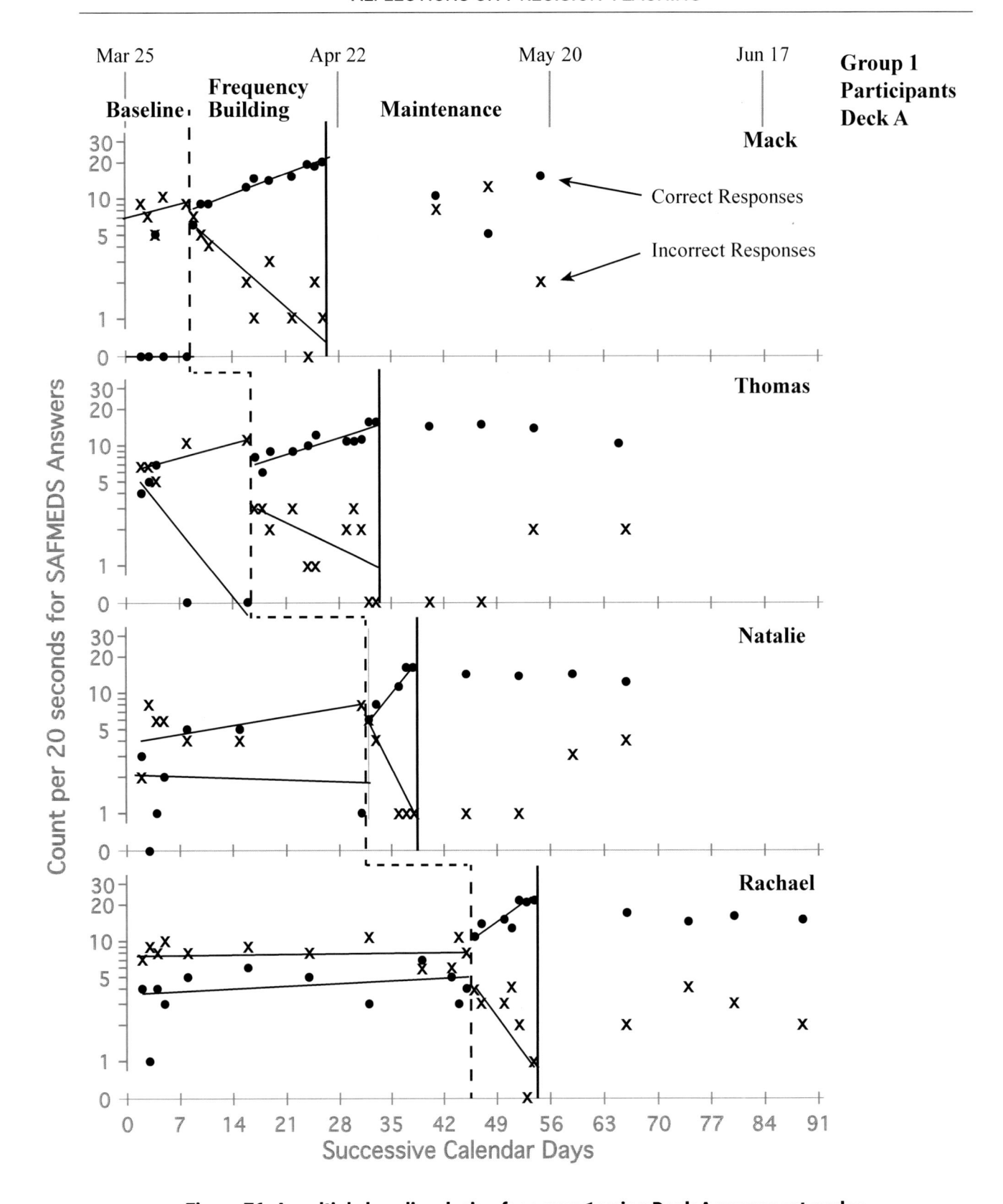

Figure 76. A multiple baseline design for group 1 using Deck A movement cycles.

The experimenters applied the SAFMEDS intervention and the same picture emerged: correct responses grew rapidly while incorrect responses decelerated quickly.

The SAFMEDS study had several important findings. 1. SAFMEDS offers a reliable method to help adult learners quickly gain competency with the targeted content (e.g., movement cycles); 2. Participants retained information across time; 3. SAFMEDS facilitates extension of content to novel content (i.e., participants tested with a novel deck performed much better than they did before the study began); 4. A performance criterion or frequency aim can specify how fast and accurately participants must respond in order to achieve their goal; and 5. Analyzing performance results on a Standard Celeration Chart provides a wealth of visual and statistical information.

Conclusion

SAFMEDS supports the learning of simple and complex content for young and older learners. SAMFEDS also gives rise to important learning outcomes such as long-term retention and maintenance, application or extension of content to novel material, and social validity seen in meaningful participant behavior change and stakeholder satisfaction.

Chapter 8

PT Inspiration

My long association with Precision Teaching, 34 years at the time of this writing, has endured not just because I find the system technically sound but also because PT inspires me. And by PT, I mean the effects I see when I or others use it. I wanted to become a clinical psychologist to help people way back in my high school years. I didn't go the route of clinical psychology, but I found a way to help people in a spectacular fashion.

PT works so well because it allows teachers, therapists, parents, or whoever employs the powerful system a means to function as an applied scientist. And science delivers the goods. But the applied component means science directly impacts people.

Without going into all the past PT literature showing dramatic successes, I have seen PT work wonders on a personal level. And those outcomes give rise to excitement at conducting experiments, publishing articles, writing books, and blogging. I reacted to news stories or other issues that inspired me in the following entries. I believe you may find that inspiration infectious.

Entry: All testing is not evil

The headline read: Test scores 'will not tell you everything.' A parent received a letter from faculty that accompanied her son Charlie's standardized test scores. The letter moved the parent, Alison Owen, so much she took a picture of it and posted it on Facebook. The post immediately went viral. Even the folks in the Twitterverse caught wind of the letter and began commenting, the letter went viral on Twitter as well.

Figure 77. Letter sent to student that went viral

What moved people so much in the letter? From the letter:

"...we are concerned that these tests do not always assess all of what it is that make each of you special and unique. The people who create these tests and score them do not know each of you the way your teachers do, the way I hope to and certainly not the way your families do."

The letter goes on and makes a direct case that the school faculty see each student in a different light:

"They do not know that you can be trustworthy, kind or thoughtful, and that you try, every day, to be your best…the scores will tell you something but they will not tell you

everything. So enjoy your results and be very proud of these but remember there are many ways of being smart."

The letter strikes a chord with so many because of the regard for students as fellow human beings who possess individuality, dignity, and intelligence. But to make the message profound, there needs to exist a profoundly bad entity. The test makers wear the black hats according to the faculty of Barrowford Primary School. When the faculty wrote, "They do not know that you can be trustworthy, kind or thoughtful, and that you try, every day, to be your best." The "they" in the previous sentence refers to test makers.

In an era of high stakes assessment, it would seem students have only one role: to score well on tests. Such a role reduces students from people to just a number. And who wants their child, brother, sister, neighborhood kid that cuts your grass, to lose their uniqueness and value as a person?

And yet assessment and measurement form the cornerstone of any scientific procedure geared towards understanding subject matter. Clearly, in chemistry and physics scientists must impartially, but systematically measure particles, energy, and motion. When it comes to education, however, the science of measurement shifts to organisms who smile, cry, occasionally have accidents, and tell jokes (or in my case bad jokes). What to do?

The answer: collect data intelligently, individually, with the goal of meaningful performance improvement. Let's look at the difference between a one-time high stakes achievement test and an agile, learner focused system like Precision Teaching (PT):

	High Stakes Assessment	**PT Assessment**
Measurement priority	Summary evaluation (Judge achievement)	Ongoing, formative evaluation. Monitor ongoing performance and change if data indicate slow or a lack of learning
Measurement frequency	Typically once a year	As frequently as daily, other times weekly
Content focus	General. A collection of different content in reading, math, or the specific academic subject area	Specific. Pinpoint of selected skill or behavior
Goal	To classify a student's performance by level (e.g., Basic, Proficient, Advanced)	To build performance to a level of fluency or competency
Materials	Created by test makers	Created by teachers or students in the local curriculum

Table 15. A comparison of high stakes assessment and PT assessment along several dimensions.

As Table 15 shows, high stake assessments differ along a number of dimensions from Precision Teaching. PT chiefly focuses on using the most precise data metrics to affect change and enhance performance improvement, a different purpose from high stakes assessment. Also, the targeted content comes from the local curriculum and has a teacher directly tailor content for the specific learner.

Thinking of Charlie above or any learner you know clearly reinforces one point: everyone deserves an insightful data monitoring/assessment/problem solving system focused on past, present, and future performance. PT offers metrics and analytics including growth milestones, positive learning achievements, learning struggles, attempts and solutions that remedy learning struggles, and the analysis of individually customized programs and interventions.

A nuanced approach to testing warrants we do not throw the baby out with the bathwater. By examining what necessary function high stakes assessment possess, and how they may benefit students, parents, teachers, administrators, and society at large, a better system may emerge. But for the here and now, enriching and deepening public education, focusing on learning and performance excellence, all learners can win with a system rooted in the science of individual measurement.

The educational literature and almost every other education professional from teacher to professor touts individualization or personalization of instruction. It makes sense and seems fair. As they say, "the devil is in the details." Many schools and teachers say they offer individualization, but sadly that could mean calling on individual students and providing an explanation for why they don't understand something. True individualization can take different forms, from instruction to measurement and decision making. After all, when we go to doctors, we expect individual tests, individual measures, and personalized recommendations based on our unique set of data. Precision Teaching delivers individualization. Indeed, individualization forms the entire foundation of PT. I tried to make that point in the following entry.

Entry: On individuality

In education, we cherish the individual, and rightfully so. For example, the term "Personalized Learning" refers to a wide range of educational programs, instructional practices, learning experiences, and different support strategies for addressing the varied learning needs and interests of students.

The United States Department of Education has defined Personalized Learning, also called Competency-Based Learning, as "a structure that creates flexibility, allows students to progress

as they demonstrate mastery of academic content, regardless of time, place, or pace of learning."
(Source: http://www.ed.gov/oii-news/competency-based-learning-or-personalized-learning)

For many years, educators have tried different teaching methods, educational structures, and class arrangements in order to promote individualization. At the heart of individualization lies the idea that by addressing each student's unique needs, academic success and personal fulfillment will rise; all noble goals worth pursuing. How might the science of individual measurement, Precision Teaching, view treating an individual?

Individualization = individual measures

We could talk about the many ways Precision Teaching addresses individuality. But let's start with measurement. Every student learns at a different rate or speed. Precision Teaching measures the rate with a celeration line and a metric called a celeration value. Celeration specifies the speed and direction of learning. As an example, a student who learns math facts at a x1.4 celeration grows by 40% each week (when measured on a daily Standard Celeration Chart or SCC).

Every other student in the room will have their own celeration values precisely depicting the speed at which the student has or has not learned math facts. How liberating to use the science of measurement to uncover the pace of each individual's learning rate. A teacher can make discrete adjustments for students who have not learned fast enough or not at all.

The celeration line also offers an accurate projection of future learning. By extending the celeration line, the student and teacher can see how long it will take to meet the academic goal. Celeration treats each individual with dignity and respect by providing a visual representation of every single student's own learning rate.

Bounce on the SCC represents the efficiency with which an individual student learns something. The larger the envelop the more variable the learning. Variable learning indicates inefficiencies with the instructional program.

By measuring bounce for each learner, a teacher learns whether instructional program has produced smooth or choppy learning. Imagine having an actual number telling you the ease or difficulty with which your student has learned. Well you don't have to imagine if you use the SCC!

Real science, real individualization

Health science measures body temperature and can definitively state if a person has a fever (and the severity of the fever through quantification). Furthermore, everyone has a pulse and the quantified beats per minute tells the physician if the person has an elevated, Tachycardia, or depressed, Bradycardia, heart rate. Meaningful health metrics serve as key indicators for the health of an individual.

Likewise, the science of individual measurement expands our vision beyond conventional boundaries and allows us to see further. Celeration and bounce show each individual's speed and efficiency of learning. Using a Standard Celeration Chart to produce student specific visual patterns of behavior and sensitive, precise metrics epitomizes the pursuit of individualization.

The topic of high stakes assessments regularly boils up in the media and certainly raises the ire of many in the educational establishment. Some people have valid points. One issue of testing or assessment debate falls to accountability. How do parents, teachers, administrators etc. know if students have learned? Testing supposedly provides an answer. And it does in its own way. But therein the problem lies. In the past, states and the initiatives have tied standardized test scores to school funding, people's jobs, and not to mention students' progress to the next grade, thus the name high stakes assessment. But we have other options beyond just standardized tests. And this entry offers one.

Entry: What is accountability?

In a recent Washington Post story, "School standardized testing is under growing attack, leaders pledge changes," we learn that many people have started to revolt against standardized tests (Source: http://www.washingtonpost.com/local/education/school-standardized-testing-is-under-growing-attack-leaders-pledge-changes/2014/10/15/bd1201b8-549b-11e4-ba4b-f6333e2c0453_story.html). Examples uncovered from the Post:

- Four states have delayed or repealed standardized testing necessary for graduation.
- Over 60,000 students in New York flat out refused to take standardized tests.
- Former President Bill Clinton commented on the frequency of standardized testing saying, "I think doing one [test] in elementary school, one in the end of middle school and one before the end of high school is quite enough if you do it right."
- Top education leaders representing 100s of schools vowed to eliminate standardized tests lacking quality or needlessly repeating content.
- Secretary of Education Arne Duncan made promises to examine the state of standardized testing and do something about it.

The sore spot

Much of the angst over standardized tests finds its roots in the 2002, No Child Left Behind Act or NCLB. NCLB requires states to test all grade 3 through 8 students in reading and math in every year. High schoolers also have to take a standardized test but only once.

People have become upset not just at the frequency of the tests but at what happens if a school doesn't do well. NCLB metes out consequences if schools don't meet "adequate yearly progress."

Adequate yearly progress differs by states but involves minimum levels of improvement as measured by standardized tests (and these vary from state to state). If after two years a school finds itself "in need of improvement," consequences occur. The consequences include giving parents

1. School transfer options; they can take their children out of the failing school and have them enroll in a better one;
2. Providing students with supplemental services involving tutoring or other educational services;
3. Corrective action, which often means school staff and curricula get replaced;
4. Restructuring where the entire school undergo a serious transformation - like getting rid of the principal, most of the staff, and changing the school into a charter school or other dramatic shifts.

NCLB had a basic idea, provide a clear set of guidelines for improvement, enforce those guidelines with standardized testing, and deliver consequences for those who do not meet the goals. Thus, accountability has teeth.

Accountability Precision Teaching style

As the news story in the Post goes, many people have reacted strongly to how accountability has played out. While it might seem easy to quickly take a side and reduce the issues to "Testing is bad, get rid of all of them!" or "Fire all the teachers who don't produce results!" (you can find both of those sides in articles and blogs), a thoughtful perspective examines the good and bad in accountability driven systems.

To begin, a problem resides with the direct link between standardized tests and teacher action.

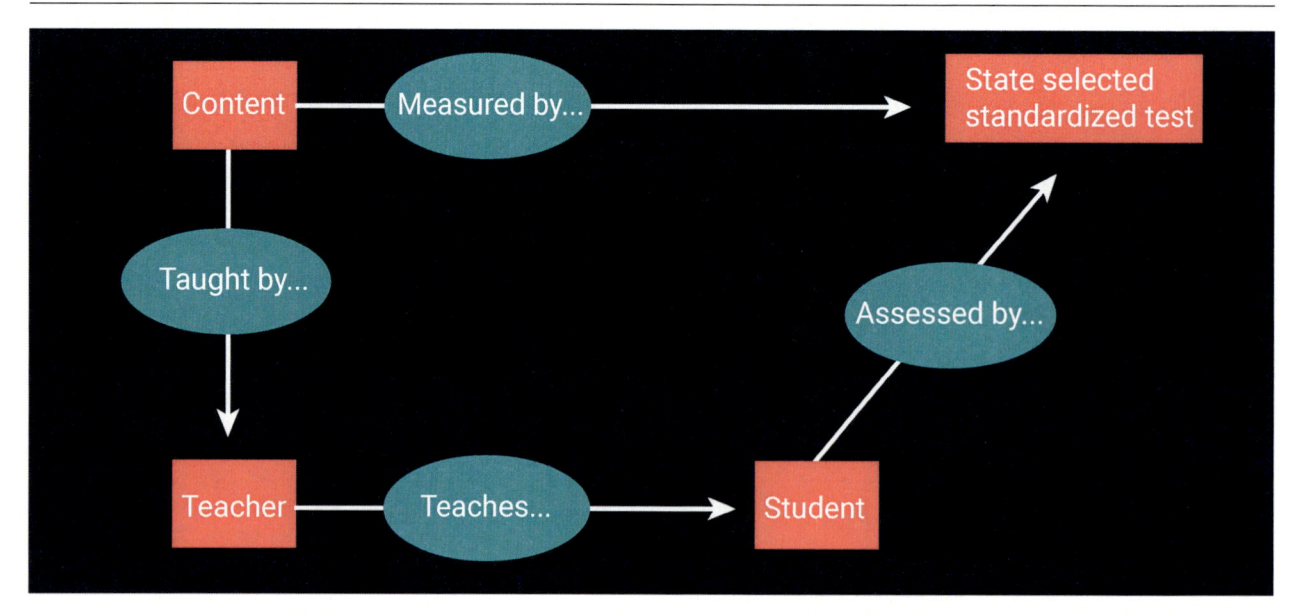

Figure 78. A diagram showing the relationships between content taught and assessment.

Students attend school to learn content (first grade math, second grade reading, fifth grade science etc.). At each local school a teacher teaches the subject matter for the selected content area to a student. Then, at the end of the year the student may take a standardized test that evaluates what the teacher taught and what the students has learned.

The academic content taught by the teacher and the standardized test might significantly differ. Therefore, if a student performs poorly on the standardized test the state passes judgement that the teacher did a poor job teaching (because the student didn't learn according to the standardized test result). Accountability seems hit or miss in a system where teachers don't have a clear idea on the assessment standards.

The education system has attempted to rectify the problem of differing standards with a "Common Core." But that content remains a post for another day. What does PT have to offer when it comes to accountability?

We find the key ingredients of PT in a standard measurement and decision making system, not a standardized test. The standard measurement and decision making system involves:

- Pinpointing a behavior (highest and most accurate level of describing behavior)
- Measuring and recording a behavior's (pinpoint's) frequency
- Displaying the recorded counts (frequency) of behavior on a standard visual display (called a Standard Celeration Chart)
- Carefully inspecting the results on a Standard Celeration Chart to determine the need for a change to the current educational program

As described above, accountability has a different flavor with PT. Figure 79 shows how each individual's performance links to teacher action.

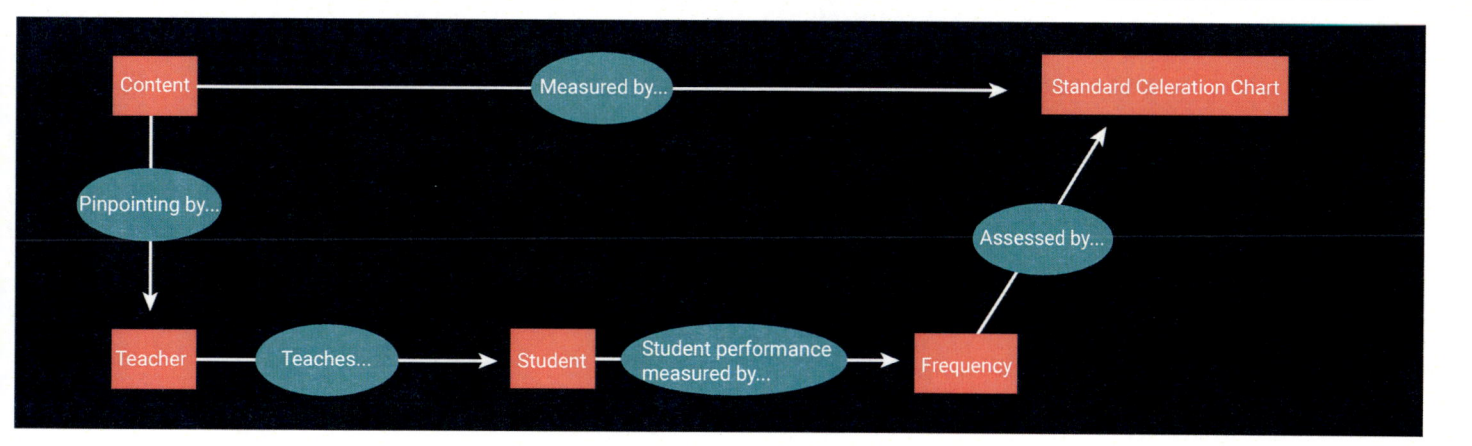

Figure 79. PT assessment system

With PT, teachers employ a measurement system with standards defining what they will label as a measure, the precise metric they will use to capture performance and learning, and how to display the data. Therefore, student progress directly reflects the instructional environment arranged by the teacher. Additionally, the focus on changing and improving student performance pervades the Precision Teaching system.

∽

I entered the field of special education in 1992 when I officially started my degree at The Ohio State University. My station in life changed from a green psych undergrad to a green special education grad student. But I learned about PT from my dear mentor Steve Graf. And then I went to my second mentor John Cooper and learned even more. I had the chance to work in an urban school using PT to tutor students. Some of the students I worked with had IEPs or Individualized Education Programs. Even as a green special education grad student, I succeeded because I used what I learned about PT and consistently allowed the Standard Celeration Chart to guide my decision making. The gains my students made inspired me to practice PT when I graduated. And that success working with students with special needs inspired me to go back to school as a green doc student and learn more about the robust measurement and decision making system.

- Entry: How do we help students with disabilities?

- Working with students with disabilities requires patience, compassion, precise measurement systems, and above all, powerful methods capable of producing remarkable change. When teachers lack any of the previously mentioned attributes or processes, trouble can follow.

- The news story "Are NOLA Schools Failing Students with Disabilities?" (Source: http://www.npr.org/blogs/ed/2014/11/20/365282978/are-nola-schools-failing-students-with-disabilities) describes some of the struggles both students and school systems can face. The story reported troubling problems students have encountered:

- The school blames a student's behavioral problem on parenting

- Rather than address a student's behavioral problems with a careful assessment and a tailored behavioral program, the school continues to suspend the student
- The charter schools that took over New Orleans have not delivered on "innovation and change" for students with disabilities

Joshua Perry, the executive director of the Louisiana Center for Children's Rights, said, "Right now we are seeing a lot of schools here that are simply unable to serve the most vulnerable and highest-need kids."

Where to start - pinpointing

What needs to happen to help students with disabilities? Many changes. But from a basic perspective, certain tactics can help both teachers and students alike quickly. For behavior or academic problems, the first issue starts with pinpointing the problem behavior. While it may seem like a simple proposition, so many people struggle identifying and labeling the problem behavior.

"Aggressive, noncompliant, disrespectful, lazy and oppositional" not only serve as terrible behavioral targets, they place the blame on the student. For example, let's say we have a student who fails to turn in their homework, scores poorly on tests, and doesn't participate in classroom instruction. If the teacher picks "lazy" as the target behavior, we now have a problem.

Lazy means the student "shows a lack of effort or care." Lazy also reflects a personality characteristic of the student. So, to fix the problem the teacher must come up with an intervention that changes the student from a lazy person to a hard-working person.

Aside from the difficulty of changing personality traits, pinpoints like lazy serve as a judgment and can color how the teacher feels about a student. As humans, teachers may have a hard time liking a lazy, angry, mean student.

Pinpointing solves the problem on multiple levels. 1. Counting behavior such as "places homework on desk" falls within the purview of what teachers can address and change (versus changing someone's personality traits). 2. Counting "says swear word when given instructions" makes it less personal than focusing on "verbal abuse." 3. Pinpoints focus on accelerative behavior versus only decelerative behavior.

More help – Standard Celeration Charting (SCC). Monitoring a student's behavior over time requires a display system sensitive to change. Big changes and small changes need represented clearly so that the teacher can carefully observe the magnitude of change occurring. If a student has a serious behavior problem, then the teacher must know the impact of any and all interventions aimed at ameliorating the problem behavior. Nonstandard linear graphs just don't cut it when teachers can have Standard Celeration Charts. Which nonstandard linear graph depicts the slope correctly?

CHAPTER 8: PT INSPIRATION

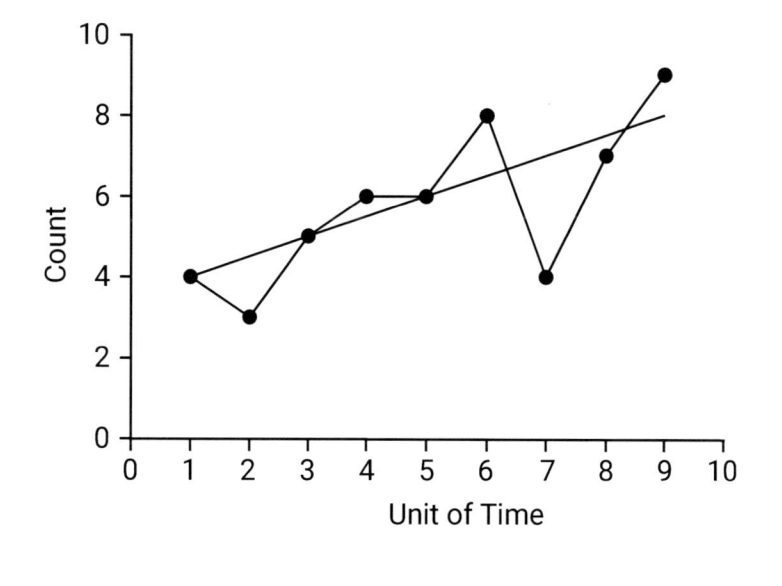

Same data, three differently scaled graphed, three different trend lines leading to different interpretations

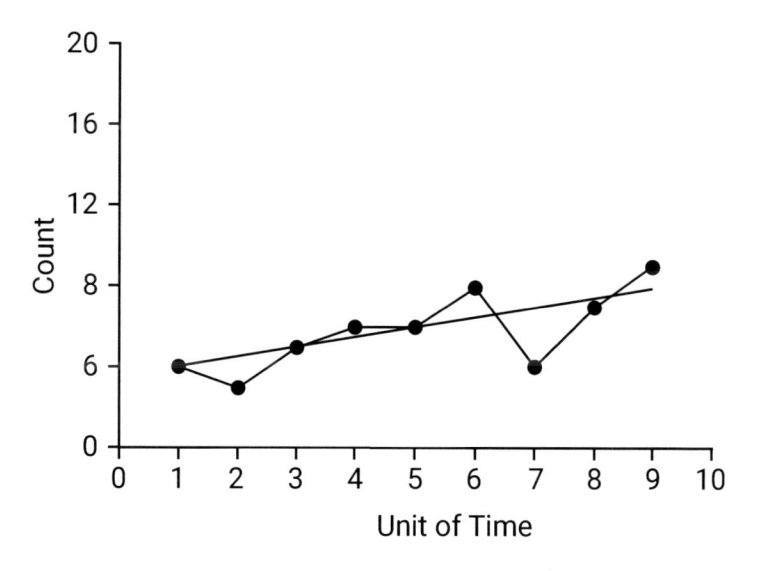

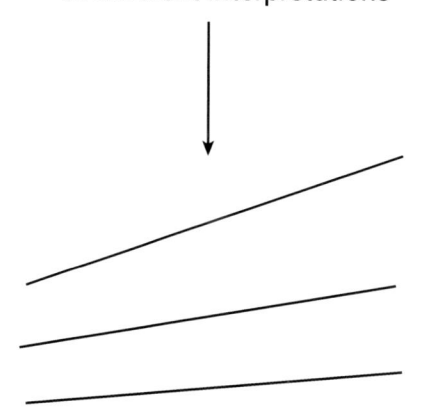

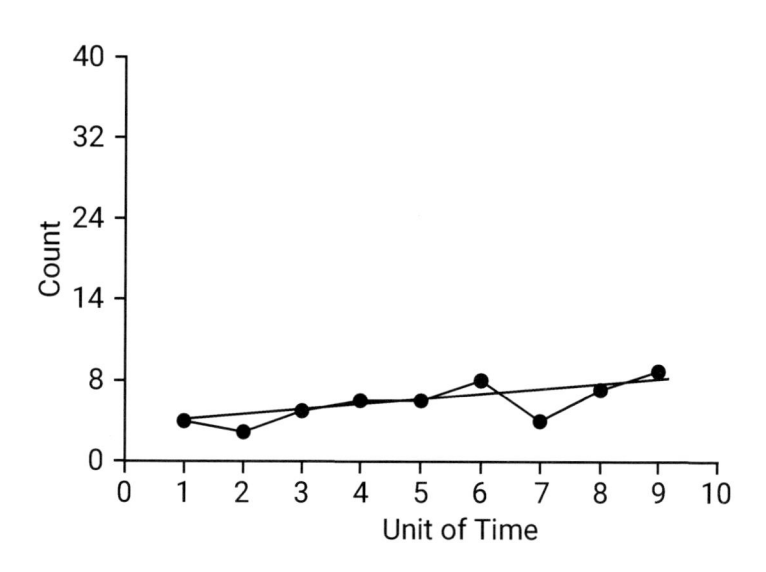

Figure 80. Three nonstandard linear graph depicts with same data.

The Standard Celeration Chart always shows change properly. The slope (celeration line) will not change like nonstandard linear graphs do (they change because people make graphs like they want to without following standards).

Also, nonstandard linear graphs do not quantify learning and change like the Standard Celeration Chart. The SCC puts a number on the multiplicative and divisional change (expressed at x2.0 per week or 100% weekly growth; ÷2.0 per week or 50% weekly decay).

Students with disabilities deserve the most sensitive measures and visual display system.

Behavioral fluency

Another facet of student improvement comes in the form of behavioral fluency. Behavioral fluency refers to behavior that reaches high levels of accuracy and speed. Fluent behavior means masterful, competent behavior.

1-BF-S1 Slice 1.1 AS   AIM: 60-80 digits correct with less than 2 digits incorrect/60 secs

$$\begin{array}{cccccccccc}
7 & 1 & 3 & 9 & 3 & 5 & 8 & 9 & 0 & 7 \\
-0 & -0 & -1 & -0 & -0 & -0 & -1 & -0 & -0 & -0 \\
\hline
7 & 1 & 2 & 9 & 3 & 5 & 7 & 9 & 0 & 7
\end{array}$$
(10)

$$\begin{array}{cccccccccc}
6 & 4 & 9 & 1 & 8 & 2 & 4 & 5 & 7 & 6 \\
-1 & -0 & -1 & -1 & -1 & -0 & -0 & -1 & -0 & -0 \\
\hline
5 & 4 & 8 & 0 & 7 & 2 & 4 & 4 & 7 & 6
\end{array}$$
(20)

$$\begin{array}{cccccccccc}
5 & 6 & 2 & 3 & 10 & 4 & 8 & 10 & 5 & 2 \\
-1 & -0 & -1 & -1 & -1 & -1 & -0 & -1 & -0 & -0 \\
\hline
4 & 6 & 1 & 2 & 9 & 3 & 8 & 9 & 5 & 2
\end{array}$$
(30)

$$\begin{array}{cccccccccc}
8 & 10 & 7 & 4 & 3 & 0 & 9 & 7 & 6 & 4 \\
-0 & -1 & -1 & -1 & -0 & -0 & -1 & -1 & -0 & -1 \\
\hline
8 & 9 & 6 & 3 & 3 & 0 & 8 & 6 & 6 & 3
\end{array}$$
(40)

$$\begin{array}{cccccccccc}
2 & 0 & 5 & 10 & 6 & 8 & 6 & 4 & 2 & 1 \\
-1 & -0 & -0 & -1 & -1 & -1 & -0 & -0 & -0 & -1 \\
\hline
1 & 0 & 5 & 9 & 5 & 7 & 6 & 4 & 2 & 0
\end{array}$$
(50)

$$\begin{array}{cccccccccc}
1 & 3 & 3 & 3 & 4 & 10 & 1 & 8 & 9 & 4 \\
-1 & -0 & -1 & -0 & -1 & -1 & -0 & -1 & -1 & -0 \\
\hline
0 & 3 & 2 & 3 & 3 & 9 & 1 & 7 & 8 & 4
\end{array}$$
(60)

$$\begin{array}{cccccccccc}
7 & 1 & 2 & 6 & 9 & 1 & 7 & 3 & 8 & 7 \\
-1 & -0 & -1 & -1 & -0 & -1 & -0 & -1 & -0 & -1 \\
\hline
6 & 1 & 1 & 5 & 9 & 0 & 7 & 2 & 8 & 6
\end{array}$$
(70)

$$\begin{array}{cccccccccc}
9 & 5 & 9 & 8 & 6 & 5 & 3 & 0 & 1 & 6 \\
-0 & -1 & -1 & -0 & -1 & -0 & -0 & -0 & -0 & -1 \\
\hline
9 & 4 & 8 & 8 & 5 & 5 & 3 & 0 & 1 & 5
\end{array}$$
(80)

Copyright 2018 Greatness Achieved Publishing Company. *Pathways to Mastery: Math.* Authorized individuals may copy this page.

Figure 81. A practice sheet for -0 and -1 subtraction facts.

To reach fluency a student must engage in systematic practice or what Precision Teachers call frequency building. And to practice, students must have materials. Figure 81 shows a properly formed practice sheet for subtraction facts.

Students with disabilities have many challenges. But with systems like Precision Teaching, teachers can learn to pinpoint meaningful behavior, measure behavior with precise metrics, have students practice to fluency, and monitor all data on a powerful visual display – the Standard Celeration Chart.

※

The Great Falls Precision Teaching Project has always inspired me. An excellent description of the project appeared in *The Journal of Precision Teaching* in 1991. The highlights from the school-wide implementation included measured improvements in concentration and work habits, self-esteem, and 20 to 40 percentile gains on standardized tests.

However, the results of what U.S. schools could achieve always seem tamped down by media stories showing the current state of affairs. A piece discussing countries in terms of educational rankings caught my attention. Finland routinely turns up as one of the best educational systems in the world. People try to deconstruct Finland's success and show how only if the U.S. adopted their practices, America would then lead the world. Such analyses seldom work for such a massive system like the U.S.; that doesn't mean we can't have it all! The U.S. educational system needs Precision Teaching. And in the following entry, I say as much.

Entry: We have an answer

News reports about the United States ranking in world of education (Source no longer functioning: http://www.cnn.com/2014/10/06/opinion/sahlberg-finland-education/) strike a mix of emotions in me. I always first feel exasperated because we can do so much better. I don't mean marginally better; I mean number one in the entire world! In fact, I believe we can do a 10x better job than anyone in the world if we change the system based on what the science of behavior and individual measurement tells us.

A recent CNN Opinion piece by Pasi Sahlberg addresses the point of why Finland, number 1 in International comparisons, does a way better job in education than the United States (number 21, but so happens to rank number 1 in the world on money spent for education). Sahlberg asks "What are the main factors that prevent American students from achieving the kind of success that Finnish students attain?"

He offers three answers:

1. Educational equity: Finland provides early childhood education to everyone and a national curriculum offering the same content to all students.
2. Lighter teaching load: Finnish teachers can network with fellow teachers and improve upon their own teaching quality. The extra time facilitates access to best practices.
3. Physical activity: Students in Finland have more time to play and work on outside activities during school.

Sahlberg makes some good points. But if we changed the entire US system based solely on the three points outlined above would we then catapult to number 1? Perhaps. But if we want a 10x separation between what our education system provides compared to everyone else world, educational equity, lighter teacher loads, and more student play will likely not enable such a distinction.

What else do we need?

1. A national curriculum means everyone has access to the same content. While not addressing the exact nature of the content, how well do we design the curriculum? First, we need a curriculum that meets the tenets of instructional design. The science of instructional design has rules governing the scope and sequence of content. And a focus on generalizable strategies rather than only memorization of facts (though I by no means disparage memorizing facts; pretty hard to sound out and fluently decode a word if a student has not memorized letter-sound correspondences).
2. All students must reach a very high level of competence on instructional content. The only way to determine how well students do is to apply world class measurements standards, not another test. We have enough of those and, as Sahlberg noted in his Opinion piece, Finland has one test at the end of high school. Using dynamic, informative assessment measures on students' performance offers a very different level of insight and decision making. Standardized tests run counter to direct powerful metrics such as frequency or rate.

    My colleague and I conducted a descriptive study comparing a group of 5th graders from the United States, Taiwan, and Japan (Lin, Kubina, & Shimamune, 2011). We did not use a test. Instead, we compared how fluent (fast and accurate) students could multiply basic facts. The results follow.

    Percentage of students who hit the fluency aim for basic multiplication fluency:

    Japan   25%
    Taiwan   32%
    United States   14%

When we did the comparison for complex multiplication facts, how many students hit the fluency mark, we found:

Japan   19%

Taiwan   38%

United States 1%

Staggering differences appeared, not by assessing students with a test that covers a multitude of skills, but instead by using a measure that offers precision and direct measures of a student's performance.

3. A variety of metrics can inform teachers on the following:
   - Speed of learning - celeration
   - Efficiency of learning - bounce
   - Quality of the overall learning process - Accuracy Improvement Measure (or A.I.M.) (Authors note: As mentioned before, Improvement Index has replaced Accuracy Improvement Measure).

Each of the previous metrics come from a student performing a behavior in a specified time (like reading 120 word correctly with 1 incorrect per minute - the previous example we call frequency or rate). Frequency measures taken repeatedly across time lead teachers to celeration, bounce, and A.I.M.

Imagine the decisions made for each individual student. No longer would teachers have to deal with ambiguity. They would see exactly how well their instruction helps their students.

Finland has done a number of things right in their education system. You don't get to number 1 in the world without students learning and showing strong transfer and application of the content. The United States can learn from other countries but even more so from the science of individual measurement and decision making (Precision Teaching).

The first sentence reveals this entry took place in 2013. The new year always finds people preparing for the year ahead, making all sorts of aspirational goals. Setting goals seemed natural as a Precision Teacher. As I look back, I can report that I worked on all the goals I set out to achieve. Of course, some of my more lofty ambitions might take a lifetime to complete. But PT and its ability to better the lives of the people it touches affirms my lifetime commitment.

Entry: Using Precision Teaching for a better future

For my 2013 New Year's resolution I chose a loftier goal: help as many people as possible learn Precision Teaching (PT). I chose this as my resolution because I firmly believe PT embodies a life altering behavioral/measurement system. In essence, PT has the following advantages:

1. Precision Teaching helps define the critical pinpoint (problem or target) in need of change. While advantage number one may seem commonplace, most people have a difficult time producing a precise pinpoint. Often, people use verbs that disguise or obfuscate the true active behavior. For example, "understanding the civil war," "solving problems," or "verbally aggressing to others" provides three inadequate descriptions of behavior. Instead of "understanding the civil war," Precision Teaching pinpoints exactly what the person does such as "says fact about civil war." Rather than "solving problems," "writes answer to multiplication problem" offers a much more explicit description. And "verbally aggressing to others" misleads people. A much better target uses the pinpoint "yells insult at teacher."

    Notice also how most people often describe behavior in the "Present Progressive tense" which communicates the activity in progress: hitting, smiling, running; when do the behaviors end? Pinpoints use the "Simple Present tense" to express the idea that the action repeats. And we care more about behavior that repeats than behavior that continues when we count pinpoints. Without a proper pinpoint, reliably detecting and counting the behavior turns into a challenge.

2. Precision Teaching has one of the most advanced recording systems for human behavior. People who use PT learn how to precisely count behavior in time. The resulting data often take the form of the workhorse measure "frequency." Frequency epitomizes a sensitive, informative measure. Think about one student who answers 8 math facts correct with 2 incorrect in a minute and another student who answers 16 math facts correct with 4 incorrect in a minute. Both have a score of 80% correct, but who has a better grasp on math facts? Incidentally, most everyone uses percent correct for decision making. Would you feel comfortable saying both students who had 80% correct have the same level of competency? Of course not, one student has answered twice the amount as the other even though both have the same accuracy. Frequency matters because our decision making matters.

3. Only Precision Teaching has the one-of-a-kind Standard Celeration Chart. The alternatives pale in comparison. Two major advantages; the Standard Celeration Chart allows chart readers to see how fast learning occurs (called celeration) and how easily, or difficultly, learning progresses (called bounce or variability). Furthermore, we can quantify those two measures. We can live in the world where we know the value of how fast and how easily someone has learned something. We can make exquisite comparisons for any intervention. No longer do we have to rely on adjectives (e.g., describing trend changes

Chapter 8: PT Inspiration

as rising slowly, moderately, or steeply) for communicating progress. No longer must we base our decision making based on the vagaries of the nonstandard graph design which will always change depending on the whims of the graph maker causing potential problems in interpretation and communication.

Additionally, a plethora of quantified change measures tell us if the intervention has produced significant or insignificant results. We owe it to our learners and ourselves to use the best possible charting system out there for time series analysis. The Standard Celeration Chart provides so much more information than typical linear line graphs. Let's arm all teachers, psychologists, and behavior change professionals with weapon of mass instruction!

Weapon of Mass Instruction

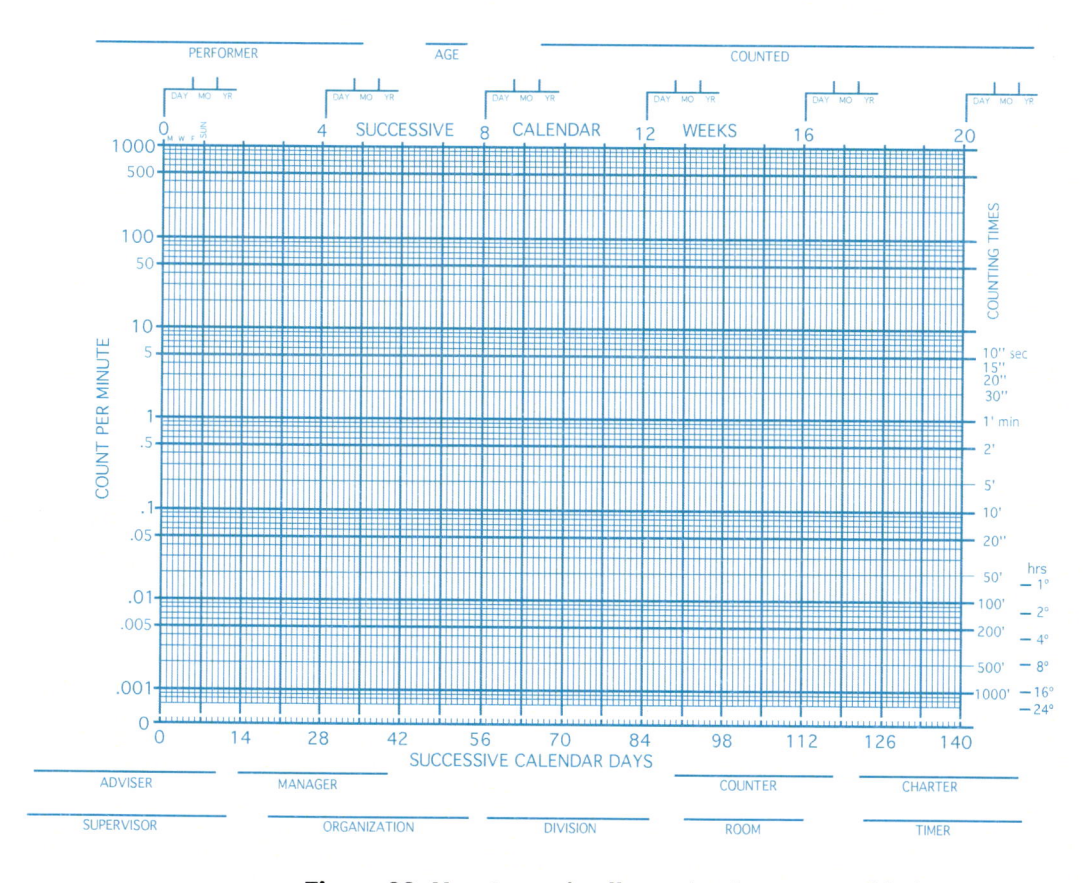

Figure 82. How to equip all people who want real behavioral change.

4. Precision Teaching has a series of interventions and analytical techniques prompting us never to give up on the learner. Indeed, the PT system exudes problem solving solutions starting with the pinpointed behavior, precise measures, carefully displayed behavior on the Standard Celeration Chart, and covering quantitative and qualitative measures telling the chart reader exactly what has, and what will, happen with the pinpointed behavior.

Rick Kubina | 201

Join me

If you read this blog I hope you have actively started using Precision Teaching (or call yourself a veteran Precision Teacher). But if you find yourself on the fence or want to learn PT you can do the following:

- Join the SClistserv with over 350 members

- Make friends and professional connections with different Facebook groups: The Standard Celeration Society, The Fluency Channel, SCC Chart Share

- Ask professional questions and receive direct answers on the Forum at The Precision Teaching Book. (Author's note: That forum no longer exists but it had a nice run).

The stakes for educational and personal change have hit an all-time high. From global competition with jobs to helping people become contributing members of science, business, and other important sectors of society, we need a method to foster competency and greatness. Consider Precision Teaching an important piece of the puzzle. Namely, PT helps measure behavior and make decisions. Those data judgements concern whether an intervention helps or hinders personal learning growth. And in the end, failure to make good decisions can mean failure to thrive. I believe people attracted to Precision Teaching share the personal urgency to discover sensible and robust solutions for learners. I hope you join me in my News Year's resolution, teaching others, or learning yourself, how to use Precision Teaching.

Chapter 9

PT Miscellany

My blogging behavior spanned from 2010 to the time of this writing, 2020. In those ten years, I learned much. One lesson of importance, how to write less technically, and more conversationally. I will admit I still try to master such a writing style. I also realized I needed to know some topics better than my then-current understanding. I learned the veracity of the saying, "You never really know something until you teach it to someone else." Teaching means writing in the case of blogging.

The previous chapters had themes where all the blogs shared commonalities. But the following entries didn't quite fit into a theme. I spent time talking about PT topics like chart shares, inner behavior, and technical details about applied science and how they related to practice. Those assorted gems appear in the following chapter.

The first and second entries share similarities; both blogs cover the technical details of where science bumps into practice. Most notably, how understanding variables and different data practices teachers and other practitioners use could fit into a better structure.

Entry: Which trial should I chart?

I get this question a lot: "Which trial should I chart?" In other words, a teacher may work with a performer who generates a number of data points with multiple practice trials. Take the example of see-write answers basic addition facts sums 0-18.

1-BF-A1 Slice 21.4   AIM: 80-100 digits correct with less than 2 digits incorrect/60 secs

8	7	6	8	9	9	9	6	7	8
+ 8	+ 9	+ 9	+ 8	+ 9	+ 6	+ 9	+ 9	+ 8	+ 7

(20)

8	9	8	9	8	7	8	9	7	9
+ 8	+ 9	+ 7	+ 8	+ 9	+ 8	+ 8	+ 8	+ 9	+ 7

(40)

9	9	8	9	9	7	6	8	9	9
+ 8	+ 8	+ 9	+ 7	+ 6	+ 9	+ 9	+ 7	+ 9	+ 7

(60)

8	9	9	6	8	6	7	9	7	7
+ 7	+ 7	+ 8	+ 9	+ 8	+ 9	+ 8	+ 6	+ 8	+ 9

(80)

8	9	7	9	8	9	9	9	7	9
+ 7	+ 6	+ 8	+ 6	+ 8	+ 8	+ 8	+ 6	+ 9	+ 9

(100)

7	8	8	8	9	8	9	9	6	7
+ 9	+ 9	+ 9	+ 9	+ 7	+ 7	+ 9	+ 9	+ 9	+ 8

(120)

7	8	8	9	6	8	9	8	9	9
+ 9	+ 8	+ 9	+ 9	+ 9	+ 7	+ 6	+ 9	+ 7	+ 8

(140)

7	6	9	7	9	9	8	9	8	8
+ 8	+ 9	+ 6	+ 8	+ 7	+ 7	+ 9	+ 9	+ 7	+ 8

(160)

Copyright 2020 Greatness Achieved Publishing Company. *Pathways to Mastery: Math.* Authorized individuals may copy this page.

Figure 83. A practice sheet for see-write answers basic addition facts sums 0-18.

The performer may do a 30-second practice trial. After one practice trial the performer receives corrective feedback and then does another practice trial. After that practice trial feedback again ensues. If the performer does a total of 6, 30-second practice trials the teacher now has 6 data points. If the teacher uses a digital Precision Teaching platform like Chartlytics, the screen shot in Figure 84 shows the data.

Chapter 9: PT Miscellany

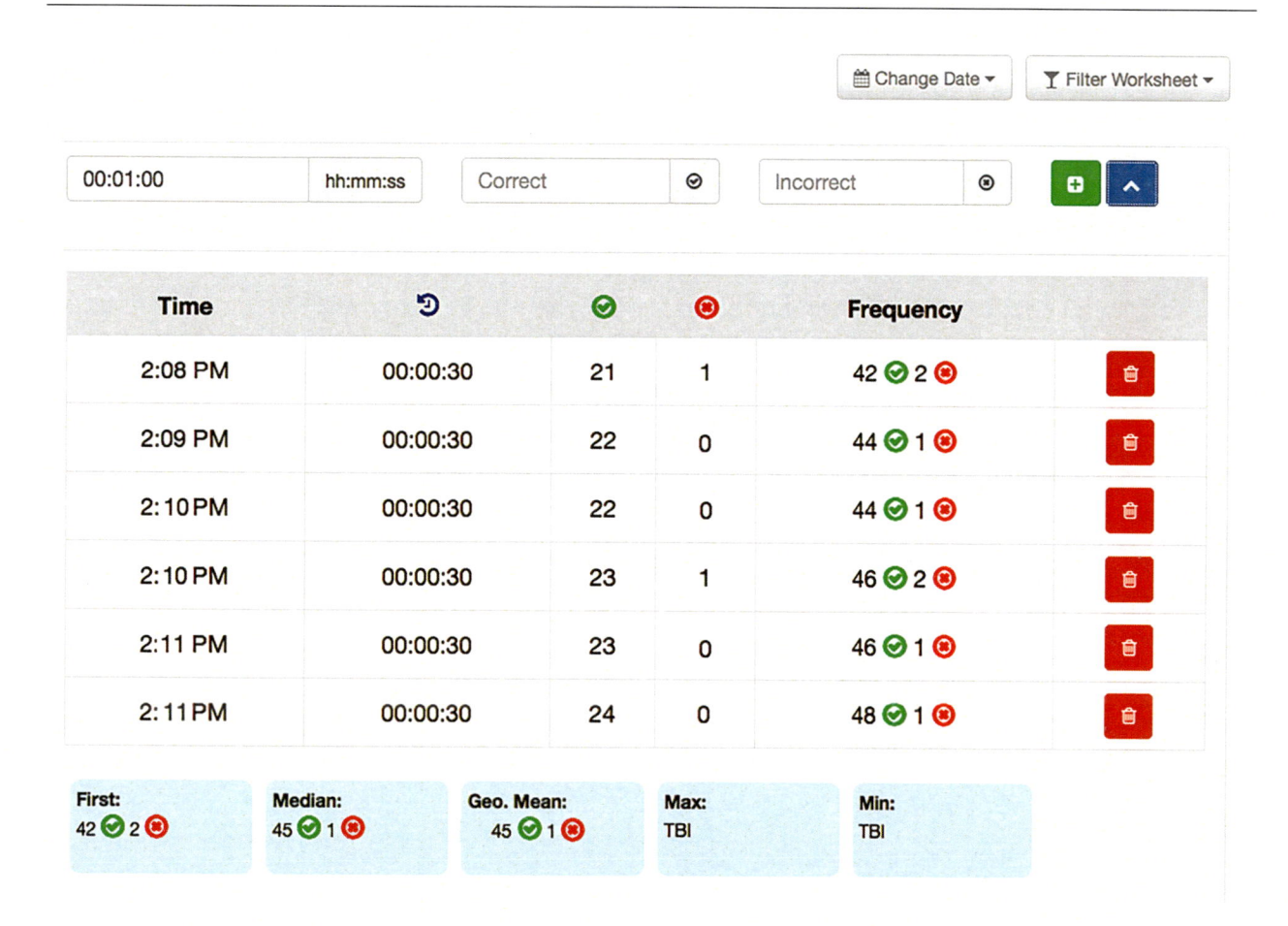

Time	↺	✓	⊘	Frequency
2:08 PM	00:00:30	21	1	42 ✓ 2 ⊘
2:09 PM	00:00:30	22	0	44 ✓ 1 ⊘
2:10 PM	00:00:30	22	0	44 ✓ 1 ⊘
2:10 PM	00:00:30	23	1	46 ✓ 2 ⊘
2:11 PM	00:00:30	23	0	46 ✓ 1 ⊘
2:11 PM	00:00:30	24	0	48 ✓ 1 ⊘

First: 42 ✓ 2 ⊘   Median: 45 ✓ 1 ⊘   Geo. Mean: 45 ✓ 1 ⊘   Max: TBI   Min: TBI

Figure 84. Part of a worksheet in Chartlytics.

(Author's note: Chartlytics has a new name, called PrecisionX. And the software still serves over 5,000 people at the time of this writing).

Notice the Time column. The data show efficiency. The performer does a 30-second trial, receives feedback, records the trial in Chartlytics, and then starts the next trial. All in all, the practice for the day took only 6 minutes.

Sidebar: While 4 minutes might seem like a lot of time the performer made 135 correct responses with only 2 incorrects in one day! Imagine the amount of production in just a week; an extrapolation shows the performer making 675 correct responses in only 20 minutes! Compare that to a student who does no systematic practice and perhaps only homework; such a performer might have a total of 100 or less correct responses per week in 30 or more minutes at best.

OK, back to worksheet interface. Notice the icon for the counting time, in that column you see 00:00:30, 30 seconds for each practice trial. Then the next two columns display the counts of correct and incorrect answers respectively. We can see the performer has 6 data points from 6 different practice trials. Which trial should we place on the chart?

The difference between practice and assessment

The answer to the question we previously asked follows from the difference between practice and assessment.

Practice, or as we call it in Precision Teaching frequency building, refers to performing (repeating) a behavior in time and then providing feedback after the trial ends. The goal of practice directly involves ameliorating performance. And if we chart those daily performances across time, we have a celeration line, which permits us to evaluate learning. Teachers use practice to help improve daily performance and, more importantly, learning.

Assessment deals with "the process of using tests and other measures of student performance and behavior to make education decisions" (Venn, 2000). With assessment we have a goal of understanding the effects of a method, procedure, or variable on performance and learning.

With our performer above, we have a problem if we treat all 6 trials as practice. Namely, we allow the performer to do each trial and then provide performance feedback afterwards. What clearly did we miss? An assessment trial.

Without an assessment trial, a dilemma now exists; out of the 6 practice trials which one represents the performance?

Solving the problem with assessment

To solve the problem, we must add an assessment trial. For our six trials, if we have 1 assessment trial (no feedback, just a timed 30 second trial) and then 5 practice trials, we clearly have a dependent and independent variable. The independent variable (the variable manipulated by the teacher) and the dependent variable (the measured behavior) now exist.

- Independent variable or IV (practice trials) - 5 timed trials of practice or frequency building (includes feedback; goal = improving performance).
- Dependent variable or DV (assessment trial) - 1 timed trial (does not include feedback; goal = assessing performance).

Now the question becomes, which assessment trial would best represent the effects of the independent variable? And which trial you select for the DV also alters the practice trial intervention (IV).

You have several options to understand your data set in Precision Teaching.

Option 1 - First. We could chart the first trial. If we provided no feedback, we would call that the assessment trial and it would also serve as a DV. The first trial of the day has the advantage of showing how the performer does without the benefit of previous practice (the performer hasn't practiced since the last day). Charting the first trial also serves as the most conservative of the trials.

Option 2 - Median. Displaying the median data point would capture the middlemost performance. Charting the median would tell the chart reader how the practice performance typically changes, another IV indicator. Median performance has advantages over the arithmetical mean (the average of all performances - see below).

Again, choosing option 2 means we no longer have a true assessment trial (DV). In other words, a teacher may have done 6 practice trials and uses one of those practices to judge the effects of the intervention. In essence, a practice trial represents all 6 practice trials.

Option 3 - Geometric Mean. The geometric mean would show the average of all 6 performances. The typical value of the practice would lead the chart reader to judge the effects of all trials. But like the median, the geometric mean lacks a designated assessment trial.

Sidebar: While the arithmetic mean and the geometric mean both display the average, the geometric mean better represents data for a few reasons. Outliers not skewing the data represent the biggest advantage. The arithmetic mean works well when scores occur independent of one another. However, the geometric functions best with values that affect one another (not independent of each other). One timed trial and feedback will affect the next one. Therefore, the geometric mean works better for depicting the average performance better than the arithmetic mean.

Option 4 - Minimum. The minimum refers to the lowest score among the data set. For the values in Figure 84, 21 correct and 1 incorrect would appear on the chart. The minimum value would conservatively represent progress. Using the minimum means not having a predetermined assessment trial and again examines practice data.

Option 5 -Maximum. The maximum refers to the highest score among the data set. For the values in Figure 84, 24 correct and 0 incorrect would appear on the chart. The maximum value would liberally represent progress. Maximum data points charted also do not have a pre-established assessment trial.

Option 6 - User Selected. The user chooses any practice trial as representative of the others, another method of inspecting the practice or IV data instead of assessment or DV data.

Option 7 - Stacked. Stacked data points result in displaying all corrects and incorrects on one line. Some charters like seeing all data visual dispersed. The advantage of stacked data points comes in having access to each trial the performer did. A disadvantage lies in determining the celeration line and not having an assessment trial.

Which chart option should you use?

We chart data to observe, analyze, interpret, and communicate changes in behavior. Depending on your situation, different options will serve you and the performer well. In a research setting, clearly an assessment trial (dependent variable) and set number of practice trials (independent variable) must exist prior to beginning to chart. Order and tight experimental protocols must take place in research in order to uncover secrets of nature.

In clinical practice or teaching settings, however, different options may appeal to the educational team. The teacher should weigh the advantages and disadvantages to determine which data point best achieves the objective of understanding what the data have to say.

Bloggers have different styles. One general distinction involves the length of the blog: short-form versus long-form. Short form blogs have anywhere from 300 to 600 words, while long-form can range from 1,000 to 10,000 words. The majority of my blogs take the long-form structure. I found I had too much to say and could not contain my thoughts to a mere 300 words. Looking back, I feel I exercised good judgment in explaining content versus providing brief nuggets of information.

The following entry typifies one of the long-form blogs. I tackled a technical PT subject, the distinction among different kinds of variables, and how they could impact analysis. To this day, I see many charts that do not adhere to the point I discussed. Specifically, having an assessment data point versus having only practice data. The following entry makes similar points to the previous blog. But in the following more recent entry, I went into greater detail and created some visualizations I hope emphasize the crux of the matter.

Entry: Data, variables, applied science, and Precision Teaching

Data functions as the lifeblood of behavior analysis. How does a practicing behavior analyst know if an intervention worked? Data. By what means do behavior analytic journals evaluate the effectiveness of experiments? Data. And in what manner do insurance companies assess the medical necessity for behavior analytic services? If you said data, right again!

Asserting that data permeates behavior analysis would evoke nods of agreement from fellow behavior analysts (and maybe a beverage of your choice at the conference if you said it enthusiastically). From Skinner to contemporary behavior analysis, data plays a pivotal role in basic research and applied practice.

Yet the sheer amount of data and how to use it properly can pose an overwhelming task for those entering the field. Functional assessment, single case design, and social validity all require data. And the ways each one of the previously mentioned events uses data differ significantly.

Many practitioners of the science of behavior, behavior analysts, concern themselves with working directly with individuals. The behavior analyst conducts an assessment to determine areas of need and a client's strengths. From the assessment data, a behavioral plan or program would emerge. Then the behavior analyst or some other person (e.g., parent, registered behavioral technician, teacher) applies the intervention. Someone collects data and evaluates the intervention. Collecting intervention data and analyzing assessment data, however, sometimes get mixed up.

IVs and DVs

What people examine in science can vary considerably. But all scientific experiments share commonalities. Namely, the concept of variables. Behavior analysis qualifies as a science and has several variables: independent variables, dependent variables, extraneous variables, confounding variables, controlled variables.

The independent variable (IV) and the dependent variable (DV) form the basis of understanding a functional relation (i.e., one variable operates in a specific manner as a function of another variable).

The IV represents the event or variable the behavior analyst controls. In applied practice, those IVs go by the name of "interventions.»

On the other hand, the DV constitutes a variable measured or tested. The DV will show what, if any, effects the IV has. Some example IVs and DVs in behavioral experiments:

- A person may smoke fewer cigarettes (DV) when exposed to negative images portraying the terrible health effects of smoking (IV).
- A child may raise their hand more often in class (DV) when the teacher praises them for hand raising (IV).
- A telemarketer may keep a potential caller on the phone longer (DV) if they compliment the caller (IV).

The above examples illustrate the ease with which people can identify IVs and DVs. Sometimes behavior analysts have so much data collection in practice the lines between data collection can blur.

Accuracy building interventions

Many behavioral interventions help learners acquire or become accurate with content. Examples include Discrete Trial Instruction (also called Discrete Trial Training, and Discrete Trial Teaching), Natural Environment Teaching, or Pivotal Response Treatment to name a few.

Discrete Trial Instruction (DTI) has become a very popular accuracy building intervention, especially for those working with children with autism. With DTI the behavior analyst implements five components: 1. Presenting the discriminative stimulus; 2. Providing a temporary prompt if necessary; 3. Waiting for the behavior to occur; 4. Providing a reinforcer; and 5. Finishing with a brief pause before beginning the next trial (Mayer, Sulzer-Azaroff, & Wallace, 2012). One discrete trial would capture the application of steps 1 through 5.

A behavior analyst working with a client would have a goal for DTI. The intervention may target color identification, gross motor imitation, or matching kitchen utensils. The behavior analyst would use DTI to help the client attain the goal (often expressed in percent correct such as "The child will imitate 25 two-step chains of motor behavior with 80% accuracy on 2 out of 3 sessions across a variety of trainers"). The question becomes, what data should the behavior analyst chart? A review of program books or program binders reveals several practices.

Some behavior analysts chart prompt levels. The prompt levels display prompt level data. Did the behavior analyst (BA) or RBT (Registered Behavior Technician) use physical (full or partial), modeling, gestural, verbal, or visual prompts?

Other behavior analysts record plus/minus (i.e., plus for a correct, a minus for incorrect response). The plus/minus data then convert to a percentage. For example, for five trials of matching yield 3 + (pluses) and 2 - (minuses). The data transform to 60% correct (3 correct out of 5 trials).

In both previous cases, the data tell a story. For the prompt levels, the data speak to BA or RBT behavior. Prompts come from the BA or RBT and the data communicate what staff did, not what the learner did.

In the second example, the percent correct report the accuracy of the learner's behavior. Specifically, how accurately did they perform with the set of discrete trials. The learner participated in 5 discrete trials and correctly completed 3 of them (60% correct).

The recorded data on a graph will show trend, level, and variability of the data. But does any of the data answer the question, "Did the learner meet the performance goal?" In other words, if a behavior analyst set a goal for a learner that involved matching the five primary colors, do the recorded and graphed data answer the question? Prompt data certainly do not get at how well a learner can match the colors. And the discrete trial data reflect progress with the accuracy building intervention itself, not necessarily an independent assessment of client behavior.

Data options

The behavior analyst must first decide which data to chart. A review of the IVs and DVs may help. Imagine the following experimental question:

- What effect does the accuracy building intervention discrete trial instruction have on the learner's ability to label five primary color swatches?

The previous experimental question offers options. The behavior analyst could record data on the IV (DTI), the DV (labeling the five primary colors), or both. Monitoring data on the DV or IV provides the BA or RBT with different information.

Dependent Variable	Independent Variable
Did the intervention (IV) affect the measured data (DV)?	How efficiently has the intervention (IV) worked? In other words, do the charted IV data show high celeration or low bounce?
To what extent did the intervention (IV) affect the measured data (DV)?	Do early signs point to a problem with the intervention (IV)?
Does a functional relation exist between the intervention (IV) and the measured data (DV)	How long or how many trials did you apply with the intervention?

Table 16. Difference between data monitoring and analyzing the DV and IV

Table 16 does gets at advantages to recording, graphing, and analyzing data on the intervention (IV). And while the behavior analyst can learn about the intervention, not having any data on the DV means not knowing or understanding the effects on a learner's behavior. The behavior analyst must decide when, on what, and how much data to collect.

The decision to collect data doesn't end with a data binder. In Precision Teaching, several options for displaying data exist. The choices include Geometric Mean, First, Last, Stacked, Median, Summative, Best, and Worst. Each provides different information for the DV and IV.

What does each option mean and when should a behavior analyst use each? Table 17 provides the answers. Deciding whether to use First, Best, or the Geometric resides with the BA, RBT, and in some cases the client. Part of the data process involves different people looking at the data. The options for focusing in on one particular aspect of data display will depend on clinical circumstances.

Points to Display	Definition	Advantages
Geometric Mean	A special mean where all the observational data in a set undergo transformation by means of taking the *n*th root of the product of *n* numbers (observations).	(DV and IV) Takes all data points into consideration and provides a very good representation of all observational data.
First	The first data point in the set of observational data.	(IV) Offers a conservative view of performance. First data points show performance "as is" from the last day's intervention.
Last	The last data point in the set of observational data.	(IV) Illustrates performance primed from all other intervention trials. Does not necessarily put forward "Best." Fatigue or endurance issues can affect last performances.
Stacked	All the observational data stacked on one line.	(IV and DV) Visually displays all data points showing entire range of performances. Best practice to not have IV and DV on same line.
Median	The middle value in the set of observational data.	(IV) Good measure for capturing the middlemost performance. Not affected by outliers like arithmetical mean for representing data set.
Summative	Totaling all the observational data which results in a summed value.	(IV and DV) Avoids a representative measure and instead combines all data. May provide insight into overall performance of the IV or DV but loses any singular performance.
Best	The best data point in a set of observational data.	(IV) Used to motivate the Performer. The Performer tries to beat or surpass the last best score.
Worst	The worst data point in a set of observational data.	(IV) Captures the lowest performance for a data set. Reveals the floor or lowest performance of the dataset. Across time offers a perspective of poorest quality behavior. The behavior analyst will see the least desirable performances produced by the IV.

Table 17. Definition of different points to display with advantages for each.

The options for displaying intervention or measurement data make for a different narrative. An example of multifaceted data appears in Figure 85. In one session an RBT ran five discrete trials that produced five sets of data points. Figure 85 shows the total data and the accel and decel data for each trial and the different data display option.

Chapter 9: PT Miscellany

Five trials of data collected

Trial #	Accel	Decel
First	4	3
Second	6	2
Third	5	2
Fourth	8	1
Fifth	7	1

First Trial 4, 3

Last Trial 7, 1

Geo Mean of Five Trials 6, 2

Best Trial 8, 1

Worst Trial 4, 3

Summative Count of Five Trials 30, 9

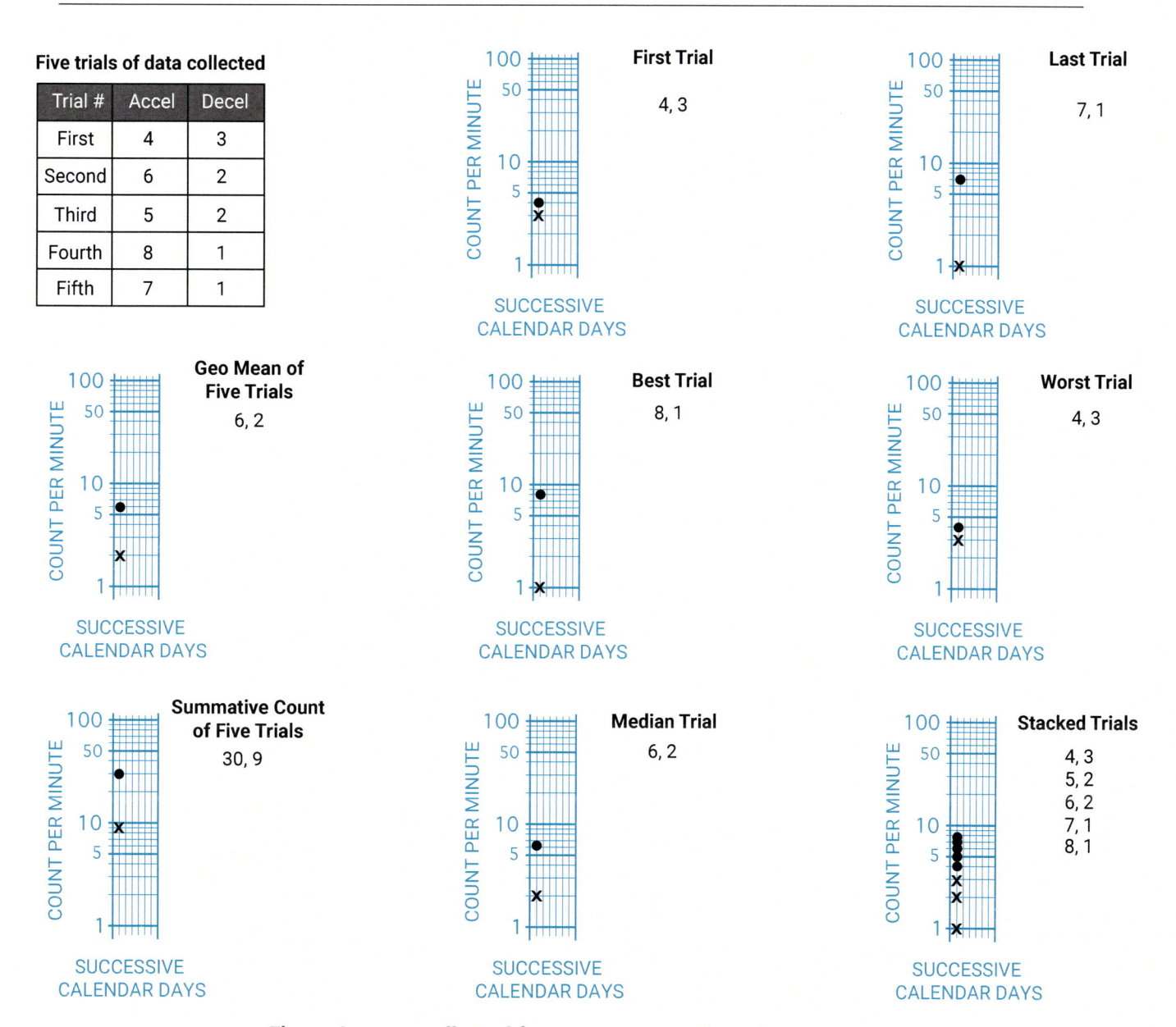

Median Trial 6, 2

Stacked Trials
4, 3
5, 2
6, 2
7, 1
8, 1

Figure 85. Data collected from one session of DTI (Five trials).

The BA can inspect the data with any of the previously mentioned options (Figure 85). Each chart segment has a Count Per Day vertical axis and Successive Calendar Days horizontal axis.

Contrast the First and Last data displays. The First discrete trial had barely more incorrects than corrects while the Last trial provides a much different performance. The Geometric Mean and Median look the same, suggesting the mean or average for the data set lie at six correct and two incorrect. The Best and Worst also drastically differ from each other demonstrating the margins of improvement in the overall session. And Stacked paints a picture of all performance data on one view. The dispersal of corrects and incorrects reveal the variability and accuracy of discrete trials.

The data views in Figure 85 all speak to the IV or intervention (DTI) and not an independent assessment of the skill (labeling five primary colors). The ability to see all the different displays and Points to Display contextualize the data. A behavior analyst gains understanding and insight when inspecting the data with different options.

Conclusion

Single day and weekly displays of behavior express the extent of change across time. Focusing on intervention data communicates how special conditions arranged by the behavior analyst may affect client behavior. The answer to how much learner behavior changes becomes visible with an independent assessment of target behavior outside of the intervention. Having different options to display IV and DV data lead a data analyst (e.g., BA, RBT, learner, stakeholder) down a fruitful path - discovering functional relations and what works best for each client.

My Master's thesis at The Ohio State University had me working with two senior citizens. The two women, aged 88 and 83, lived in assisted living. I would visit them and collect the data they took on their self-counts of negative feelings and thoughts. I helped them define what they would count. After obtaining baseline, I taught them both an intervention to accelerate their number of positive thoughts and feelings. The result of my thesis ended in two seniors self-reporting fewer negative thoughts and feelings.

The previous story illustrates my first foray into inner behavior or what some call private events. People who can think and feel have inners. Sometimes the inners bother people and require adjustment. The work on inners done in PT struck me as liberating. We have a method that people can use to balance their thoughts and feelings if they wish. I saw it during my thesis, and since I have conducted many inner interventions on myself. The following entry describes inners in more detail.

Entry: Inners

All people travel a path that forms their life's journey. Along the way each person has a unique set of experiences that shape their behavior. Outside observers can witness many events that come to impact a person. Examples include:

- A mother complimenting her daughter for using manners.
- A dog barking and chasing at a child on their way to school.
- A man telling a tasteful joke and his date laughs.

The science of behavior, behavior analysis, has uncovered laws of learning through years of experimentation (Cooper, Heron, & Heward, 2020). The systematic observation of behaviors drove the understanding that behavior operates in a lawful manner just like all other parts of nature people understand (e.g., physics and motion, chemistry and chemical reactions).

However, an entire set of experiences takes place throughout each person's life that no one else can see: thoughts, feelings, and emotions. Surprising to many, the founder of contemporary behavior analysis, B. F. Skinner, not only recognized the need to understand private events (i.e., thoughts, feelings, and emotions), but to embrace and study them.

For example, Skinner wrote: "No entity or process which has any useful explanatory force is to be rejected on the ground that it is subjective or mental. The data which have made it important must, however, be studied and formulated in effective ways (Skinner, 1964, p. 96).

Precision Teaching has done just that: provided a means for people to bring private events into the public. And the only requirements involve a pinpoint, a timing device, and counter.

Figure 86. Telling a joke and its public effect.

Inner behavior

Abigail Calkin championed the study of private events from a Precision Teaching perspective. She used the term "inner behavior" to note that what happens inside the skin does not differ from what happens publicly. In others, public and private behavior both fall under the domain of the science of behavior.

Calkin (1981) examined inner behaviors as a case study where she counted seven pinpoints. Her counts focused on positive and negative feelings about herself. After Calkin defined what a positive and negative feeling meant, or an inner behavior, she then went about self-counting.

The procedure involved counting positive and negative inners for 1,000 minutes or about 16 and 1/2 hours, a full waking day. After counting for nine days, Calkin could then observe the record of her inner behavior on the Standard Celeration Chart. She made her inner behavior public by visually displaying her counts.

Calkin proceeded to intervene on negative and positive inners by using a one-minute timing intervention. She would sit for one minute and write as many positive things about herself as she could.

The upshot? Across time, the frequency of positive inners rose while the frequency of negative inners greatly declined. As Calkin wrote: "I considered the project completed because I felt good about myself for the first time in my life. Twenty-two of the 24 positive thoughts I wrote on my list in During 1 had now become positive feelings. Fourteen of the 18 initial negative thoughts and feelings were no longer there" (Calkin, 1981, p. 20-21).

More research, more positive inners

In recent decades, a number of articles appeared that demonstrated the constructive application of examining inner behavior.

McCrudden (1990) charted his inner behavior so he could "learn, discover, and change" feelings that bothered him. As his self-counting and self-charting project unfolded a salient feature of measuring inner behavior became apparent: "…it respects the learner enough to allow his/her to define an inner according to his/her own unique criteria" (McCrudden, 1990, p. 19).

In another article, Cooper (1991) described how self-pity, agitated thoughts about his mother-in-law, and strong thoughts about sexual activity for other women threatened to end his marriage of 25 years. The inner behavior project involved a one-minute intervention accelerating the number of loving thoughts and feelings about his wife and family members.

Intervening on private events jeopardizing a marriage required immediate help. Having a method such as the one-minute timing procedure along with self-counting inners provides a remarkable boon to those suffering. The relief and humor come through in Cooper's summary comments: "Destructive thoughts and feelings are no longer a personal or potential family problem. Best of all, I did not have to pay a marriage counselor" (Cooper, 1991, p. 45).

Action

Many disciplines of psychology and the sub-discipline of counseling offer interventions to help people with disturbing private events. Different methods of counseling range, for instance, from Adlerian and Cognitive Therapy to Psychoanalysis and Eclectic Counseling.

The Precision Teaching method of self-counting inners for addressing private events or inner behavior has grown considerably. Applications have expanded to helping senior citizens (Cobane & Keenan, 2002; Kubina, Haertel, & Cooper, 1994), people with depression (Patterson & McDowell, 2009), and college students' low self-esteem (Clore & Gaynor).

Changing the self-counted frequency of inners or private events does not mean an associated public behavior will also change. A Precision Teaching discovery of 1,000,000s of charts show behaviors occur independent of one another (Lindsley, 1992). Nevertheless, making the private public shines light on a topic in desperate need of study. The 14 articles below show the growing literature and database for the study of inner behavior.

The promise of successfully, systematically, and scientifically changing inner behavior has widescale appeal. Many disorders that cause great personal pain fall within the purview of inners: post-traumatic stress disorder, bulimia, depression, and generalized anxiety disorder. Therefore, pinpointing behaviors that occur within one's own skin, self-counting such targets, and then placing them on a Standard Celeration Chart offer an elegant solution to helping people.

I remember my first conference chart share with great fondness. It happened back in 1997 in Hartford, Connecticut. I felt super nervous because a cast of legendary Precision Teachers sat in the audience with no less than Ogden Lindsley himself attending. Chart shares have a long history in PT, and as I soon learned, evoked excitement and pleasure, not anxiety or distress. Chart shares allow anyone to take center stage and share their data on a Standard Celeration Chart. For many years people used overhead projectors and charts on transparencies to share their data. Technology has led more people to use digital projectors, but many old-schoolers still go the route of the overhead. The exciting data, thoughtful contemplations, and occasional humor in the short SCC presentations have endured. The following entry describes the delightful PT social event called chart share.

Entry: Chart shares are fun

Look at the following graphs. What do you notice about each one?

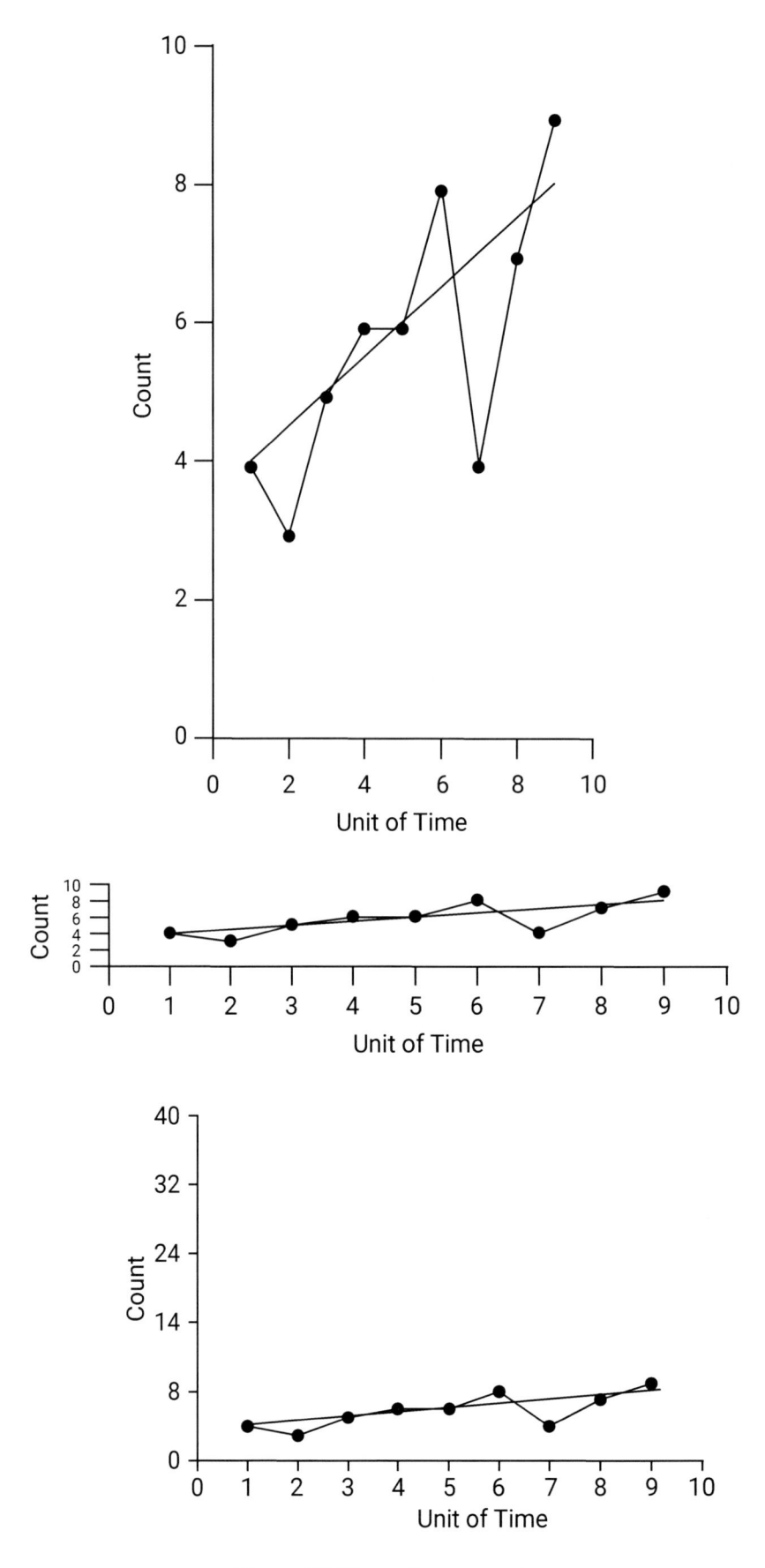

Figure 87. Three linear graphs.

If you said, "They look different" you win! Yes, they look different but guess what? The graphs all have the same data. You might have thought "Wait a minute, why do we have such widely discrepant versions of graphs with the same data?" Many answers exist to explain why each person makes their visual display differently. But they all share a common trait. Namely, the graphs arise from within a system of nonstandardization.

Problems with nonstandardization

Let's start with standardization. Standardization means applying world-class specifications governing the delivery and construction of services, systems, and products (International Organization for Standardization, 2014).

Standardization leads to a standard or "...an agreed-upon way of doing something" (Spivak & Brenner, 2001, p.1). When we lack standards or do things in a nonstandard manner, we get different results. Always.

The lack of standards shows up in the three differently constructed linear graphs with the scaling of vertical and horizontal axes, size of the axis lines, and the slopes of the line for each trend. One of the consequences befalling people who use nonstandard graphs comes in the form of communication.

It takes time to acclimate people to new graphs. Furthermore, with varying graphs decision making also can suffer. People who use nonstandard linear graphs no doubt want the best visual display for rapidly discerning effects. What to do?

Standards have benefits

The previous question has an easy answer, standard graphs. Standardizing graphs solves many problems. For example, doctors and technicians who read electrocardiographs (ECGs) experience the following benefits from a standard graphic display (Dubin, 2000):

- Deep understanding of cardiac physiology
- Develop a lifetime of practical knowledge
- Rapidly comprehend the ECG (electrical output of the heart)

The same benefits hold true for standard graphs. Graph readers can develop a deeper understanding of the subject matter. Practical knowledge of the subject matter occurs more quickly and systematically. And the speed of graph comprehension accelerates.

For years, Precision Teachers have enjoyed the previous benefits of looking at the world through the lens of a standard ratio (also called semilogarithmic) chart, the Standard Celeration Chart.

Simply stated, people who use Standard Celeration Charts never have to deal with differently sized axes. Also, the scaling will not once shift. As a result, the slope of the line on each chart (when the same angle) means the same thing to every person who sees it. Without having to spend time figuring out the chart dimensions or what the symbols mean, Standard Celeration Chart (SCC) viewers rapidly get to the business of analyzing and interpreting the data.

Chart shares

A long history of good will and a positive focus spurred mottos such as "accentuate the positive," and "Celerate, then celebrate." In conjunction with Standard Charts, Precision Teachers developed a wonderful social practice called "Chart Shares."

A chart share works just as its name implies, people share charts. Charting sharing began with overhead projectors and transparencies of charted data. Figure 88 shows Og (the founder of Precision Teaching) sharing a chart.

When someone shares a chart, the protocol involves going to an overhead projector, or now an LCD projector or document camera, and talking about a chart for 1 or 2 minutes. People can communicate so much information about the data because of the standard view afforded by the SCC.

If you would like to experience a chart share many different formal and informal opportunities exist. Formal opportunities occur at conferences such as the International Precision Teaching Conference. Informal meetings occur at learning centers, university and college courses, and even online. Hopefully you have an opportunity to participate or soak in the goodness of Standard Celeration Chart share.

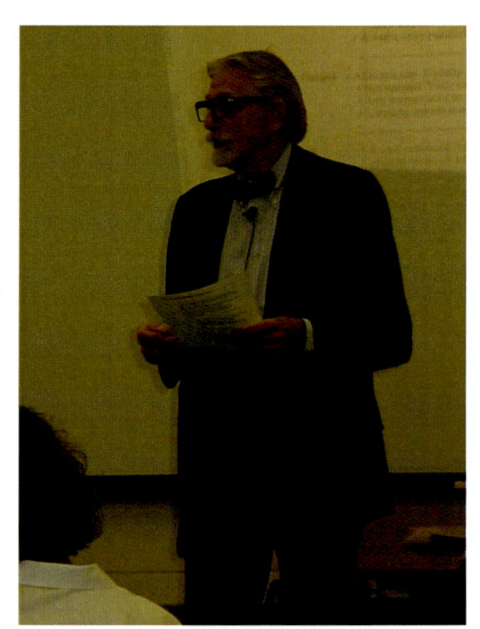

Figure 88. Ogden Lindsey talking about a chart at the 2003 International Precision Teaching Conference.

I began the following blog during the New Year and wrote to a behavior analytic audience. I believed writing a blog and encouraging people to adopt PT might match up to their new ambitions. The following entry makes the case that should resonate with many in the behavioral community. Namely, Skinner founded the entire behavior analytic enterprise with standards. Skinner used a standard unit of measurement, rate or frequency, and a standard visual display, a device called the cumulative recorder, which produced cumulative records. Other sciences adopt standards, but perhaps some behavior analysts forget the rich history in the science of behavior. In the following entry, I celebrated standards and called upon colleagues to embrace them once again.

Entry: Cumulative Record → Standard Celeration Chart

Ogden Lindsley always gave credit to his mentor B. F. Skinner for two important components of Precision Teaching: rate of responding and the cumulative recorder (Lindsley, 1971, 1991a, 1991b).

The cumulative recorder helped Skinner discover laws of behavior. The cumulative recorder had a number of elements for recording real time behavior. The cumulative recorder produced a cumulative (increased quantity of successive additions of responses) record (a piece of paper recording responses in time).

The actual records produced standard visual displays. Even without knowing the specifics, such regularity produced easily identified and recognized patterns of behavior in different animals who underwent the same experimental procedures.

Why did lines only go up or stay flat? The cumulative record worked by a rat (pigeon or any other animal) responding in an experimental chamber (aka Skinner Box). If the rat activated a level by depressing it with its paw, that sent a signal to the cumulative recorder which would move the pen one unit in the same direction (once it reached the end it would reset). The marks on the cumulative record show when food (a reinforcer) was delivered. The marks, called pips, along with the pattern revealed by the shape of the line allowed Skinner and all other behavioral scientists to understand nature – namely behavior. As Lattal said:

"The history of the cumulative recorder is the story of gaining control over the four aforementioned functions: step, pip, reset, and event mark. Thus it is a history of striving to achieve an ever more accurate and precise picture of behavior in real time, the primary subject matter of the discipline. In the broader scheme of things, it is also in microcosm the story of the experimental analysis of behavior and how the reciprocal interaction between the scientist, the subject matter, and its measurement has led to change and progress" (Lattal, 2004, p.330).

The gift of standardization

The standardization of visual display conferred by the cumulative records to the young science of behavior analysis inspires wonder and reverence. An entire science came into being when Skinner deliberated over visual patterns of behavior. The magnitude of changes he saw occurred due to the variables systematically implemented. The magnitude of the changes was not influenced by a shifting design of the cumulative record, they stayed the same because there were standard. When other scientists examined the magnitude of changes of their animals, they saw regularity because each scientist did not have to manually create a separate cumulative record, the standardized visual always came from the cumulative recorder. The reliability and quality of the standard visual displays reduced interpretation errors and enhanced productivity; anyone trained to understand cumulative records could immediately understand the visible data patterns.

Ogden Lindsley got it. He saw the power of standardization his mentor Skinner gave the world. Lindsley spent part of his early career using cumulative records with people at the Metropolitan State Hospital in Waltham, Massachusetts, one of the first people to do so (Potts, Eshleman, & Cooper, 1993). The moment-to-moment behavior changes shown in all their standardized splendor led Lindsley to discover conjugate schedules of reinforcement. He made many other important discoveries. But the standard visual display of the cumulative records showing changing frequency measures (i.e., count over time) profoundly influenced Lindsley. The glory of science stood before him: a standard, absolute, universal measure of behavior (frequency) could appear on a standard visual display.

The Standard Celeration Chart

Fast forward to the 1960s and Lindsley moved from the State Hospital to the University of Kansas. Lindsley decided to devote the rest of his professional career to helping students in education. He had a vision for education – bring science to the field and many discoveries would follow. Armed with the knowledge of what a standard visual display offers, Lindsley created the Standard Celeration Chart or SCC. The cumulative record differs in purpose from the SCC, thus Lindsley needed a new graphic.

	Cumulative Record	Standard Celeration Chart
Standard Visual Display	Yes	Yes
Measurement Displayed	Moment-to-moment behavior change	Frequency-to-frequency behavior change
Analytic	Frequency change	Celeration, bounce

Table 18. A brief comparison of the cumulative record and the Standard Celeration Chart.

Table 18 compares the features of the two visual display systems. Both have their place in understanding behavior change. The cumulative recorder shows a pattern of behavior changing moment-to-moment. If we want to understand how our behavior may change in a given situation, the cumulative record offers an exquisite view. Figure 89 shows a person gambling on slots. If we measured the rate at which he activated the machine, we could see a cumulative record of behavior. Under similar circumstances if we took another measure, we would likely see the same behavior pattern, pretty powerful stuff!

The SCC shows behavior on a different scale, not moment-to-moment but frequency-to-frequency. Let's say we gave a child a sheet of addition problems and measured how many they completed in 1 minute. We have a frequency measure for that day. If the next day we do the same and continue taking a frequency for 7 days in a row, we now have a frequency-to-frequency measure. We call that measure (unit of change) celeration. Not only do we have a standard visual display with a line that gives us a standard visual picture, but we can also quantify the change, again, pretty powerful stuff!

As you move through the year, ask yourself if a standard visual display would help you do your job better. Whether that job involves working with children, teenagers, adults, or improving yourself. Would celeration improve analysis?

Figure 89. A person playing slots.

The chart would not change. The visual picture emerging has the same flavor of standardization that Skinner and Lindsley marveled at; differential visual patterns resulting from different variables.

Good luck in the new year and may all your charts accelerate. Unless you want to decelerate behavior, then may all your charts decelerate!

∽

I previously mentioned I first learned about, and used, Precision Teaching way back in 1986. At the same time, I also encountered applied behavior analysis (ABA). Since that time, I have practiced PT and ABA. I freely admit I love both sciences. ABA has its mission set squarely on helping people change their behavior for the better and reach their personal goals. PT has the same purpose. The mixture of the two truly forms an impressive cocktail of amazing behavior change. But few behavior analysts use PT. I have tried to change the usage in ABA for as long as I can remember. I became more effective at sharing information with colleagues as my knowledge increased. The following blog, the last in this book, shows another attempt to convince my behavior analytic peers to adopt PT.

Entry: ABA and PT

Problem behavior requires the best applied science available, applied behavior analysis or ABA. ABA developed from the work of B. F. Skinner and his experimental work with animals in tightly controlled laboratory settings.

Skinner observed rats responded in lawful ways to a set of events. For example, when a light came on, if the rat pressed a bar, the rat immediately received a food pellet. In the future, when the rat entered the experimental chamber it would behave in a similar manner; when the light came on, the rat pressed the bar and received food. Skinner called his discovery positive reinforcement.

It turns out all the experimental findings Skinner and his colleagues made in the laboratory also applied to humans. Many people have heard of "time out." But the time out procedure came straight out of the experimental chamber and works on laboratory animals the same the way it works on humans. Of course, that assumes people actually do time out correctly! Sadly, some people use distorted procedures of time out which don't always work.

People also warped Skinner's advice on using punishment; he adamantly warned against it! Skinner and his colleagues discovered what punishment procedures do. As a result of seeing the harmful effects, Skinner spent his entire career encouraging people to use positive reinforcement and other non-punitive measures to change behavior.

ABA grew from its humble laboratory beginnings and many practitioners wanted to harness the powerful science of behavior (i.e., Applied Behavior Analysis) to better humankind. Flash forward to today and an embarrassment of behavior change riches has now made its way into journals, parenting magazines, conference, classrooms, board rooms and even popular media.

Old school experimental behavior analysts used standard graphics

The methods of ABA rest on careful observation and experiment. Therefore, many people call behavior analysis the science of behavior. But like any science, progress depends on the quality and precision of a measurement system.

B. F. Skinner and his contemporaries had the advantage of a sensitive monitoring device providing standard real time data. Everyone who used a "cumulative recorder" would see data forming distinctive patterns. Just like going to a doctor who interprets standard views of heart activity on ECGs, Skinner quickly deduced what specific change patterns meant.

Skinner loved standard graphs and said the following, "... the curve revealed things in the rate of responding, and in changes in that rate, which would certainly otherwise have been missed" Skinner, 1956, p. 225). Without a standard view and a standard data metric called frequency (or rate), ABA would likely not exist today.

New school applied behavior analysts use nonstandard graphics

Along the way to developing ABA almost all the practitioners and experimenters abandoned standard graphics like the cumulative record in favor of nonstandard graphics like the nonstandard linear graph. However, one of Skinner's graduate students (who later would go on to make amazing contributions), Ogden R. Lindsley, took the lessons he learned from his dear ole mentor and created a standard visual display called the Standard Celeration Chart (SCC). What Lindsley offered the world, and especially behavior analysts, may one day completely change how people measure and view data.

The scope of features

The following infographic displays a number of visual features offered by Standard Celeration Chart. The discernible properties of behavior appear to SCC users helping elevate the practice of ABA. Those using nonstandard linear graphics not only have none of the visible characteristics of behavior available to them, but must contend with the chaos of nonstandardization (widely variable sizes of axes, scalings, scale labels, and graphical symbols).

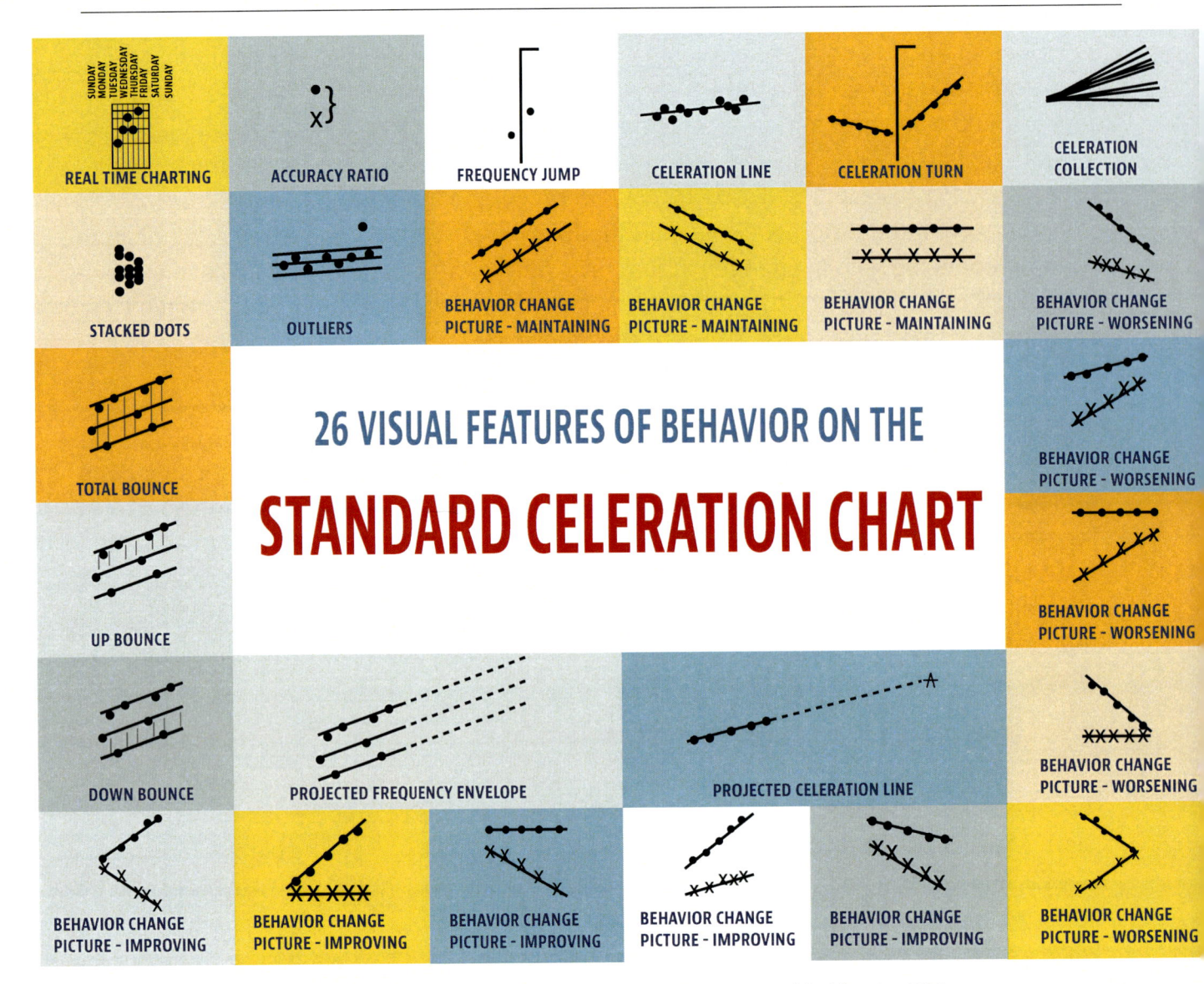

Figure 90. Twenty-six visual features of behavior provided by the SCC.

While covering all the visual features falls beyond the scope of the present blog post, I will highlight a few essential for ABA.

Real time charting. When we visit the doctor with either an injury or illness we ask the doctor how long the treatment will take. We all want to know how long we must suffer pain or inconvenience caused the malady or harm.

The SCC has four different charts with different time scales. The daily SCC, for instance, presents data in the scale of days. Behavior analysts who use the daily SCC will see how the intervention they applied to behavior changes across each week (seven days = a "celeration period").

If more behavior analysts used the SCC, we would know generally how long procedures such as time out, positive reinforcement derived interventions, or differential reinforcement take to change behavior.

In other words, behavior analysts could tell parents or insurance how long an intervention would likely take. Furthermore, real time charting shows the effects of illness, vacation days, and time spent away from an intervention.

Celeration line. Skinner and his colleagues used frequency or rate (the count or number of behaviors over a specific time period) to measure behavior. Lindsley and Precision Teachers also used frequency to measure behavior. Placing successive frequencies across time gave rise to a new, powerful unit called celeration.

The celeration line shows the direction and speed of behavior change. The steeper the celeration line the faster the behavior has changed. Applied behavior analysts who use celeration lines can see if a pinpointed behavior such as "calls out answer in class without permission" changes quickly or slowly as a result of an intervention.

In Applied Behavior Analysis a hallmark of the science resides in a characteristic called "Effective." According to the authors, Effective means "If the application of behavioral techniques does not produce large enough effects for practical value, then application has failed" (Baer, Wolf & Risley, 1968, p. 96).

A celeration line flashes a red or green light in the face of the behavior analyst. Effective interventions change behaviors in the right direction and do so quickly. Without celeration lines and real time behavior monitoring, behavior analysts have no way of knowing, or communicating to others, the precise effectiveness of any intervention.

Using the celeration line also permits behavior analysts to match up individual interventions and their efficiency. On a daily Standard Celeration Chart, a x1.5 per week celeration value (the quantification of the celeration line) means the behavior grew 50% per week. Behavior analysts could report the effects to parents, teachers, insurance companies, and other people who wish to know the speed at which a behavior has changed.

Projected Celeration Line. The celeration lines become possible because of the special architecture of the Standard Celeration Chart. The vertical ratio scale shows behavior changing by equal ratios instead of equal intervals (as they do on linear graphs).

The properties of the ratio scale result in very nice projections of future behavior. Straight line projections on ratio charts like the SCC can turn into curvilinear lines on linear graphs. The ability to accurately project the future course of behavior facilities the analysis, evaluation, and planning of interventions.

Bounce. Lindsley used the plain English word "bounce" to communicate the concept of "variability" to teachers, parents, and students. When measured across time, behavior bounces around. Bounce always occurs because humans never perform a behavior the exact same way. Those variations, or bounce, may take place very slightly (low bounce) or quite significantly (high bounce).

The SCC not only shows bounce clearly; it also allows behavior analysts to explicitly quantify the degree of influence. A student with a bounce of x2 compared to a student with a bounce of x11 jumps out at the chart reader. The x2 bounce makes obvious the degree of influence an intervention has on student 1's behavior. Student 2's x11 bounce has more variability, indicating the intervention in place does not have very strong control (influence) over the targeted behavior. In fact, student 2 has 11 times more behavioral variability when compared to student 1.

Conclusion

The previous three attributes of the SCC markedly enhance the power of behavior analysts' ability to detect meaningful changes. Furthermore, the analysis, interpretation, and communication of applied data outcomes greatly improve. More information means better analysis, better decisions, and better outcomes.

We made it to the end of the book. And I hope you, my dear reader, have found my blog entries compelling and convinced you to adopt PT if you have not done so yet. And if you have, then I hope this book expanded your knowledge or contributed in some other way to enhance your understanding and practice of Ogden Lindsley's gift to humanity.

References

*Indicates an inner behavior Precision Teaching article

All, P. (1977). *From get truckin' to jaws, students improve their learning picture.* Unpublished master's thesis, University of Kansas, Lawrence.

American Cancer Society (2014). Questions About Smoking, Tobacco, and Health. Retrieved at http://www.cancer.org/acs/groups/cid/documents/webcontent/002974-pdf.pdf

American National Standards Institute & American Society of Mechanical Engineers (1960). Time-series charts. New York: American Society of Mechanical Engineers.

American National Standards Institute & American Society of Mechanical Engineers (1979). *American national standard: Time-series charts.* American Society of Mechanical Engineers.

American Society of Mechanical Engineers. (1938). *Time series charts: a manual of design and construction.* Committee on Standard for Graphic Presentation, American Society of Mechanical Engineers.

Baer, D. M., Wolf, M. M., & Risley, T. R. (1968). Some current dimensions of applied behavior analysis. *Journal of Applied Behavior Analysis, 1,* 91–97. doi: 10.1901/jaba.1968.1-91

Binder, C. (1996). Behavioral fluency: Evolution of a new paradigm. *The Behavior Analyst, 19,* 163-197. doi: 10.1007/BF03393163

Bowen, R. (1992). *Graph it! How to make, read, and interpret graphs.* Prentice-Hall.

Branch, A., Hastings, R. P., Beverley, M., & Hughes, J. C. (2018). Increasing support staff fluency with the content of behaviour support plans: An application of precision teaching. *Journal of Intellectual & Developmental Disability, 43*(2), 213-222. doi: 10.3109/13668250.2016.1267334

*Calkin, A. B. (1981). One minute timing improves inners. *Journal of Precision Teaching, 2*(3), 9-21.

*Calkin, A. B. (1992). The inner eye: improving self-esteem. *Journal of Precision Teaching, 10*(1), 42-52.

*Calkin, A. B. (2002). Inner Behavior: Empirical Investigations of Private Events. *The Behavior Analyst, 25,* 255-259.

*Calkin, A. B. (2009). An examination of inner (private) and outer (public) behaviors. *European Journal of Behavior Analysis, 10*, 61-75.

*Clore, J., & Gaynor, S. (2006). Self-Statement Modification Techniques for Distressed College Students with Low Self-Esteem and Depressive Symptoms. *International Journal of Behavioral Consultation and Therapy, 2*, 314-331.

*Cobane, E. F., & Keenan, M. (2002). A senior citizen's self-management of positive and An Examination of Inner (Private) and Outer (Public) Behaviors negative inner behaviours. *Journal of Precision Teaching and Celeration, 18*(2), 30-36.

*Conser, L. (1981). Charting: The quick picker upper. *Journal of Precision Teaching, 2*(3), 27-29.

*Cooper, J. O. (1991). Can this marriage be saved? Self-management of destructive inners. *Journal of Precision Teaching, 8*(2), 44-46.

Cooper, J. O., Heron, T. E., & Heward, W. L. (2020). *Applied behavior analysis* (3rd ed.). Pearson Education.

Dubin, D. (2000). *Rapid interpretation of EKG's*. Cover Publishing Company.

*Duncan, A. D. (1971). The view for the inner eye: Personal management of inner and outer behaviors. *Teaching Exceptional Children, 3*, 152-154.

Ericsson, K. A. (2006). *The Cambridge Handbook of Expertise and Expert Performance*. Cambridge University Press.

Gast, D. L., & Lane, J. D. (2014). *Single case research methodology: Applications in special education and behavioral sciences* (2nd ed.). Routledge.

Giesecke, F. E., Mitchell, A., Spencer, H. C., Hill, I. L., Loving, R. O., Dygdon, J. T., & Novak, J. E. (2001). *Engineering graphics* (8th ed.). Prentice Hall.

Guild, J. (2015, July). *Accelerating classroom learning by teaching students how to use the standard celeration chart to efficiently collect, analyze, and select appropriate interventions based on their own performance data*. Paper presented at the annual meeting of the Northeastern Federation for Precision Teaching, Pittsburgh, PA.

Graf, S., & Lindsley, O. (2002). *Standard celeration charting 2002*. Graf Implements.

International Organization for Standardization (2014, June 4). *What are standards?* Retrieved from http://www.iso.org/iso/about/discover-iso_meet-iso/about.htm

Johnson, K., & Street, E. M. (2013). *Response to intervention with precision teaching: Creating synergy in the classroom*. Guilford.

Johnston, J. M., & Pennypacker, H. S. (1980). *Strategies and tactics of human behavioral research*. Erlbaum.

Johnston, J. M., & Pennypacker, H. S. (2009). *Strategies and Tactics of Behavioral Research* (3rd ed.). Routledge.

*Judy, M., Malanga, P. R., Seevers, R. L., & Cooper, J. O. (1997). A self-experimentation on the detection of forgets using encouraging think/say and hear/tally statements. *Journal of Precision Teaching and Celeration, 14*(2), 37-46.

Karpicke, J. D., Butler, A. C., & Roediger III, H. L.(2009). Metacognitive strategies in student learning: Do students practise retrieval when they study on their own? *Memory,17*, 471-479.

Kennedy, C. H. (2005). *Single-case designs for educational research*. Allyn & Bacon.

*Kostewicz, D., Kubina, R. M., & Cooper, J. O. (2000). Managing aggressive thoughts and feelings with daily counts of non-aggressive thoughts: A self-experiment. *Journal of Behavior Therapy and Experimental Psychiatry, 31*(3-4), 177-187.

Kubina, R. M. (2019). *The Precision Teaching Implementation Manual*. Greatness Achieved.

Kubina, R. M., & Yurich, K. K. L. (2012). *The Precision Teaching Book*. Greatness Achieved.

*Kubina, R. M., Haertel, M. W., & Cooper, J. O. (1994). Reducing negative inner behavior of senior citizens: The one-minute counting procedure. *Journal of Precision Teaching, 11*(2), 28-35.

Kubina, R. M., Kostewicz, D. E., Brennan, K. M., & King, S. A. (2017). A Critical Review of Line Graphs in Behavior Analytic Journals. *Educational Psychology Review, 29*, 583-598. doi 10.1007/s10648-015-9339-x

Kubina, R. M., Yurich, K. L., Durica, K. C., & Healy, N. M. (2016). Developing behavioral fluency with movement cycles using SAFMEDS. *Journal of Behavioral Education, 25*, 120-141.

Lin, F. Y., Kubina, R. M., & Shimamune, S. (2011). Examining Application Relationships: Differences in Mathematical Elements and Compound Performance Between American, Japanese, and Taiwanese Students. *International Journal of Applied Educational Studies, 9*, 19-32.

Lindsley, O. R. (1964). Direct measurement and prosthesis of retarded behavior. *Journal of Education, 147*, 62-81. https://doi.org/10.1177/002205746414700107

Lindsley, O. R. (1967). *Theoretical basis of behavior modification*. University of Kansas Bureau of Child Research.

Lindsley, O.R. (1971). From Skinner to precision teaching The child knows best. In J. B. Jordan & L. S. Robbins (Eds.), *Let's try doing something else kind of thing* (pp. 1- 11). Arlington, VA: Council for Exceptional Children.

Lindsley, O. R., (1990). Precision teaching: By teachers for children. *Teaching Exceptional Children, 22*(3), 10-15.

Lindsley, O. R. (1991a). B. F. Skinner (1904-1990): Thank you, grandpa Fred! *Journal of Precision Teaching, 8*, 5-11.

Lindsley, O. R. (1991b). Precision teaching's unique legacy from B. F. Skinner. *Journal of Behavioral Education, 1*, 253-266.

Lindsley, O. R., (1992). Precision teaching: Discoveries and effects. *Journal of Applied Behavior Analysis, 25*(1), 51-57.

Lindsley, O. R. (1997). Precise instructional design: Guidelines from Precision Teaching. In C. R. Dills & A. J. Romiszowski, (Eds). *Instructional development paradigms* (pp. 537-554). Educational Technology Publications.

Lindsley, O. R. (1999). From training evaluation to performance tracking. In H. Stolovitch & E. Keeps (Eds.). *The handbook of human performance technology* (2nd ed.). (pp. 210-236). Jossey-Bass.

Lindsley, O. L. (2000, August 16). Re:Plotting celeration lines-Zero line [Electronic mailing list message]. Retrieved from http://lists.psu.edu/archives/sclistserv.html

Lindsley, O. R. (2010). *Skinner on measurement*. Behavior Research Company.

Lydon, S., Burns, N., Healy, O., O'Connor, P., Reid McDermott, B., & Byrne, D. (2017). Preliminary evaluation of the efficacy of an intervention incorporating precision teaching to train procedural skills among final cycle medical students. *BMJ Simulation and Technology Enhanced Learning, 3*, 116-121. doi: 10.1136/bmjstel-2016-000154

Malott, R. W., & Shane, J. T. (2014). *Principles of Behavior* (7th ed.). Pearson.

Mayer, G. R., Sulzer-Azaroff, B., & Wallace, M. (2012). *Behavior analysis for lasting change* (2nd ed.). Sloan.

*McCrudden, T. (1990). Precision teaching: feeling fixer. Journal of Precision Teaching, 7(1), 19-20.

McTiernan, A., Holloway, J., Healy, O., & Hogan, M. (2016). A Randomized Controlled Trial of the Morningside Math Facts Curriculum on Fluency, Stability, Endurance and Application Outcomes. *Journal if Behavioral Education, 25*, 49–68. https://doi.org/10.1007/s10864-015-9227-y

National Institute of Standards and Technology (2014, June 2). *Unit of time (second)*. Retrieved from http://physics.nist.gov/cuu/Units/second.html

Parsonson, B., & Baer, D. (1978). The analysis and presentation of graphic data. In T. Kratochwill (Ed.), *Single subject research* (pp. 101–166). Academic Press.

Parsonson, B. S., & Baer, D. M. (1986). The graphic analysis of data. In A. Poling & R. W. Fugua (Eds.), *Research methods in applied behavior analysis: Issues and advances* (pp. 157–186). Plenum Press.

*Patterson, K., & McDowell, C. (2009). Using precision teaching strategies to promote self-management of inner behaviours and measuring effects on the symptoms of depression. *European Journal of Behavior Analysis, 10*, 283-295.

Pinker, S. (2011). *The Better Angels of our Nature*. Viking.

Potts, L., Eshleman, J. W., & Cooper, J. O. (1993). Ogden R. Lindsley and the historical development of precision teaching. *The Behavior Analyst, 16*, 177-189.

Robbins, N. B. (2005). *Creating more effective graphs*. John Wiley & Sons.

Schmid, C. F. (1976). *The Role of Standards in Graphic Presentation*. In Graphic Presentation of Statistical Information: Papers Presented at the 136th Annual Meeting of the American Statistical Association (pp. 69-78). U.S. Department of Commerce.

Schmid, C. F. (1992). *Statistical graphics: Design principles and practices*. John Wiley & Sons.

Schmid, C. F., & Schmid, S. E. (1979). *Handbook of graphic presentation* (2nd ed.). John Wiley & Sons.

Skinner, B. F. (1938). *The Behavior of Organisms: An Experimental Analysis*. B.F. Skinner Foundation.

Skinner, B. F. (1956). A case study in scientific method. *American Psychologist, 11*, 221–233.

Skinner, B. F. (1984). The Shame of American Education. *American Psychologist, 39*, 947-954. doi: 10.1037/0003-066X.39.9.947.

Spivak, S. M., & Brenner, F. C. (2001). *Standardization essentials: Principles and practice*. Marcel Dekker.

Steinhausen, H. -C., Mohr Jensen, C., & Lauritsen, M. B. (2016). A systematic review and meta-analysis of the long-term overall outcome of autism spectrum disorders in adolescence and adulthood. *Acta Psychiatrica Scandinavica, 133*, 445-452. doi: 10.1111/acps.12559

*Stromberg, G. (1974). Pinpointing helps teens end self-destructive feelings. *Special Education in Canada, 48*(3), 19.

Touchette, P. E., MacDonald, R. F., & Langer, S. N. (1985). A scatter plot for identifying stimulus control of problem behavior. *Journal of Applied Behavior Analysis, 18*, 343-51. doi: 10.1901/jaba.1985.18-343

Tufte, E.R. (1983). *The visual display of quantitative information*. Graphics Press.

Van Time, D. M., Moseley, J. L., & Dessiger, J. C. (2012). Fundamentals of performance improvement: Optimizing results through people, processes, and organizations (3rd ed.). Pfeiffer.

Venn J. (2000). *Assessing Students with Special Needs*. Prentice Hall International.

White, O. R. (2005). Trend lines. In M. Hersen, G. Sugai, & R. Horner (Eds.), *Encyclopedia of behavior modification and cognitive behavior therapy. Volume III: Education applications* (pp. 1589–1593). Sage.

Index

A

absolute change 73–74, 78, 234
acceleration 45, 53, 86, 86–88, 95, 99, 108, 121, 127, 129, 134, 148
accountability vi, 190, 190–192
accuracy 5, 24, 30, 49, 86-87, 114, 127, 155, 165, 179, 196, 199-200, 210–211, 213
accuracy pair 127
action verb 8, 39, 48–49, 180
aim 27, 55, 97, 115, 127, 134, 165-166, 171, 176, 183, 198
analytics vi, 23-25, 36, 141–142, 145, 188
Applied Behavior Analysis 224, 227, 229, 232, 234
arithmetically scaled 77–80, 82–84, 137–138
assessment 25, 47, 105, 168–169, 179, 181, 187–193, 198, 206–210, 207-209, 211, 214

B

behavioral fluency 6, 30, 155, 162, 165, 178, 196, 231
behavior change 1-2, 6, 13, 25, 30, 34, 36-37, 40-41, 46, 52, 59, 61, 67, 90-91, 97, 100, 105-106, 108, 111, 116, 127-129, 132, 134, 136-139, 141-146, 149, 166, 168, 170-171, 180, 183, 201, 222, 224, 227
bounce vi, 17, 37, 53, 75, 84, 86, 87-88, 108-109, 110-114, 117-118, 121, 122-123, 143-145, 189-190, 199, 200, 211, 222, 228
bounce envelope 109-110, 113, 117-118

C

celeration v-vi, 10, 23, 25, 27-28, 32, 37, 52-53, 55, 75, 84-88, 94-95-97, 99-101, 103-108, 110-112, 115, 118, 121-123, 127, 134-136, 143-144, 148-149, 152, 189, 196, 199-200, 206-207, 211, 223, 226-227, 230, 232
celeration analysis 84
celeration fan 27
celeration line projection 123
celeration multiplier 84, 148, 149
celeration period vi, 97, 106-108, 148, 226
change v-vi, 1-2, 5-6, 9, 12-14, 17, 20, 23-27, 29-30, 32-34, 36-37, 40-41, 46-47, 52-53, 59, 61, 63, 67-75, 77-79, 81-106, 108, 111-113, 115-117, 120-121, 125, 127-129, 132, 134, 136-146, 148-149, 151-152, 161, 166-168, 171, 180, 183, 187-188, 192-194, 196-197, 200-202, 214, 216-217, 221-225, 227, 232
charting 22, 84-86, 94, 129, 132, 141, 178, 201, 216, 226-227, 230
Chartlytics 2, 175, 204-205
Chart Share 202
component 49, 136, 142, 155, 167, 185
component-composite analysis 167
composite 167
compound 155, 166-171
condition change 91, 93-94
conventions v, 7, 84, 87
corrects 9, 53, 55, 88, 114-115, 127, 207, 213
correlation 34, 75
Cumulative Record vi, 221-222

D

data 6, 9-10, 14, 16-17, 19, 22-25, 27, 33-37, 43, 47, 56-58, 61, 63-75, 77- 79, 83-89, 91, 93, 100-101, 103, 105-110, 112, 113-122, 124-125, 127, 128-134, 136,

139-146, 148-155, 159-161, 166, 172-173, 175, 178, 180, 187-188, 193, 196-197, 200, 202-215, 217, 219, 220, 222, 225-226, 228, 230, 233
data analysis 35
data change 17, 27, 79, 115
data display 103, 211-212
data path 115
data point 37, 56, 88, 105, 107-109, 114, 116, 128, 134, 144, 148, 207-208, 212
decay 27, 53, 55, 83, 97-100, 105, 108, 115, 121, 141, 196
deceleration 45, 53, 86-87, 90, 95, 97, 99, 108, 120-121, 127, 129
decision making vi, 2, 5, 6, 9, 16, 19, 23-25, 33, 35, 46-47, 57, 61, 66-67, 74, 78, 81, 101, 125, 128-129, 151, 160, 180, 188, 192-193, 198-201, 219
defining behavior 5
Dependent Variable 211
diagnosis 82
discontinuous 55-56
Discrete Trial Instruction 210
Discrete Trial Training 210
doubling 27, 75, 77, 84, 108
down bounce 84, 109-110
drill vi, 156, 161-162
duration 23, 33, 130-132, 134-136, 165

E

education iii, 5-6, 13-14, 18, 20-22, 28, 35, 37, 39-40, 46, 51-53, 55, 61, 62, 72-73, 75, 79, 81, 82-85, 95, 155-156, 162, 166, 172-173, 180, 187-188, 190, 192-193, 197-199, 206, 222, 230
element 43, 59, 155, 166, 167-171
element-compound analysis 166-167, 169, 171

F

feedback 157, 161-162, 164-165, 172, 178, 204-207
fluency 6, 30, 155, 157, 159-160, 162, 164-166, 173, 178-179, 187, 196-199, 229, 231
fluency aim 165-166, 198

frequency 8-9, 11, 19, 23, 33, 52-53, 55, 57, 84, 86-90, 97, 109-112, 125, 143, 148-149, 155, 158, 164-165, 171, 181, 183, 187, 190-192, 197-200, 206, 216-217, 221, 222-223, 225, 227
frequency building 155, 158, 197, 206
frequency multiplier 84, 86, 88-90, 148-149

G

Geometric Mean 207, 211-213
goal 41, 47-48, 55, 85, 97, 115, 127, 134, 137, 157, 166, 169, 171, 174-175, 177, 183, 187, 189, 200, 206, 210
graphing 62, 69, 74, 211

I

improvement index 86, 113-116, 118, 148-149
incorrects 9, 30, 40, 53-55, 114-115, 127, 205, 207, 213
Independent Variable 211
individualization 188-190
intervention 1, 10, 17, 24, 27, 41, 51-52, 55, 58, 64, 77, 84, 91-92, 100-101, 105, 125, 127, 132-134, 136, 141-145, 148-149, 178, 182, 194, 200-202, 206-212, 214, 216, 226-228, 230, 232

L

labeled blanks 132
learner iii, 5, 7, 8, 11, 22-23, 52, 55, 76, 187-188, 189, 201, 210-211, 214, 216
learning channel 40, 43, 49, 132
learning picture 9, 124-125, 127-229
learning pictures 125, 127-129
level lines 134-135
Lindsley 35-37, 85-86, 90, 101, 104, 113, 117, 125, 127, 179, 217, 221-225, 227-228, 230-233
linear graph 16, 26, 62, 67-71, 75, 77, 79-81, 83-84, 100, 103-104, 106, 113, 132, 148, 194, 195, 225

M

magnitude 1, 67, 82, 88, 94, 105, 138-141, 147, 152, 166, 194, 221-222

math 7, 23-24, 30, 42-43, 57, 59, 76, 89, 97, 116, 139, 141, 155-56, 158, 164, 187, 189, 191, 192, 200
measurement 2, 5-6, 11-12, 22-23, 25, 30, 33, 35, 46-47, 51-52, 55, 61, 84, 86-88, 101-103, 106, 116-117, 127, 132, 136, 152, 180, 187-190, 192-193, 197, 199-200, 212, 221, 224, 231-232
metrics v, 23-25, 27-28, 36, 85, 113-114, 141-145, 148-149, 188, 190, 197-199
momentary time sampling 55
monitoring 23, 25, 37, 108, 127, 129, 166, 174-175, 177, 188, 211, 225, 227
movement cycle 39-40, 43, 48-49, 180-181

N

Natural Environment Teaching 210
nonstandardization 14-18, 69, 73-75, 82, 106, 219, 225
nonstandard linear graphs 15-18, 24-26, 75, 82, 106, 111, 196, 219

O

outcomes 2, 28, 30, 36, 41, 47, 50-51, 69, 75, 95, 100, 136-137, 156, 158, 162, 183, 185, 228
outliers 75, 111, 116-118, 212

P

PEAK v, 46-50, 168-169
percent v, 5, 32, 52, 55, 57-59, 98, 166, 200, 210
percentage 52, 57-59, 70, 74, 79, 83, 97-98, 114, 210
performance iii, 1, 5, 7-9, 11-12, 20, 23, 25, 27, 30, 36-37, 46, 50, 55, 58, 70, 72, 84, 90, 101, 105, 108, 111, 113, 117, 125, 127-128, 144, 155, 157, 159, 161-162, 164-165, 179, 183, 187-188, 192-193, 198-199, 206-207, 210, 212-213, 230, 232, 234
performance improvement 1, 12, 155, 187, 188, 234
phase change v, 91, 93
pinpoint 8, 9, 27, 39-47, 49, 69, 86, 91, 97, 105, 109-110, 122, 170-171, 180, 192, 197, 200, 215
pinpointing behavior 8
Pivotal Response Treatment 210
practice vi, 2, 6, 8-12, 20-21, 27, 28, 32-33, 39, 44, 46-47, 52, 55, 67, 86, 115, 149, 155-166, 172-173, 178-181, 193, 196-197, 203-209, 212, 220, 225, 228, 233
practice trials 159-162, 165, 179, 203,-208
Precision Teaching i, v-vi, 1-2, 3, 5-9, 11, 16, 19, 21-22, 25, 29-33, 35-41, 43, 47, 50, 55-57, 61, 69, 76, 83-88, 90-91, 94-95, 99, 101, 105, 107, 109, 114, 116-117, 125, 127, 137, 139, 141, 144, 145-146, 155, 167-169, 178, 180, 185, 187, 188-189, 191, 193, 197, 199-202, 204, 206, 208, 211, 215-217, 220-223, 229-232
PrecisionX 175, 205
prediction 24, 122, 145
Private Events 229
problem-solving 5
proportional change 67, 77, 79
proportional construction rule 63-64, 74

Q

quantification 105, 108, 134, 143, 148, 189, 227

R

ratio scale 34, 227
record v, 9, 40-41, 53, 55-56, 210-211, 215, 221-223, 225
record ceiling v, 55-56
record floor 56
recording behavior 5
relative change vi, 59, 74-75, 78, 94, 137-138, 143

S

SAFMEDS vi, 100, 178-183, 231
science vi, 5, 6, 11-12, 14, 19-23, 25, 39, 40, 43, 44, 46-47, 51-52, 55, 59, 61, 75, 81, 85-86, 91, 100, 102-103, 106, 110, 113, 136-137, 146, 149, 158, 161, 167, 171, 178, 185, 187, 188-190, 192, 197-199, 202-203, 208-209, 215, 221-222, 224, 227

science of behavior 20, 43, 46-47, 110, 136, 171, 197, 209, 215, 221, 224
self-chart 9
self-improvement 1, 46
self-monitor 9
sessions 64-65, 160-161, 164-165, 210
Skinner 37, 43, 46, 125, 208, 215, 221-225, 227, 232-233
slope 16-17, 27, 53, 63, 100, 104, 108, 134, 194, 196, 220
special education 61-62, 72-73, 162, 166, 172-173, 180, 193, 230
Standard Celeration Chart vi, 6, 9, 12, 19, 23, 25, 27-28, 32-35, 37, 53, 56, 68, 75, 79, 80-84, 86-87, 89, 91, 94-95, 97, 99, 101, 103, 104, 107-109, 113, 115-117, 119, 120, 125, 129-131, 136-140, 141, 143, 145-146, 149, 150, 152-153, 159-160, 166, 175-178, 183, 189, 190, 192-193, 196, 197, 200-201, 215, 217, 219-222, 225, 227
standardization 219, 221-223
standards v, 6, 11-15, 33, 62-63, 65, 192-193, 196, 198, 219, 221, 230

T

testing vi, 37, 185, 188, 190-191
tick mark 66
time bar 56-57, 86-87, 89, 90, 127, 131
time series 6, 14, 16, 33-34, 61, 65, 69-75, 77, 79, 82, 101, 142, 152, 201
time series data 6, 33-34, 61, 73, 101, 152
time series graph 65, 70-71
timing v, 23, 51-52, 64, 132, 155, 162, 215-216, 229
total bounce 109-110
trend 10, 24-25, 37, 61, 67, 70-71, 74, 79, 101, 103-106, 115, 119, 121, 134, 143, 145, 200, 210, 219
trials 159-162, 165, 179, 203-208, 210-213

U

up bounce 84, 110

V

variability 17, 24, 42, 63, 70, 74, 84, 109, 111-114, 116, 143-145, 200, 210, 213, 228
visual analysis 134, 143, 145
visual display 6, 33-34, 78, 80-81, 83, 84, 125, 129, 142-143, 150, 152, 192, 196-197, 219, 221-223, 225, 234

W

within condition analysis 113
writing 1-2, 5-6, 8, 10, 13, 40, 42-43, 76, 114, 119, 155, 158, 162, 165-166, 172-178, 185, 203, 205, 220

Z

zero v, 86-87, 89-90, 139